CONDO CONQUEST

LAW AND SOCIETY

LAW AND SOCIETY SERIES
W. Wesley Pue, General Editor

The Law and Society Series explores law as a socially embedded phenomenon. It is premised on the understanding that the conventional division of law from society creates false dichotomies in thinking, scholarship, educational practice, and social life. Books in the series treat law and society as mutually constitutive and seek to bridge scholarship emerging from interdisciplinary engagement of law with disciplines such as politics, social theory, history, political economy, and gender studies.

Recent books in the series:

L. Jane McMillan, *Truth and Conviction: Donald Marshall Jr. and the Mi'kmaw Quest for Justice* (2018)

Sarah Grayce Marsden, *Enforcing Exclusion: Precarious Migrants and the Law in Canada* (2018)

Jasminka Kalajdzic, *Class Actions in Canada: The Promise and Reality of Access to Justice* (2018)

David Moffette, *Governing Irregular Migration: Bordering Culture, Labour, and Security in Spain* (2018)

Constance Backhouse, *Claire L'Heureux-Dubé: A Life* (2017)

Christopher P. Manfredi and Antonia Maioni, *Health Care and the Charter: Legal Mobilization and Policy Change in Canada* (2018)

Julie Macfarlane, *The New Lawyer: How Clients Are Transforming the Practice of Law,* 2nd ed. (2017)

Annie Bunting and Joel Quirk, eds., *Contemporary Slavery: Popular Rhetoric and Political Practice* (2017)

Larry Savage and Charles W. Smith, *Unions in Court: Organized Labour and the Charter of Rights and Freedoms* (2017)

For a complete list of the titles in the series, see the UBC Press website, www.ubcpress.ca.

Randy K. Lippert

CONDO CONQUEST

Urban Governance, Law, and Condoization in New York City and Toronto

UBCPress · Vancouver · Toronto

27 26 25 24 23 22 21 20 19   5 4 3 2 1

Printed in Canada on FSC-certified ancient-forest-free paper (100% post-consumer recycled) that is processed chlorine- and acid-free.

Library and Archives Canada Cataloguing in Publication

Lippert, Randy K., author

Condo conquest: urban governance, law, and condoization in NewYork City and Toronto / Randy K. Lippert.

(Law and society)
Includes bibliographical references and index.
Issued in print and electronic formats.
ISBN 978-0-7748-6035-2 (hardcover). – ISBN 978-0-7748-6037-6 (PDF).
ISBN 978-0-7748-6038-3 (EPUB). – ISBN 978-07748-6039-0 (Kindle).

1. Condominiums – Law and legislation – Ontario – Toronto. 2. Condominiums – Law and legislation – New York (State) – New York. 3. Real estate management – Law and legislation – Ontario – Toronto. 4. Real estate management – Law and legislation – New York (State) –New York. I. Title. II. Series: Law and society series (Vancouver, B.C.)

KEO240.L57 2019	346.713'5410433	C2018-905870-6
KF581 L57 2019		C2018-905871-4

Canadä

UBC Press gratefully acknowledges the financial support for our publishing program of the Government of Canada (through the Canada Book Fund), the Canada Council for the Arts, and the British Columbia Arts Council.

This book has been published with the help of a grant from the Canadian Federation for the Humanities and Social Sciences, through the Awards to Scholarly Publications Program, using funds provided by the Social Sciences and Humanities Research Council of Canada.

UBC Press
The University of British Columbia
2029 West Mall
Vancouver, BC V6T 1Z2
www.ubcpress.ca

FOR JESSE

Contents

Tables

Acknowledgments

This book took more than six years to research and write and was easily the most challenging work I have ever undertaken. I need to thank a lot of people for helping make it happen. Foremost I am deeply grateful to my amazing partner Francine whose support of my academic pursuits, and most everything else in my life, has been unwavering for three decades.

The book also would not have been possible without the efforts of several graduate students. Stefan Treffers helped research and write an earlier version of Chapter 5 and truly went above and beyond in reviewing the manuscript early on and, throughout, in sharing his passion for urban studies and a deep concern about inequality. Rhys Steckle diligently conducted many interviews in Toronto and helped write part of what eventually became Chapter 3 and an early version of Chapter 6. Thomas Bud also aided the research and analysis for this book. It was a special honour to work with these three students and to watch their careers advance since. I sincerely thank Setha Low from City University of New York for helping to secure funding, graduate student researchers, and interviews with condo residents in New York City. I am also indebted to Holland Marshall, whom I think has at once a deep dislike of, and a contagious passion for, all things condo. I thank him for meeting over the past four years to talk about condos and for his support of the research. I also acknowledge the help of that generous property manager with thirty years' experience: over two days I accompanied him to condo buildings that he managed to see the inner workings of condo life – something of which most residents are unaware. I am also grateful to Alan Walks of the University of Toronto who went above and beyond in reviewing an early version of the manuscript and who suggested perceptive changes without which the book would be lesser than it is. Thanks are due too to Mariana Valverde for her voluminous socio-legal and urban studies scholarship, from which this book drew much inspiration, and her generous support of my own scholarship over the years. I am also grateful to the two anonymous reviewers with UBC Press for their useful and supportive comments. I also thank Kevin Walby for his steady moral support and patience from afar during this very long endeavour (amidst our other research projects) and for listening to my grumbling about it, first during lunch in Hell's Kitchen in 2013 and in untold e-mails and communications in the five years since.

Randy Schmidt, senior editor at UBC Press, is a marvel. Having experienced several publishers and editors in the twelve years between two books with UBC Press, I can say that scholars working in socio-legal studies are truly fortunate not only to have Randy doing what he does so superbly but also to still have excellent university presses like UBC Press in Canada. With regard to this book, Randy came to the rescue at a crucial juncture, with understanding, remarkable efficiency, and his regular no-nonsense grace. I sincerely thank him for that.

Canadian scholars are so fortunate to still have the publicly funded Social Sciences and Humanities Research Council of Canada in these neoliberal times, and I gratefully acknowledge a major research Insight Grant that funded the study for this book and without which it would not have been possible.

Finally, I am deeply grateful to the 160 persons who gave up their time to answer questions about owning, living in, managing, securing, designing, monitoring, and governing the condo world.

The following articles were significantly revised and supplemented to form Chapters 3, 4, and 6, respectively.

Lippert, R.K., and R. Steckle. 2016. "Conquering condos from within: Condo-isation and urban governance and knowledge." *Urban Studies* 53 (1): 132–48. Copyright (2016) by Urban Studies Journal Ltd. Reprinted by permission of Sage Publications, Ltd.

Lippert, R.K., and S.R. Treffers. 2016. "Legal knowledges and surveillance in the condo world." *Social and Legal Studies* 25 (4): 419–40. Copyright (2016) by the authors. Reprinted by permission of SAGE Publications, Ltd.

Lippert, R.K. 2012. "Governing condominiums and renters through legal knowledge flows and external institutions." *Law and Policy* 34 (3): 263–90. Copyright (2012) by the author. Reprinted by permission of John Wiley and Sons.

CONDO CONQUEST

1

Introduction

Condominiums are like sausages: they are made, sold, consumed everywhere in cities, and, with little fanfare or sophistication, promise to efficiently satisfy a need. But, like sausages, little is known about condo innards, and the less one knows, the better off one may feel. The inner workings and governance of condos remains either a distasteful topic (due to imagined conflict, acrimony, or dreariness) or a minor urban mystery easily left unexplored among weightier urban issues such as severely limited affordable housing, crumbling infrastructure, physical insecurity, crime, local government corruption, and unequal power and property relations. Yet these familiar urban issues – as well as others, such as nuisance – are closely tethered to condo governance. As more and more people are becoming its subjects and agents through "condoization," there is little appreciation of how condo governance works, the knowledge it requires, or of how it is mutating and might be set free from its conquerors. This rising, perhaps even accelerating, condoization is a special way of governing urbanites and urban space comprising various elements – processes, agents, logics, technology, and forms of knowledge – assembled and working in concert. Exploring condo governance and condoization promises to reveal much about urban governance and life and its possible futures, the condo's role in the fluctuating urban imaginary, and the value of theoretical concepts when it comes to rendering these matters intelligible. But despite its apparent import, there is little study of condo governance and how it is changing, theoretically or otherwise. Like the innards of sausages tightly assembled in casings and covered with condiments, condo governance's complex, occasionally unseemly ingredients remain masked by slick developer and other forms of commercial marketing, and perpetually promising government statutory reviews and reforms. And, like eating too many sausages, unless one dissects the innards of condo casings (if only to conceive of alternative recipes) too much condoization may be placing the long-term well-being of urban life at risk.

Few people would deny knowing what a condo is. Yet in everyday parlance "condo" and "condominium" are used without qualification to refer *both* to a unit within a residential multi-unit building and to the entire building (e.g., "I live in a condo"); both to the apartment and to the complex in which it is located. The importance of the emergence of this dual meaning of "condo" should not be overlooked since it speaks to the presumed self-evidence of the assembled elements that constitute it. "Condominium" properly refers to a legally defined, unique form of property and tenure that combines cooperative ownership (as found in cooperatively owned housing [i.e., "cooperatives" or "co-ops"]) and more traditional individual ownership (as found in detached dwellings, the staple of North American housing). Owning a "condo" thus means owning both a unit and a common share of the building in which it is situated. In *Condo Conquest* "the condo" is shorthand for this specific legally defined form of ownership and the special governing arrangements it entails in North America and beyond. This book seeks to elaborate upon and to render intelligible this form of ownership. Accordingly, in what follows "condo" is used to refer to buildings, units, and practices operating under these arrangements as well as to the increasingly specialized agents and organizations (e.g., condo lawyers, condo property management firms, condo boards, etc.) they enlist.[1]

The urban imagination presumes limited residential living space and thus a need to share it, and this is precisely what, from the outset, the condo proposed to accomplish. The condo's common ownership capacity, governing board, and bylaws and rules promised the sharing of space, related resources, and responsibility for their governance. These arrangements depended on enabling legislation (Risk 1968), and the condo ascended through special state and provincial statutes passed in the 1960s in North America. These statutes have undergone continuous reform ever since. The condo's uncommon marriage of common and individual ownership, and the ostensibly private governing arrangements to oversee this union, however, comprise not only its ongoing potential but also its perpetual frailty and its source of scholarly intrigue.

Presently the condo dominates growing swathes of the North American urban landscape and is found, albeit in slightly varying form and ranging proportion, in cities the world over, including those in Australia and Asia (see Easthope et al. 2014; Huong and Sajor 2010; Pow 2009; Zhang 2008; McKenzie 2006). One of the most under-recognized and discussed aspects of urban China, for example, is that it undoubtedly already has more condos – is more condoized – than the rest of the world combined due to conversions from public housing and new-builds during its rapid capitalist economic growth in recent decades. Indeed, authors of a rare study of condo governance in China recently observed that "the conclusion that the condominium is the principle housing feature of urban China is inescapable" (Chen and Kielsgard 2014, 22n). Limited residential land has been maximized by extending condo buildings vertically with more and more floors – verticality being a rarely noted feature of much condo governance and life – as well as by further increasing the number and often decreasing the size of units. Consonant with apparent efficiencies stemming from sharing space and elements, the condo has been touted at various junctures and by diverse sources as a solution to urban problems. This may be one reason this form of property has relentlessly converted and carved out urban spaces by horizontally and vertically displacing older forms and their inhabitants, including private and publicly owned rental complexes and industrial workplaces the world over.

Used first in the 1970s, the term "condoization" meant converting and dividing rental apartment complexes into multi-owned condo units and common elements for private sale and purchase. This is the conversion process undergone by a rental apartment building "going condo." Beginning in 1977, this has been particularly prevalent not only in American cities like New York (Lees, Slater, and Wyly 2008, 28; see also Chambers 2006) and Chicago, which led the United States in conversions in the 1970s (Gallun 2006), but also, over the past thirty-five years (Steele 1993), in Toronto and smaller Canadian cities like Winnipeg (Hildebrand 2013). These "condo conversions" of existing rental housing are often used by building owners to avoid municipal or other local taxes as well as to engage in profiteering, and by other developers as opportunities to transform older, relatively affordable rental housing into luxury units that are for sale.[2] While this process is relevant to what follows, this book expands "condoization" to mean a governing,[3] constitutive process in cities that enlists a wide but mutually supporting array of agents, processes, knowledges, and other elements. Thus, condoization includes building-specific condo governance – the inner ordering of condo complexes – as well as condo conversions and "new-build" development. Much of this book is about this inner ordering; but, upon closer inspection, it shows that any inner-outer distinction, or any distinction between condo governance and development, based upon the varied governing agents and knowledges brought to bear on condo governance, becomes blurred. "Condoization" is thus a summary term referring to all the agents, knowledges, logics, and processes that have arisen, been repurposed, or continue to emerge and are assembled in spaces and times to make the condo and its governance possible.

Upon passage of the first North American condo statutes, the condo was to be governed by a volunteer board of unit owners residing in a condo building. At this juncture, there was little to no anticipation of the role,[4] for example, of property management, security, or law firms in managing condo affairs. But since then condo governance has been slowly, almost imperceptibly conquered by these and other commercial agents and knowledges that now profoundly influence how any given condo building and unit is governed and, arguably, what statutory reforms that seek greater accountability and transparency of condo governance are possible. This gradual shift means, too, that the common knowledge of residents informing condo governance is increasingly being supplemented or displaced by expert, commodified knowledges and technologies. Concurrently, since its arrival in North America, the condo is becoming more and more an investment commodity and less and less an urban residential community in which to live, with units being increasingly purchased to rent to others rather than to use as a residence. This contrasts with provincial/state and federal levels of governments' imaginings of condo corporations and buildings, which, by and large, were meant to be communities. As McKenzie (2011, 37) writes, mostly about the United States, condo arrangements "are viewed by many as having the potential to create strong communities" and, when compared to municipal governments, to have "greater flexibility to do the things that might promote community."[5] This is a crucial assertion for following chapters and requires further elaboration.[6]

This community emphasis is evident, for example, in the 1977 statutory review preceding a revised Ontario Condo Act the following year: "*Community life* is an integral part of condominium living. Since the condominium concept is based on common property ownership, it involves owners in the problems as well as the rewards *inherent in community life*" (Ontario 1977, 9; emphasis added). Later this review foresees condo living enlisting residents "interested in a high level of *community* involvement ... [and] relying on formalized cooperation" (Ontario 1977, 105; emphasis added). The federal Canada Mortgage and Housing Corporation's (2017) *Condominium Buyers' Guide* suggests to would-be condo owners: "Whether it's compulsory or not, you have a responsibility to yourself and to other owners to become involved in your condominium *community*" (emphasis added). A prominent Toronto condo lawyer and one of the architects of Ontario's 1998 revised condo statute explained during the latest statutory review that there was a "condominium *community* environment that government originally anticipated would be there when condominium *communities* were built. Condominium *communities* were intended to have people of like mind who shared the running of their home" (Miller Thomson LLP 2012, 324; emphasis added). And this latest Ontario statutory review process explains: "To say the [condo] corporation is a *community implies that its members share common interests and the relationship among them is essential to promoting those interests.* In short, they need one another" (Canada's Public Policy Forum 2013c, 14; emphasis added). This review further reports that "a central challenge" "is to find ways of encouraging condo owners to look on their homes as part of self-governing *communities*" (Canada's Public Policy Forum 2013c, 6; emphasis added; see also 2013c, 10).

Like "community," this notion of "self-governing" contrasts sharply with the current character of condo governance that surfaced in the accounts of often isolated resident owners interviewed in this book. This governance is evinced as operating instead through an assemblage of agents, forms of knowledge (hereinafter "knowledges"), and technologies, mostly from beyond and outside a given building, rather than primarily from owners and board members residing within it. The assumption that a condo building and its governing corporation is a viable urban form that *fosters* or at least *promises community* due to the communal aspects and knowledge upon which it relies, including but not limited to shared property ownership and board participation, is revealed as increasingly dubious, though perhaps not yet beyond hope.

Condo Conquest is about how condo arrangements are governed and changing. It attends to varied elements that converge to make possible, shape, and police seemingly separate private condo worlds hidden to all but those implicated in them. In adopting a distinctive sociology of governance approach to the subject matter, this book insists that condo governance be viewed as a loose collection of governing agents, knowledges, logics, technologies, and processes – that is, as an "assemblage." One underlying aim of this approach is to render the familiar condo strange. The seemingly self-evident condo of everyday discourse that is built or converted, priced, bought, sold, rented, occupied, insured, secured, surveilled, measured, renovated, repaired, and managed nearly everywhere in cities, is revealed to be more an unfamiliar, shifting, contingent, tenuous accomplishment than a permanent, fixed edifice or space therein. The following chapters reveal the condo as less a physical structure built or converted by developers and more a mutating, assembled set of legal, social, and (often vertical) spatial relationships among various elements and a form of urban governance. To study condo assemblages and how their seemingly disparate elements work together is to begin to understand how property is born and continuously reconstituted.

The condo, as a special set of relationships, is also deemed to have a capacity to solve perpetual urban problems. Through this study the condo will begin to look a little familiar to scholars since, as a rich realm of governance awash with law and knowledge, they will recognize that analytical concepts with purchase elsewhere are also relevant to the workings of the condo. For example, this book demonstrates that risk management and surveillance are growing perhaps as much in the condo world as in municipal and other realms of public government. Given this and the condo's influential and proliferating urban presence, it is inadequate to merely use empirical research to describe condo governance and how it might be changing, however expertly governments (e.g., Ontario 1977) and scholars (e.g., Easthope et al. 2014) may conduct that research. The study of condo governance promises to extend, refine, or underscore the value of key analytical concepts from overlapping governance, urban, socio-legal, and surveillance literatures and to itself assemble these literatures into a common thought space. What is needed is to relate condo governance, where possible, to analytical concepts informed in some manner by social theory, especially but not exclusively by the multidisciplinary literature inspired by the writings and ideas of French philosopher and historian Michel Foucault. To neglect to nurture the fertile empirical ground (and air) of the condo in this way would waste a fruitful opportunity. However, consistent with Foucault's spirit, the aim here is not to introduce a new universal theory of condo governance or condoization but, rather, to introduce a modest but conceptually engaged intervention to trouble what has arrived in such an apparently self-evident form in our urban present. *Condo Conquest* seeks to make the condo and its governance intelligible by deploying concepts rather than by merely describing the condo, however valuable description might be for the immediate concerns of policy makers, industry practitioners, and some condo owners.[7] It is especially for this reason that I pay attention to these concepts here before proceeding to explore condoization and condo governance. The following analysis avoids detailed prescription,[8] but it can nonetheless inform condo governance policies and practices in North American cities. While this book is not intended as a condemnation of the condo, in studying its governance, I discover troubling trends pertaining to how it has become arranged, conjoined, and constituted, and I discuss some of the effects thereof. Thus, condo governance has been mutating, not spectacularly, but gradually in ways discernable through detailed study. The condo is becoming less and less controlled by an elected board of owners representing, residing in, and acting in the interest of the long-term well-being of a residential community and is more and more being conquered by external commercial and private agents. These agents include non-resident investors, property managers, lawyers, security providers, and real estate agents who often operate to the detriment and/or literally at the expense of resident owners and largely excluded urbanites who are able only to rent a roof overhead (but who nonetheless foot the mounting bill) and perhaps also municipal governments if, in coming years, many condo corporations should become financially unsustainable or declare bankruptcy.

Condo Conquest draws on extensive empirical research conducted over several years. This research entailed numerous interviews with condo residents and industry representatives, and the collection and analysis of myriad documents from condo buildings (e.g., rules and contracts) as well as condo owner advocacy websites, professional trade magazines, developer marketing materials, formal submissions from owners and industry representatives to statutory reviews, mass media accounts, legislation and case law, and many other items related to condo governance. The empirical focus is on condo governance in Toronto and, to a lesser extent, New York. Toronto is Canada's most populous city, a dense and diverse urban centre. The metropolitan Greater Toronto Area, which includes the cities of Brampton and Mississauga, has over 6 million people. New York is the most densely populated city in the United States, with more than 8 million people distributed across five "boroughs" – Manhattan, Brooklyn, the Bronx, Queens, and Staten Island. These two metropolitan areas have among the largest condo concentrations in North America. Toronto and New York are also both economically "polarized" (Walks 2014) or "divided" (Florida 2014) cities, with shocking and rising inequality in income and wealth distribution. This inequality is reflected in, among other shared features, the severe lack of affordable housing and the need for millions to rent a space in which to live while condo high-rises for purchase are erected all around, especially in downtown Toronto and Manhattan. As such, these cities provide two urban locales for the study of condo governance, with populations of slightly differing ethnic diversity and legal cultures but with unmistakable similarities in legislation, agents, and issues related to this distinctive form of governance.

The condo form is concentrated in these cities, but elements of its governance and condoization are largely applicable to other North American cities as well as to cities being condoized elsewhere. For example, condo buildings in Belgium and Australia predate their appearance in North American cities, and there are now far greater numbers of them in China than in North America. Yet all of them have somewhat similar specialized legislation, governing arrangements, agents, and knowledges. *Condo Conquest*'s major topics, including legal knowledge, elevators, and nuisances, are relevant to condo governance and condoization the world over. Indeed, what has been happening regarding condo governance and condoization in Toronto and New York, and the focus of this book, might best be termed "condo conquest."

CONDO CONQUEST

Condo Conquest, the title of this book, looks at the extension of condoization – an extension that takes the form of a conquest, a take-over of condo governance and the condo by commercial or profit-seeking agents, especially representatives of condo law, real estate, insurance, security, and property management firms, and growing legions of non-resident owners who purchase condo units exclusively as commodities. It also explores the affiliated processes and knowledges that accompany this conquest. *Condo Conquest* offers a summary assessment of these conditions. Although the elements to which condoization and condo conquest refer have become aligned and, at numerous points in an assemblage, are mutually supporting, I do not suggest a grand conspiracy among the various identified agents, much less the other elements mentioned. I chose the term "conquest" because it presumes a quest for a reward using this collection of elements rather than another and thus connotes that there is much at stake for cities and urbanites. But, like all conquered territory, including the air space far above condo high-rises, it is never permanently and wholly captured. Rather, conquests must be continuously assembled, governed, and maintained, and there are perpetually emerging cracks and holes through, and ways around, the physical walls and increasingly surveilled barriers of condo buildings as well as through and around unending house rules and statutory reforms that seek to at once provide for and control condo life. Certainly, the elevator emerges as one space where this resistance grows and becomes evident, while conduct deemed to be a nuisance in the way it defies space and rules is another. And whether the condo can be or is worth sustaining in the urban is not a given.

Condo development in Toronto and New York and the remarkable rise to dominance of the condo form has not occurred without some organized opposition. The politics of condo development is complex and differs in the two cities. Yet, like all organized resistance predating the conquering of a realm, in retrospect it seems limited in scope and aim. Often it has entailed opposition to the imagined effects of the erection of a specific building on the part of adjacent neighbours, businesses, or renters, sometimes appearing as NIMBY reactions (e.g., Powell 2017) rather than as being generalized across sites. In Toronto there has been growing organized resistance from several sources concerning the effects of rapid condo growth, including its mounting pressure on public infrastructure to the benefit of developers and to the detriment of local taxpayers, not to mention its gentrification effects (O'Neil 2017). But the results of this resistance have been limited. In New York resistance was especially significant in the 1970s, when rental buildings were increasingly converted, which was often claimed as gentrification and which saw long-standing renters fight back, with some success, to prevent the conversion of their buildings. To mention one example, in New York in the 1970s, in an estimated 10 to 15 percent of cases condo (and co-op) conversions were effectively resisted by long-term renters who were preoccupied less with decentralization issues and more with keeping a place in which to live (Lasner 2012, 267). Not everyone has seen the condo as worth embracing, nor has it been seamlessly imposed. However, no "anti-condo" organizations have emerged in either city during the condo's ascendency.

The elements of condoization and this conquest increasingly constitute the fabric of condo life in ways that may threaten the condo's long-term viability and that are mostly inconsistent with the notions of community that governments and some early advocates (e.g., Teaford 1969) intended to accompany the condo and other cooperative forms of residential housing.[9] The title *Condo Conquest* also highlights the way the condo promised to conquer various urban problems (e.g., Risk 1968), the notion of urban governance *through* the condo. Thus, from its outset, agents ranging from municipal and other political authorities, to local businesspersons in urban retail strips, to low-income urban housing advocates thought the condo possessed the capacity to respond to issues inherent to the urban world, the foremost of which was lack of housing space and affordability. This justification for the condo is plainly evident, for example, in the first legislative debate and discussion about enacting condo statutes in Ontario and New York State in the 1960s. As well, when condo conversions increased, particularly in New York but also in other US cities like Chicago, Denver, and Houston in the late 1970s (United States Congress 1981), the condo was a way of helping to solve the US urban problem of "decentralization" (see Fine 1980, 314) and related urban decay. That problem entailed the creation of a spatial "doughnut," the hollowing out of populations and wealth in the centres of major US cities, and the movement of middle-class and upper-class (often white) families to the suburbs, leaving a residential hole in the city with a corresponding tax base vacuum. Through the 1980s and 1990s, the economic decline of urban areas and reduced public funding for municipal infrastructure and services due to major reductions in federal, provincial/state, and municipal government taxation and spending emerged as a problem. In North America, the condo promised either to offer its own services/infrastructure in place of municipal arrangements or to stand as high-density housing to reduce municipal service delivery costs (Nelson 2005; Warner 2011). At this juncture new-build condo complexes also promised to enhance consumption, especially in declining retail zones and downtowns increasingly overseen by business improvement associations (Lippert 2012). This was because they ensure the arrival of many new consumers in a targeted area and even, if condo developers' marketing is to be believed, function to reduce carbon emissions through more efficient energy use (Tridel 2017). More recently, as discussed in Chapter 8, the condo has been deployed to house lower-income city residents (Mah and Hackworth 2011, 72) in Toronto and New York. The condo's common, shared elements and spaces promise to reduce demands for horizontal residential space (as they often expand vertically into urban skies) as well as reliance on state expenditures for urban public housing and residential services. These two senses of "condo conquest" overlap and intermingle in practice. For example, juridification that entails increasing the influence of condo law firms, lawyers, and various forms of legal knowledge regarding the condo world as well as the influence of condo developers on governance – both examples of the conquest of condo governance – are not easily separable from using the condo to solve urban problems. One entails the other.

CONDO GOVERNANCE RESEARCH

Seldom taken up as a topic in its own right,[10] condo governance is usually a subject – when remarked upon at all – within a broader but somewhat mottled collection of legal, socio-legal, and urban studies. In these otherwise insightful literatures, condo governance is typically approached obliquely or subsumed in discussions of "homeowner associations" (e.g., Chen and Webster 2005), "co-operative homeownership" (e.g., Lasner 2012), "property owner associations" (e.g., Kress 1995), "common interest communities" (e.g., Barton and Silverman 1994; McKenzie 2003, 2011), "multi-owned properties" (Sherry 2017), as well as "gated communities" in the US (e.g., Kennedy 1995; Low 2003, 2013), Canada (Grant 2005), the United Kingdom (Atkinson and Flint 2004), and globally (Atkinson and Blandy 2013). These various, somewhat poorly delineated (see Levi 2009) forms and spaces of private governance have been proliferating since the early 1970s. Significant works focusing more on condo governance are Barton and Silverman (1994) in the US and a recent significant collection about condo governance in Australia (Sherry 2017). Both move beyond describing the emergence, legal details, and requirements of condo statutes for governance to empirically discover further characteristics and consequences in practice. Barton and Silverman offer an account of condo life and governance in California. They ultimately argue that the condo is flawed because it creates conflict between the notion of private property as commodity and property as community. They assert that condo owners' low participation in governance and conflict results "from contradiction between the complex reality, in which private and public life are interrelated, and people's privatized understanding of their individual rights" (Barton and Silverman 1994, 130). Sherry's work, which is more recent, concentrates on the financial, political, and social consequences of condo law arrangements in Australia, especially relating to how bylaws must be enforced against a diverse set of owners. This account has broader relevance since the Australian condo statutes influenced those developed elsewhere, including in British Columbia. While neither work engages with social theory to any extent (though Sherry [2017, 229] draws on legal theorist Joseph Singer's democratic theory of property law to consider how condo governance is undemocratic), these significant studies are nonetheless relevant to Toronto and New York condo contexts and vice versa. For example, the revision and enforcement of bylaws in condo buildings in both Toronto and New York have encountered the economic and political barriers described in these two books. As in California and Australia, so in Toronto and New York a lack of participation on condo boards is evident. Indeed, this suggests the following chapters may be of relevance to condo buildings and governing arrangements well beyond Toronto and New York.

Besides periodic provincial statutory reviews (Canada's Public Policy Forum 2013a) and market studies (Skaburskis 1984), most existing Canadian scholarly research on condo buildings is written by urban geographers: it deals with complex issues of condo development (see Kern 2010a; Lehrer, Keil, and Kipfer 2010; Rosen and Walks 2013; Webb and Webber 2017) and only obliquely with condo governance,[11] if at all. Condo development is the process of investing to convert existing, or to build new, residential structures as condos. For Toronto, municipal- and provincial-level planning, land-use, and zoning laws and policies increasingly encourage such forms of development (see Lehrer 2008) and discourage others, such as homeless shelters (Ranasinghe and Valverde 2006) and subsidized rental apartment buildings (Kern 2010a, 34, 62). What is understood as development is part of the condo story in major cities like Toronto and New York, but it is only part. Neglected in urban geography is condo governance and its significance in ordering urban space and life (but see Kern 2010a; Rosen and Walks 2013). Some recent theoretically engaged research on the condo in Canada centring on new-build condo development has emerged concerning Toronto (Kern 2007, 2010a, 2010b; Rosen and Walks 2013, 2015a, 2015b; Rosen 2016, 2017; Webb and Webber 2017) and, to a lesser extent, Vancouver (Harris 2011), where, in the past decade or so, condo growth, mostly of high-rises, has burst upward and across skylines. This theoretically engaged work on the condo provides keen insights into the mutating political economy of the expanding condo world. It includes attention to powerful private interests – mostly developers (Rosen 2017) – which condo development represents, as well as to the legal aspects that fuel it (Harris 2011).

The rapid expansion of the condo is sometimes asserted to reflect accelerating privatization consistent with the onset of urban neoliberalism (e.g., Kern 2007; see also McKenzie 2011, 3) and "gentrification" (Lehrer and Wieditz 2009; Ley 1996, 70). Neoliberalism is generally understood to entail "the embrace of public-private partnerships, deregulation, fiscal austerity, cross-subsidies and market solutions" (Blomley 2004, 29–74; see also Brady and Lippert 2016). The neoliberal roll-back of Keynesian welfarism (Peck and Tickell 2002; Hackworth 2008) means that, as urban space is increasingly redeveloped, it results in the expulsion of low-income and homeless persons (see Catungal and Leslie 2009). This gentrification entails increasing class inequality through exclusion and displacement (Brash 2011; Atkinson 2004; Smith 1996, 2002) or socio-spatial polarization (Walks 2014). With regard to Toronto's condo growth specifically, Kern (2010a, 2) discusses "condo development as an expression of neo-liberal ideology," and Lehrer and Wieditz (2009, 4) use the term "condoification" to describe condo development "as the latest phase of gentrification in Toronto" (see also Smith [2002, 441] on a condo development in New York). In the same vein, Kern (2010a, 2010b) cogently examines gender dynamics within Toronto's neoliberal-oriented condo development. She explores how women are targeted by developers and sold not only condo units but also a contrived, impoverished, commodified urban lifestyle thought to befit their gender. This account includes limited attention to governance (Kern 2010a, 118–24) by drawing on twenty-one interviews with women condo owners.

This insightful, small body of work tends to view the condo as an economic and cultural force of urban development, an argument perhaps most persuasively articulated by Rosen and Walks (2013; see also Rosen and Walks 2015a; 2015b) drawing on innovative research in Toronto. Rosen and Walks (2013) introduced "condo-ism" into the urban studies lexicon to help explain Toronto's condo growth. For Rosen and Walks (2013), condo-ism, beyond involving condo development in the form of new high-rise buildings in Toronto, is "a new way of urban life" (Rosen and Walks 2015a) that accompanies a penchant for privatization of public services consistent with neoliberal sentiments and, more broadly, with a collection of forces, logics, and ways of life (Rosen and Walks 2015a, 2015b). Clearly, condo-ism complements condoization. They are not conflicting concepts but, rather, mutually reinforce a focus on different but vital aspects of the condo (i.e., development and governance). Condoization underscores a *constitutive process* that, in the spirit of Foucault, relies upon various processes, agents, technologies – and especially knowledges – to bring governing relations, and thus the condo itself, into being.

While informative and critical, these various accounts of development are perhaps less helpful in illuminating condo governance within and across the boundaries that supposedly demarcate the inside and the outside of the purview of condo buildings and corporations, though admittedly this is not their stated aim. For example, it is almost never noted in these or other accounts that condo buildings have internal forms of inequality that are represented foremost by the condo renter's presence. And, indeed, the suggestion that condoization might be equivalent to gentrification belies the fact that many condo units are now rented (see Chapter 4). This book seeks to extend and complement rather than to critique the mostly insightful and critical work detailing condo development in urban geography, which often, but not exclusively (e.g., Rosen and Walks 2013), presumes the influence of neoliberal ideology.[12] To this end, Chapter 3 shows how condo development and inner governance are not easily separable, that the latter is more relevant to understanding development than might first appear, and that development entails elements of inner condo governance.

Other work by legal scholars in Canada tends to outline the development and details of condo statutes (see Risk 1968; Harris 2011). Similar scholarship in the US usually suggests that condo governing arrangements entail excessive rule making on the part of boards and conflict between boards and owners (e.g., McCabe 2005; McKenzie 2011; Low 2003; Elberg 2001; Kim 1998; Kress 1995; McKenzie 1994; Mittelbach and Ebin 1975; see also McLellan 1978; Blandy, Dixon, and Dupuis 2006). While relevant, these accounts neglect some key features of condo governance. Condo boards and other owners are especially vital governing agents, but previous scholarship neglects to examine not only increasingly influential commercial and other private agents beyond boards but also related knowledges, technologies, processes, and logics. In other words, it neglects to explore and problematize the full range of elements that make condo governance possible. Examination of knowledges in urban governance, following Foucault's influence, is essential (Valverde 2005). As a form of urban governance, condoization relies fundamentally on knowledges from diverse sources, including the multiple processes enlisting legal, real estate, insurance, property management, and security agents – processes that, themselves, are heterogeneously constructed. These agents, and the related role of knowledge, have been missing in previous accounts of condo governance.

More broadly, almost no scholarly work has explored condo governance in North America in a theoretically engaged manner. None has approached condo governance as an assemblage of multiple agents, knowledges, processes such as commodification and securitization, and related governing logics, nor has any recognized the benefit of doing so. *Condo Conquest* seeks to begin to encourage further research along these channels and, ultimately, to bridge the gap between urban geography's focus on development and socio-legal studies' focus on legal and related private urban governance.

SOCIOLOGY OF GOVERNANCE

The chapters that follow examine condo governance using a sociology of governance approach that is loosely based upon and overlaps with the voluminous, multi-disciplinary, Foucault-inspired "governmentality" literature and its concepts, which includes a focus on knowledges and technologies (for overviews, see Hunt and Wickham 1994; Rose, O'Malley, and Valverde 2006; Dean 2010; Lippert and Stenson 2010; Walters 2012; Brady and Lippert 2016).[13] In this literature, which spans several disciplines, governance (or "government") is conceived variously as "act[ion] upon action" (Rose 1999, 4) or, more broadly, as "any attempt to control or manage any known object" (Hunt and Wickham 1994, 78).[14] Governance includes laws, policies, and strategies of public and private agents, and it targets and involves both conduct and things. Governing is not easily distinguishable from "policing," and for this reason the terms are sometimes used interchangeably (see Chapter 6). Overall, this body of research focuses on detailed practices of state governance as well as of governance by private (Rose and Miller 1992) and hybrid agents that lie beyond the state and that are neither exclusively public nor exclusively private. Many persons quoted in the following chapters – owners, board members, lawyers, and property managers – are precisely such agents. Governance is constitutive: it brings its agents and targets into being as it operates (Hunt and Wickham 1994). Governing and constituting happen at once. Governance also always involves power relations and resistance at each site of connection (Hunt and Wickham 1994, 80) among elements. And, as is shown, there are multiple forms of resistance in relation to these elements. Thus, owners have resisted some condo governance arrangements by joining associations beyond their building – typically during times of statutory reform (see Chapter 2) – and, based on interviews, do so within condo corporations and in relation to specific rules and bylaws or board actions. But inanimate objects also resist. For example, tobacco smoke can "resist" condo rules and spatial divisions when it travels through floors and walls, and its ugly remnants – cigarette butts – jump from balcony to balcony outside both the condo building envelope and the house rules (see Chapter 6); technologies such as elevators, that aid condo governance, can acquire new purposes in ways that resist the plans of boards and property managers (see Chapter 7); and condo owners – often isolated from one another and their boards – can form resistant condo owner associations across condo buildings to share common knowledge of their experiences and to encourage statutory reforms pertaining to condo governance (albeit not especially effectively) (see Chapter 8).

Assemblages, Knowledges, Logics, Technologies, and Law

Beyond condo, condoization, and governance, five other sociology of governance concepts require elaboration. Readers familiar with them may wish to proceed directly to the research procedures and data sources section. For those unfamiliar with them, it is vital to understand them before proceeding since a key aim of this book is to move beyond mere description.

The first concept is "assemblage," a fancy term that refers to a loose assortment of elements that hang together. As Hunt (2013, 71) suggests, such "elements do not necessarily constitute a system." Rather, their conjunction is presumed to be contingent and temporary. The concept of assemblage is used in sociology of governance and overlapping socio-legal (see Brady and Lippert 2016; Hunt 2013; Dean 1996), urban (Valverde 2016; Murakami Wood 2013; Farias and Bender 2010), and surveillance (Haggerty and Ericson 2000; Lyon 2007; Lippert 2009) literatures.[15] In adopting this concept, the chapters that follow gather these literatures into a space that permits a closer conversation between and among them. Assemblage is used in relation to a range of substantive areas such as urban infrastructure (Valverde 2016), forest management (Li 2007), and immigrant settlement (Lippert and Pyykkönen 2012). In urban studies the notion of assemblage permits the "study of the heterogeneous connections between objects, spaces, materials, machines, bodies, subjectivities ... that 'assemble' the city in multiple ways" (Farias 2010, 14). Similarly, regarding the topic of urban infrastructure, Valverde (2016, 200) uses "assemblage" "to dynamically study the shifting, ever-changing articulations of heterogeneous participants and interests that one finds in all governance." One distinguishing feature of assemblage is "that it links directly to a practice, to assemble" (Li 2007, 264). This book does not seek to discern and analyze all assembling practices of condo governance and condoization. Rather, its more modest aim is to identify several vital current elements, how they shift and work in concert and provide each other with mutual support, including the knowledges (especially legal knowledges) shaping and linking them; how contestation among some elements manifests itself; and how several rudiments are excluded. The concept of assemblage is chosen based on what is revealed by the empirical study of condo governance. For Valverde "assemblage" refers to "the *only partially planned combinations* of capabilities and resources that do the work of governing" (2015, 51; emphasis added). Thus, assemblages are not tantamount to grand conspiracies: they can also entail amalgams of governing logics (often called "rationalities"), such as "precautionary logic" and its obsession with catastrophic private property loss (Chapter 5) and "police" with its peculiar fixation on details of space and time (Chapter 6). Finally, assemblages can also enlist private agents and rules exemplified by condo governance. Thus, Valverde (2011, 292) notes that to fully understand urban governance *private* realms must also be considered:

> Public laws and rules did not have a monopoly on regulation, because such private actors as insurance companies also imposed rules ... lenders as well as realtors also imposed their own private but nevertheless compelling regulations ... A full genealogy of urban governance would have to include the myriad private ... regulatory structures that converged on different kinds of property owners and different kinds of properties.

This notion can be extended to condo governance, to the practices that constitute private property (see Chapter 2), and, crucially, to various other private governing agents discussed throughout this book.

A second vital concept of the sociology of governance is "knowledges." Following Foucault, governance is anticipated to be at once informed by and dependent upon types of knowledge, including legal knowledge (Rose and Valverde 1998; Hunt and Wickham 1994; see also Lippert and Walby 2014a). Knowledge is necessary to shape and inform governance, and governance carves out opportunities for knowledge production, transfer, and use. One entails the other. As noted, explicit attention to knowledges is absent in nearly all previous work on condo governance and development. Of interest here is the relation of knowledges to governing practices and how they aid the formation of assemblages. Research reveals the wide range of this relation, from real estate value assessments and myriad property manager-run software and digitized reports (Chapter 3), to images from surveillance cameras and numbers from audits that identify rule-breaking (Chapter 5), to decibel levels from devices to measure noise nuisance to settle disputes (Chapter 6) – all related to condo buildings and the conduct of residents and boards. Bruno Latour's studies of science (e.g., Latour 1993) complement the sociology of governance in their attention to knowledges (see, among others, Williams 2012; Lippert 2007; Moore 2007; Rose, O'Malley, and Valverde 2006; Rose and Miller 1992) and embrace the concept of assemblage (e.g., Brown 2006), too. These tools can enhance the study of "knowledge flows" (Valverde 2005, 422).

Analysts are thus encouraged to focus on "*process* and *flow*" and "how actors pick through documents or discourses" (Valverde 2005, 420; emphasis in original) for their own purposes. In this way the Latourian notion of "excerpting" or reducing knowledge is valuable (see Chapter 4), as is the notion of "inscription devices" that permit material things to be represented and then more easily governed (see Chapter 3). These conceptual tools help provide insights into the role of knowledge and of external private agents in condo governance, from whom knowledge is transferred, associated, and/or produced. They help reveal how knowledge can, for long periods or only for moments, assemble disparate rudiments in pursuit of common governmental aims, including during statutory law reform hearings (see Chapter 8). In addition, Latour shows, somewhat controversially, that inanimate objects are among the agents operating within assemblages and, thus, are also agents of the condo world. Examples of these things are numerous, but cigarette butts are perhaps exemplary when they manifest as nuisances requiring policing.

The third concept is law, and I give it considerable attention. But interest here, following Foucault's influence, is mostly in legal knowledge and how it emerges and flows in relation to governance and surveillance of condo inhabitants, conduct, and spaces, and less in analyzing details of fixed black-letter legal texts like Ontario's and New York State's condo statutes per se. Legal knowledge is also deemed pluralistic (see Walby 2007) and is assumed to pertain to condo building-specific house rules as well as to municipal law and to newer forms of law such as provincial human rights codes and information privacy statutes. Thus, legal knowledge refers to everyday aspects of condo governance – for example, wearing certain religious attire in common recreational areas (human rights codes) or circulating board meeting minutes that identify owners (information privacy law) (Jaglowitz 2008). Attention here is on how legal knowledge from various sources is adopted, reduced, and repurposed across assemblages, mostly using long-term renters of condo units as an example. Legal knowledge is constantly mutating, coupling with and disconnecting from other forms of governance and knowledge. It perpetually enlists and delists non-legal strategies and ways of knowing (Rose and Valverde 1998).

One specific emergent form of law in condo governance, discussed in Chapter 5 in relation to surveillance, is "counter-law" (Ericson 2007, 207; see also Levi 2009). This is a concept adapted from Foucault (1977) and that is associated with "precautionary logic" (explained below). According to Ericson

(2007), counter-law appears in two forms: counter-law I and counter-law II. The former are "laws that counter ... traditional principles, standards, and procedures" (Ericson 2007, 207). Counter-law I entails the creation of new laws or the increased use of existing legal provisions against established law to diminish those traditional principles and procedures deemed to restrict pre-empting causes of harm – in this case to the condo corporation – consistent with precaution (Ericson 2007, 24). Exemplars of such "laws" in the condo world are (1) statutory provisions for courts to assign an emergency administrator to replace a demonstrably incompetent condo board and (2) a board's "special assessments," which are imposed on owners to cover repairs to salvage a building's integrity and to quickly compensate for acute funding shortfalls. These are condo world examples of counter-law, and they are distinguished by the often drastic, exceptional (i.e., special or emergency) nature of their deployment. In recent years, the notion of the "exception" has received greater attention in socio-legal studies and beyond but not in relation to more mundane or ostensibly private realms such as condo governance (Lippert and Williams 2012). As discussed in Chapter 5, counter-law II, the deployment of surveillant assemblages, is even more relevant than counter-law I. Counter-law II "involves broader and deeper surveillant assemblages that cast widely for signs of threat in the hope of pre-empting disasters waiting to happen" (Ericson 2007, 207). More generally, the increasing influence of legal knowledge (along with condo law firms and lawyers) in condo governance as part of condoization is termed "juridification."

The fourth concept, "rationality," or "governing logic," refers to a methodical way of enacting and conceiving of governance, a broad discourse that makes governmental practices possible. Governance is seen to be shaped by logic and to take a discernible discursive form; thus, there is a focus on discourse as constitutive, though not to the neglect of actual governmental practices (Lippert and Stenson 2010). Several logics have been elaborated in overlapping governance, socio-legal, urban studies, and surveillance literatures, with by far the most work attending to variants of neoliberalism (e.g., Barry, Osborne, and Rose 1996; Larner 2000; Rose, O'Malley, and Valverde 2006; Ericson 2007; Kern 2010a; Brash 2011; Brady and Lippert 2016). This rationality concerns shifting responsibility for the governance of all aspects of urban daily life, from public authorities to private agents and an associated market of commodified solutions. This certainly resonates with the shift from public municipal government to private governance represented by condo growth (Kern 2010a), particularly when viewed from outside. Yet there is good reason to be cautious about blithely applying neoliberalism as a rationality (or even as an ideology[16]) to condoization and related trends. Thus, the influential governmentality scholar, Pat O'Malley (2017, vi), has recently remarked that the

> master variable "neoliberalism" ... was used to explain almost every disliked political change since 1970 and which has turned out to be, at best, a kind of greasy, portmanteau term: hard to pin down and carrying a lot of hidden baggage. Such broad concepts and visions may be useful at first, when certain changes need highlighting and outlining, but they become a hindrance once it becomes necessary to focus analysis to gain theoretical and political traction with specific developments. (See also Lippert and Brady 2016)

The notion of neoliberalism may well be initially useful, but one such "specific development" concerns mutation in condo governance, and, in closely examining it, this book argues that the more mundane, older "police" logic is also relevant. "Police" is a rationality, or governing logic, highlighted both in Foucault's writings and in the sociology of governance literature that draws from them. In the latter, "police" often appears as the expired antecedent of early liberalism (e.g., Hunt and Wickham 1994; Miller and Rose 2008, 33), thus acting as a foil to Foucault's account of liberal governmentality (see Walters 2012, 28) and as a type of state power (Novak 1996). The exploration of "police" in condo arrangements shows that this logic is present not only in municipal or other state forms but also in the nominally private condo world. Earlier versions of "police" in Europe embraced the "utopian dream that all regions of the social body could be penetrated, known and directed by political authorities," but they were "abandoned" with the rise of liberalism, which backed away from such direct intervention (Miller and Rose 2008, 33). However, based upon the discovery of how nuisances are policed in condo spaces, that dream is plainly not dead, no matter how often one is awakened after 11:00 p.m. by a condo neighbour's noise. Foucault notes an early tether between "police" and the urban. Thus, he remarks in his "Security, Territory, Population" lectures, reflecting on the eighteenth-century writings of Domat, that "to police and to urbanize is the same thing" (Foucault 2007, 336). These Foucauldian reflections are suggestive for urban governance assemblages because they hint that if "police" is decidedly urban, and the condo is saturated with this logic, then so is the condo. "Police," in Foucault's sense, may be an integral part of condo governance and condoization (see also Rosen and Walks 2013), and what can be discerned through its study may be revealing of contemporary urban governance arrangements and urban futures more broadly.

Another specific development related to notions of "counter-law" is the newer "precautionary logic" (Ericson 2007). Risk avoidance is discussed in relation to private insurance in condo governance and has neoliberal variants, but precautionary logic carries this emphasis further. This latter logic presumes "worst case scenarios and form[s] ... around merely imagined disasters" (O'Malley 2017, v). It is a logic of uncertainty that presupposes a limit on the ability of science and technology to produce reliable knowledge about risk, and it may be emerging in the condo world. Precautionary logic and risk avoidance are associated with neoliberalism. But again, there is more uncovered about condo governance in this book than can be made intelligible by invoking neoliberalism. Put simply, neoliberalism in the condo world is "just one thing among other things" (Collier 2012, 191).

The fifth and final concept is "technology of government" (see Rose, O'Malley, and Valverde 2006; Lippert 2010; Dean 1996). Such technologies may range from "inscription devices," such as mundane maps (Blomley 2004), statistics (Hacking 1991), signage (Hermer and Hunt 1996; Lippert 2009), and digitized reports, to elaborate mobile spatial technologies such as high-rise elevators. As a key element of urban life, the mundane elevator has received only limited scholarly attention (see, e.g., Hirschauer 2005; Graham and Hewitt 2012; Bernard 2014). Little is known, for example, about how the elevator is governed and its functions within "skyscraper geography" (McNeill 2005). The elevator may have been overlooked because, as Graham and Hewitt (2012, 72) remark, urban studies has tended to deploy an "overly flat discourse" that neglects verticality. There remains a need to critically examine technologies of this "Z axis" in urban governance (Skayannis 2010), including in condo high-rises – vertically arranged complexes that entail unique governing arrangements.

These technologies are presumed to articulate with logics but are not permanently tethered to them on a one-to-one basis (Valverde 1996). A technology can articulate with different governing logics, depending on time and place, to activate and make governable subjects and spaces amenable to programming of one kind or another. With little justification, technologies of government have often been neglected in the sociology of governance (Lippert 2010), and the condo provides an excellent opportunity to explore the role of the elevator in urban governance.

RESEARCH PROCEDURES AND DATA SOURCES

Condo Conquest adopts a triangulation research strategy (see Singleton and Straits 2010, 431–34; Moran-Ellis et al. 2006; Miles and Huberman 1994) involving various methods, data sources, and data types compatible with the interrogation of governing assemblages (see Lippert and Stenson 2010; Valverde 2005; Hunt and Wickham 1994). While much research effort centred on interviews with owners and board members in two major North American cities and, to a lesser extent, condo industry representatives, triangulation meant that other methods were necessarily employed and other sources and data types generated and drawn upon. To investigate condo governance, beginning in 2006, intensive empirical research was conducted in the Greater Toronto Area (which includes the cities of Mississauga and Brampton and other immediate suburbs) and, much more extensively, from 2012 to 2016, both there and in Ontario as well as in New York City and New York State. Interviewees included current or former condo board members, property managers contracted to manage condo buildings, and other industry representatives in Toronto and owners and board members in New York. Because these condo buildings and owners are known to vary, beginning in 2012 I sought to interview owners and board members from buildings of varying sizes (those with fewer than 150 units, and those with more than 150 units) and units of varying values (some units valued at more and some less than CDN$600,000 in Toronto and units valued at more and some less than US$800,000 in New York, as reported by owners) to ensure inclusion of a variety of condo owners and buildings. Most interviews were generated through letters mailed to owners and board members from thirty-two such condo buildings identified through tax rolls in Toronto and via snowball sampling for other owners, board members, and industry representatives (or service providers), which resulted in 160 interviews in total. Industry representatives included condo lawyers, accountants, architects, property managers, security personnel, and real estate agents. It was discovered that these are not mutually exclusive categories: owners are of course sometimes board members and both are not infrequently also key agents of the condo industry. Owners, board members, and industry representatives are not homogenous groups and thus it is important to note that interviewees included men and women more or less equally and reflected Toronto's, and to a lesser extent New York's, ethnic diversity. Interviewees also varied by age, sexual orientation, and, to a lesser extent (since property ownership tends to exclude lower-income groups), class. These wide-ranging, open-focused (or semi-structured) interviews revealed numerous aspects of condo governance and living, such as reasons for purchasing a condo unit, relations with board members and other residents, use of legal knowledge, and everyday problems in buildings (such as nuisances). Together they provide an intimate look at condo governance and living that is unavailable through documents or other sources. What emerged as key topics, including renters, surveillance, and elevators, were not specifically targeted in interviews; rather, they emerged during the analysis of interviews and other textual data obtained from owners and board members. To be properly researched, some of these topics (e.g., surveillance and elevators) required the use of other documentary sources. Interviews with condo industry representatives, including insurance, property management, security, and law firm representatives, focused on their roles and associated knowledges in condo governance. To ensure anonymity and mask condo building locations and names of specific commercial firms and condo industry representatives throughout, interviewees are designated with pseudonyms. They are further designated by city ("TO" or "NYC") and by whether they are a board member ("Board"), resident owner ("Res."), or have condo-specific expertise ("Real Estate," "Lawyer," "Architect," "Manager"). These designations reveal interviewees' locations in condo assemblages.

As important as interviews to understanding condo governance was the collection and analysis of a wide array and sizable volume of documents. Included are documents from condo buildings, such as declarations, bylaws, rules, newsletters, and meeting minutes. Other documents are more broadly focused on condo governance and particular aspects of condoization, such as those from condo owner association or advocacy websites, condo newsletters, legal decisions, developers, condo insurance, property management, developer firm marketing materials and publications, condo law newsletters, condo law review submissions, broader condo industry publications (such as *Condo Business*), media accounts, statutes, case law, and numerous items produced by and relevant to condo governance mostly in Toronto but also in New York. These documents provided detailed insight into condo governance and overlapping processes involving property management, law, real estate, insurance, and security firms and agents. I also went to two major annual condo industry conferences attended by lawyers, insurance personnel, property managers, and a few owners. Additionally, I examined media coverage of lawmakers' debates over Ontario's first condo legislation in the 1960s and non-governmental groups and individuals' submissions and debates (i.e., the written record of the Ontario legislature known as *Hansard*) concerning the earliest (1977) and latest (2013) statutory reforms as well as accompanying reviews. These reviews are the distillation of discourses about condo governance; in governance terms they are "programmatic" (Rose and Miller 1992) and not parochial. The submissions were acquired through a Freedom of Information (FOI) request of the Ontario government ministry overseeing the review of the province's condo statute, yielding more than a thousand pages of owner, board member, and industry representatives' submissions to Ontario's legal review processes. Not normally released to the public or researchers, FOI requests have recently proven to be a valuable qualitative research method (e.g., Walby and Lippert 2011, 2015; Lippert and Walby 2014b).

I also acquired and analyzed the "bill jackets" that accompanied condo law reforms in New York State at various junctures since that statute's inception in 1964 as well as the current bill (A6941) to introduce a condo ombudsperson (New York Senate 2012). Further, I collected and thematically categorized a major condo industry organization's member internet "discussion board" and "condo advice" columns in Toronto's two major daily newspapers featuring experts' responses to governance questions from board members and unit owners from 2005 onward. The same was done for a major condo owner association's "discussion board" (comprising owner and board member postings from condo buildings in Toronto from 2008 to 2012) and an anonymous "board talk" discussion board, which collected owner and board member postings from New York during 2014 and 2015. I organized and thematically coded the interviews and documents using N-vivo analysis software. While I did not use N-vivo analysis exclusively, it provided an efficient means of organizing what became a small mountain of qualitative data from diverse sources and aided the ability to discern commonalities and trends across data sources and types consistent with triangulation.

Though these research procedures were undertaken for both Toronto and New York, it is vital to underscore at the outset that condo governance in the two cities is not systematically compared in what follows, as laudable as such an effort might be. Rather, my aim is to explore condo governance by drawing on relevant data from at least two major North American cities. Owing partially to the high cost and challenging logistics of securing interviews in New York,[17] more interviews were conducted and far more industry information was collected in Toronto. Thus, Toronto should be understood as the primary context of the research and New York as a significant supplemental context. The provincial or state statute overseeing condo governance in each city developed slightly differently. The inquiry in Ontario included provincial statutes and the wider condo industry in addition to municipal law and local condo building governance, whereas the inquiry in New York was limited primarily to the municipal and condo building level, along with limited attention to the content and reform of New York State's condo statute. The analyses that follow reflect these different foci. Yet remarkably similar issues and elements of condo governance were identified in both cities. *Condo Conquest* focuses on these similarities and draws on owners' and board members' rich accounts of condo living from both cities. In doing so, the book suggests a wider relevance to the condo world beyond Toronto and New York.

Having discussed the approach, key concepts, methods, and data sources deployed in this book, it is now time to turn to condo statute emergence and condo growth in Toronto and Ontario and in New York City and New York State.

CONDO EMERGENCE AND GROWTH

The condo continues to grow in numbers and significance in major North American cities. This section describes the emergence of condo statutes and increasing prevalence of the condo in Canada and the United States and, specifically, in Toronto/Ontario and New York City/State.

Canada: Ontario and Toronto

In Canada, the first provincial condo legislation, the Strata Property Act, appeared in British Columbia in 1966, and this is also likely where the first condo building in Canada was constructed. By 1969, the most populated Canadian provinces had condo statutes in place, and, in 1977, with its introduction in Prince Edward Island, this was true of all provinces (see Table 1.1).

Canada has seen recent rapid condoization (see Table 1.2). In Canada, by 1996 there were half a million condo units (Canada Mortgage and Housing Corporation 2012), and by 2016 this had almost quadrupled to nearly 1.9 million units (Statistics Canada 2017a). Condo units are also growing as a proportion of all Canadian housing. In 1996, condo units represented 5 percent and in 2016 more than 13 percent of all housing units. Condo units as a proportion of all housing in Canadian cities increased by almost 17 percent in the last five years alone (Statistics Canada 2017a). Of the major Canadian cities, Toronto (445,650) and Vancouver (293,765) are now the most condoized,

TABLE 1.1 Provincial condo statutes

Canadian province	Year
British Columbia (Strata Property Act)	1966
Alberta (Condominium Property Act)	1966
Ontario (Condominium Act)	1967
Manitoba (Condominium Act)	1968
Saskatchewan (Condominium Property Act)	1968
New Brunswick (Condominium Property Act)	1969
Quebec (Code Civil du Québec)	1969
Nova Scotia (Condominium Act)	1971
Newfoundland and Labrador (Condominium Act)	1975
Prince Edward Island (Condominium Act)	1977

Note: The Canadian territories also now have condo statutes.

TABLE 1.2 Condo units in Canada in millions, selected years

	Total housing units	Total condo units
1996	10.8 (100%)	0.51 (4.8%)
2001	11.6 (100%)	0.67 (6.0%)
2011	13.3 (100%)	1.6 (12.1%)
2016	14.1 (100%)	1.9 (13.3%)

Sources: Statistics Canada (2011); Canada Mortgage and Housing Corporation (2012).

closely followed by Montreal (276,455) and then Calgary (113,055), Edmonton (99,590), and Ottawa (74,830) (Statistics Canada 2017a).

Ontario borrowed heavily from US condo legislation in drafting its first condo statute, passed in 1967 (Skaburskis 1984). Like several other major North American cities in the 1960s, Toronto was experiencing an affordable housing shortage, and condo legislation was thought to encourage "empty nesters" to purchase condo units and to exit single-family detached dwellings so that the latter could be bought and occupied by younger families. This rationale is evident in media accounts at the time (see *Toronto Star* 1967; Wills 1967; Farrell 1966). The assumption, too, was that, as the urban population "greyed" and affordable urban space dwindled, more elderly Ontarians would seek condo units over larger detached dwellings. Condo buildings were thus assumed to be a more efficient use of urban space (Nelson 2005, 40).

There was a sense of urgency in the debate about the first condo statute in the Ontario legislature. James Renwick (elected member for Riverdale) remarked:

> So far as I can tell from the reading of the law on condominium ... there is very little difference in the proposed law of condominium than there was in the law which was introduced in one or two other provinces in Canada and elsewhere in the world ... We cannot wait ... eight or nine years ... for ... the Law Reform Commission ... or wherever the studies have taken place, to bring themselves up to date in matters of law which are well known and well established and functioning efficiently in a jurisdiction such as New York State across the lake. (Ontario 1967a, 1725–26)

At the time, in the Ontario legislature the doubtful opposition member also asked whether the sitting government had evidence of the condo's success in responding to urban housing shortages: "Or have we begun to adopt willy-nilly whatever particular *fad and fashion* has begun to seep through the common law jurisdictions by way of adaptation ... in ... the faint hope that it will in some way assist in solving the immediate crisis in the province of Ontario?" (Ontario 1967b, 1928; emphasis added). Whatever the effects, the condo was soon to far surpass a "fad and fashion." It could scarcely be imagined that, fifty years later, the condo would comprise nearly *one-quarter* of all residential housing in Canada's largest city, enjoy a new dominance in New York (partially at the expense of the long-established cooperative), and have an expanding industry comprising myriad condo-specific firms rising around or, perhaps more accurately, growing deep inside the condo's workings and traversing its exterior walls.

In 1967, as Renwick suggested in the Ontario legislature, the New York State condo statute was deemed successful "across the lake" (i.e., Lake Ontario). But a remaining area of concern in Ontario was whether the Canadian federal government, via the Canada Mortgage and Housing Corporation, would provide insurance for condo mortgages (i.e., whether the state would backstop condo developers and, as time went on, indirectly backstop the emerging condo industry too). Noteworthy at the birth of Ontario's statute is the fact that the burgeoning cooperative housing alternative (see Schill, Voicu, and Miller 2007) to individual detached housing, popular in New York, was framed in media and legislative discussion as the condo's ability to justify reassigning some financial risk from a collectively owned arrangement to individual owners (e.g., *Toronto Star* 1967; Wills 1967; Farrell 1966). Thus, the condo was claimed to be less financially risky for Ontario owners than the cooperative, and this was especially vital because, at this point, the federal government's Canada

Mortgage and Housing Corporation decided to mimic the US Federal Housing Administration's mortgage insurance provision (see below) for condo purchases in Canada (see Romney 1974; Rosenberg 1972; Risk 1968; Ferrer and Stecher 1967). Condo law's emergence in Canada in the 1960s was fuelled by this transfer of the financial risk posed by this new form of private ownership to governments and individual owners. Ontario's first condo statute was a short piece of legislation, numbering but a few standard pages. Shortly after passage, the first Ontario condo arrangement, a modest townhouse complex, was erected in Brampton (a Toronto suburb) in January 1968 (Davies 1969). On its fortieth birthday in 2008 it was celebrated in an article in the *Toronto Star:* "The 37 two-story townhouses built by Bramalea Consolidated Developments comprising Peel Condominium 1, were registered on Dec. 27, 1967 with the first owners moving in a month later. Monthly maintenance fees were $27" (Hanes 2008). By 2013 there were some 600,000 condo units in which 1.3 million Ontarians resided, the majority in Toronto (Canada's Public Policy Forum 2013c).

Due to their supposed more efficient use of space, condo buildings have since become particularly useful with regard to densifying urban areas like Toronto. Lehrer, Keil, and Kipfer (2010, 84) explain that condo development befits Ontario's provincial plan to intensify urban areas throughout Toronto so as to reduce urban sprawl. Here condo development, and especially the condo high-rise, is seen as positively contributing to densification.

Toronto has experienced an explosion of condo development over the past two decades (Kern 2010a; Rosen and Walks 2013) (see Table 1.3). In 1996, Toronto had slightly over 86,000 condo units, or 9.5 percent of total city housing, and by 2016 this had grown to a staggering 445,650 units, representing a remarkable 21 percent of all housing in the city. The development between 2001 and 2016 shows rapid proliferation and, if trends continue, suggests

TABLE 1.3 Condo units in Toronto in thousands, selected years

	Total housing units	Total condo units
1996	903.5 (100%)	86.3 (9.5%)
2001	943.1 (100%)	108.3 (11.5%)
2011	1,989.7 (100%)	371.8 (18.7%)
2016	2,135.9 (100%)	445.7 (20.9%)

Sources: Statistics Canada (2011, 2017a); Canada Mortgage and Housing Corporation (2012).

the condo's even greater future significance (see Statistics Canada 2017a). Lehrer, Keil, and Kipfer (2010, 84) assert that condo growth in Toronto underwent two spurts, one of which was from 1970 to about 1980, the other of which commenced at the end of the 1990s and continued through 2010, a year during which *at least* 240 new condo high-rises were under construction (McMahon 2014). This surge has continued. Toronto's downtown core and adjacent areas are now not inappropriately labelled "Condo Land" (Preville 2014). But this is not a term of endearment since rapid growth has accompanied media exposés of questionable condo building construction and, to a lesser extent, governance issues related to newer high-rise condo buildings (McMahon 2014; Preville 2014). Simultaneously, the comparative volume of affordable housing available in Toronto continues to dwindle (Florida 2014), with little or no new public or social or regular rental housing emerging in the past two decades.

The size of condo complexes has been rising in Toronto as well.[18] As one Toronto property manager involved with condo buildings since 1993 related: "Now you are getting new condos with twelve hundred people or more. So the idea of large has changed. My definition of large would be three hundred to four hundred [units]" (TO Manager 5). Based upon systematic quantitative analysis of a major condo real estate website that provides information about size and building date of condo buildings and units in Toronto (condos.ca), from 1996 to 2016 the number of condo units per building based on year of construction has been consistently mounting. Thus, in buildings erected in 1996, the average number of units was slightly more than one hundred (already nearly three times the number found in the 1968 condo townhouse in Brampton noted above). By 2006, the number of units per buildings from that year was a bit more than two hundred, and buildings built in 2016 averaged almost three hundred units, almost triple the number in only twenty years. This analysis also revealed, perhaps unsurprisingly, that the average square footage of units has been consistently decreasing. This change to more smaller units per building over time is discussed in later chapters, but suffice to say here that this developmental shift is connected not only to new developer and densification strategies but also to a concurrent growth in the capacity of governing agents and knowledges beyond boards to govern the expanding number of condo inhabitants and spaces. This essential capacity, what Foucault would call a "condition of possibility," is almost never acknowledged in accounts of condo development, which tend to grant agency in fueling condoization almost exclusively to developers and public governments.

United States: New York State and New York City

In the US, Keith Romney (later called the "father of condominiums") helped draft the first continental US legislation in Utah in 1960 and served as the developer's lawyer for its first offspring, a condo complex adapted from a planned cooperative called "Graystone Manor" in Salt Lake City (Benson 2012). In 1961, the US Federal Housing Administration (FHA) used a 1958 condo statute from Puerto Rico to draft model legislation for adoption by US states (see Nelson 2005, 40). Puerto Rico had earlier encountered a shortage of housing, high housing costs, and land scarcity. The first two of these trends was emerging in several US cities. But as vital for the condo's spread in the US were the lobbying efforts of Puerto Rican businesspersons and professionals during US Congressional hearings (Christensen and Levinson 2003). Despite condo legislation enacted in Puerto Rico, a bank mortgage for a condo unit was still difficult for average Puerto Ricans to obtain (Berger 1963). The delegation therefore encouraged Congress to arrange for the US federal government to insure mortgages for would-be condo owners (Christensen and Levinson 2003). Congress passed section 234 of the National Housing Act to insure loans for condo units (Nelson 2005, 40), meaning the US government would now backstop the financial risk created by this largely unproven form of property. This helped fuel condoization.

Following model condo legislation and the insuring of mortgages by the FHA, the condo proliferated across the US at a breathtaking rate. Condo legislation had been introduced in almost all US states by 1967 (Nelson 2005, 40). By 1980, the number of condo units in the US had reached 2.1 million (Adams 1987). By 2011, the number had more than quadrupled to 9.4 million units (ten times the number of "cooperatives" in the US). Between 1991 and 2013, the number had increased by over 5.5 million (United States Census Bureau 1991a, 2013a). In 2013, condo units represented over 7.6 percent of all housing units in the US (US Census Bureau 2013a) (see Table 1.4). New York is among the major US cities with the most condo units (270,900 units), ranking third behind Miami (585,900) and Chicago (415,700). These three are followed by other metropolitan areas like Detroit (144,800), Seattle (131,800), and Houston (87,300) (United States Census Bureau 2013a).

New York State's first condo statute was passed in the state legislature in 1964, three years before Ontario's (*Chapter 82, An Act to Amend the Real Property law or Condominium Act as Article 9-B*). But, like Ontario's statute, it was a pithy sixteen standard pages in the "Laws of New York, 1964" and similarly mostly laid out definitions (section 339e), such as what constitutes

TABLE 1.4 Condo units in the United States in millions, selected years

	Total housing units	Total condo units
1996	105.7 (100%)	4.5 (4.2%)
2001	119.1 (100%)	5.9 (5.0%)
2011	132.4 (100%)	9.4 (7.1%)
2013	132.8 (100%)	10.1 (7.6%)

Source: US Census Bureau (2004, 2013a).

"common elements" (section 339e, 3), the potential content of bylaws (including provisions for election and removal of board members), and potential responses to owners who fail to comply with bylaws and rules (section 339j). Almost immediately amendments commenced. One of the first enacted was an exception to condo bylaws and rules concerning flying a specific *size* of American flag, suggestive of the attention condo governance paid to detail (in this instance to a building's aesthetics). This gradual growth in detail of condo statutes is evident in other jurisdictions too; for example, Florida's first statute was only six pages in 1963, but, by 2005, it had increased almost eight times to forty-seven pages (Nelson 2005, 44).

Even by December 1965, a year after passage of New York State's first condo statute, mortgage financing for condo units was still via "conventional loans" provided by a bank in Brooklyn, despite available FHA insurance elsewhere (Ennis 1965). But New York City, like Toronto, nonetheless experienced significant condoization after 1965 when FHA insurance began to be adopted. Manhattan's first condo complex was, "the Saint-Tropez ... built in 1965 at 340 East 64 Street. It was not well received and took a while to sell (because people felt much more comfortable with the cooperative housing form)" (Schill, Voicu, and Miller 2007, 278). The Saint-Tropez was the first high-rise in its area, with three hundred units. Broadly speaking, it mirrored the size and style of condo buildings that emerged in the 2000s and 2010s in both Toronto and New York more than it did New York condo buildings that eventually became such – many through conversions rather than "new-build" – through the 1970s and 1980s (Schill, Voicu, and Miller 2007). While many condo buildings in New York are a result of conversion, a condo owner recently remarked: "Now you see more and more buildings that are built as condos right from the beginning" (NYC Res. 11). While New York was associated more with the cooperative than with the condo, and the former predated the latter's growth, by 2007 it was already being claimed that "the primacy of the cooperative apartment in New York has shown some signs of erosion in recent years ...

From 1998 to 2001, 9,743 condo units were built compared to only 349 cooperative apartments" (Schill et al. 2007, 280). More than a thousand rental housing and cooperative units also converted to condo arrangements during that period (Schill et al. 2007, 280n). By 2007, there had emerged a "dominance of condos ... in New York City in new construction" (Schill et al. 2007, 280). Schill et al. (2007, 281) suggest why this shift occurred in New York:

> The different legal status of condominiums and cooperatives (fee simple ownership v. ownership of shares in a corporation) is accompanied by different financing structures. The purchaser of a condominium unit typically borrows money to finance the acquisition and grants its lender a mortgage secured by the real property ... [But] the owner of a cooperative apartment typically makes periodic payments on two separate debt obligations – her own mortgage and her ratable share of the building's mortgage, whereas the condominium owner pays only one mortgage loan. Interest on all of the mortgage loans ... is deductible from income taxes under the Internal Revenue Code.

A condo owner in New York, however, suggested that his choice of a condo unit over a cooperative unit had partially to do with governing arrangements and that a condo board had less rather than more power over the investment, thus making a condo unit more attractive:

> In a condo you can sell the unit without a co-op approval so you're not dependent on the ... board to sell your unit in case you need to sell it. So, you feel a little more in control of your finances. Also, if you want to be financed, the board and the condo doesn't have control. So [regarding] the problems between me and the board in this building, at least I don't think it affects that part of my investment. (NYC Res. 12)

This also means it is easier and faster for owners to purchase and sell their units, which is not necessarily conducive to forming a longer-term sense of community. By 2015, the long-standing dominance of the cooperative over the condo in New York had ended, with the condo now representing 6.7 percent and the cooperative only representing 6.3 percent of residential dwellings in this city (United States Census Bureau 2018). While previously the proportion of condo units had been well below the US national average in New York, by 2015, with the proportion of condo units at 6.7 percent, this was no longer

TABLE 1.5 Condo units in New York in thousands, selected years

	Total housing units	Total condo units
1991	4,158.1 (100%)	118.7 (2.9%)
2004	4,849.8 (100%)	217.4 (4.5%)
2015	7,351.2 (100%)	493.2 (6.7%)

Note: The American Housing Survey statistics for 2013 for New York are not directly comparable with 2015 due to addition of urban areas to the New York category. For this reason, 2013 was left out of the table.
Source: US Census Bureau (1991b, 2004, 2013b, 2018).

the case (United States Census Bureau 2018). In New York, the number of condo units increased by 200,000 between 1991 and 2013. In 2015, of the more than 7 million total housing units in the New York metro area, 493,000 were condo units. These represented 6.7 percent of all housing compared to 4.5 percent in 2004 and 2.9 percent in 1991 (United States Census Bureau, 1991b, 2004, 2013b) (see Table 1.5).

SCOPE, SECESSION, AND COMPLEXITY

As significant as the mounting number of condo complexes in Toronto, New York, and beyond is the scope of the condo's governance of urban life. As the size of condo buildings has grown, so too has the scope of condo governance. Buildings now variously include provision of physical security, concierge services, water, electricity, waste disposal, recreation (tennis and basketball courts, party rooms, libraries, swimming pools), and transportation, traditionally associated with municipal governments,[19] as well as intensive rule-making and enforcement, financial management, and related planning for future infrastructure repair, modification, and replacement of commonly owned elements. This remarkable scope led two of the few scholars who have studied condo governance in North America to suggest, already twenty years ago, that it was something of a separate "level" of governance (Barton and Silverman 1994). Yet this book shows how condo governance draws on an emergent private condo industry and attendant knowledges and technologies as well as on forms of public law and court enforcement. Condo governance is constitutive of developments far beyond condo edifices themselves. In showing this, *Condo Conquest* complicates understanding condo governance as merely a "level" of governance. The scope of condo governance in providing services that are normally the realm of municipal governments raises the spectre of secession – that is, whether these private governments can secede from municipal governments entirely or, at least, whether they have been granted too much leeway to displace public government and service delivery. There is some evidence of a secessionist tendency in the US regarding gated communities (see Levi 2009), which often entail condo arrangements, but it can also be glimpsed in a tentative move in a Toronto suburb where condo owners are decrying what they call "double taxation" (see Chapter 8) as they are being asked to pay both condo common fees and municipal taxes for services.

CONCLUSION

Given the growing importance of the condo and its governance to the contemporary urban imaginary and their connection to issues spanning several research literatures it is perhaps surprising that they have received so little scholarly attention. *Condo Conquest* takes up this challenge by examining condo governance in Toronto and New York, two cities with among the highest condo proportions on the continent and that continue to experience significant condo growth. The book uses a sociology of governance approach, which, as its name suggests, is first and foremost about governance. Yet it considers governance broadly to include the role of agents and knowledges not always associated with it (or even located in a condo building) as well as the vital roles of other interconnected elements that ultimately form an assemblage.

2

Condo Owners and Boards

> All these condos ... they're not designed for end users; they're designed for investors. So obviously condos are cookie cutter and ... designed by numbers and they're almost treated like a commodity rather than like a place to live because it's bought and sold just like stock.
>
> – *TO BOARD 2|ARCHITECT*

> I don't really know who's on the board except for this one woman. It seems to be ... very well run ... they hired good people ... like the doorman ... so it seems like they did a good job in selecting and managing them. And then they keep our fees very low ... compared to other buildings.
>
> – *NYC RES. 1*

The two traditional agents of condo governance are owners and the boards they comprise. These two are typically presumed, both in condo statutes and outside the condo world in North America, to be, respectively, the governed and the governors of condo buildings. This chapter looks at two types of owners that have emerged in condo discourse: the resident owner and the non-resident owner. The importance of discerning the temporal fluidity of motivations and positions of condo ownership should not be understated. Much previous work in this realm (Skaburskis 1984; Nelson 2005, 44–45) is limited to providing static snapshots of condo buyers' motivations and does not acknowledge discursive shifts. This division into two types of agent has had profound, rarely acknowledged consequences for condo governance and life, and it is common to condo corporations across North America (and likely globally). A key consequence of this division is that it has additionally created the "condo renter" category (see Chapter 4) that has emerged hand-in-hand with the non-resident owner. Another effect of this division is that non-resident owners, alongside condo commercial firms, have become a condo conqueror and, as such, unlike the renter (upon whose revenue they rely), tend to avoid blame when condo governance challenges arise. Their emergence hardens the notion of the condo as a commodified property rather than as a community. Other implications include the rise of non-resident pressure to initiate unsustainable low maintenance fees; the possibility that non-resident owners might forcibly dissolve the condo corporation to profit from the sale; and how board membership is voted upon. Finally, this chapter considers boards and elaborates upon how owners relate to them (ranging from trust to distrust to conflict) as well as upon organized owner pressure for statutory reform.

TWO TYPES OF OWNERS

Governance arrangements anticipate that the condo owner will dutifully pay monthly common fees, follow myriad rules, be concerned about the building's and unit's property values, and attend the statute-mandated annual general meeting (AGM) of owners. Based mostly upon interviews, it seems that presently in many condo buildings owners are not necessarily expected to relate with other owners as though in a community, other than when they are serving on the board, which is not a common goal of most owners. This is true both for the resident owner (or "owner-occupier") and the non-resident owner, a key division that underscores that reasons for buying into the condo world vary over time and not simply with the ups and downs of urban real estate markets. But even within the resident owner category, along with growing commodification there may be a move towards seeing the condo unit as an investment rather than as a residential community.

Resident Owners[1]

Especially in the early condo years, the resident owner category was absent from condo governance discourse. Resident owners enter the condo world by purchasing units, often to downsize from a detached larger dwelling. As one owner explained: "I decided to live in a condo because I'm sort of a typical sell-the-house-kids-have-moved-on [person] ... it was time to sell the house and we had lived in a condo before so we knew that to downsize we wanted to go to a condo" (TO Res. 1). For another resident, the reduction of space associated with a condo is deemed to come with a decrease in "stress" consistent with the notion that the condo offers "care-free" living:

> That's when I decided you can't live in a house, you have to live in a condo because ... [it will be] less stressful ... so in the end the decision was to downsize, live in a condo. We chose this specific type of condo where all the amenities and utilities are built into the management fees. (TO Res. 2)

For an owner who became a board member, the condo as downsized dwelling promised reduced "labour," and, interestingly, it was thought that the collective nature of governance would "take away" responsibility, again suggesting a care-free lifestyle:

> It's a part of stage of life thing ... the children have grown up and graduated and have their own families. I came to the point of retirement and we started planning about a year or so before that to downsize. We were overhoused. We wanted to pick a certain kind of condo. We didn't want to go from a single-family dwelling to a twenty-story model ... It had some of the things we wanted ... a little back garden, it has an exercise room, and we liked the design of it ... so we said we could ... live there ... We did it in part because of the labour involved with a house. Snow removal, you know just a ton of stuff. And here I thought it would be collectivized and the responsibility [taken] away ... from us. (TO Board 1)

Others purchased condo units because they were without the finances to buy a detached house in Toronto or New York – to "upsize" – in the first place. One such owner chose a condo unit after leaving a house following a marital separation:

> This choice as I said was because of a separation and it wasn't because I chose to leave, but I mean being a single person, living in a condo, as I said I couldn't afford a house and these were very affordable at the time, they're

still very affordable, unfortunately, they haven't gone up at all. There's no comparison really. (TO Board 3)

A younger owner explained that she lived "in a condo because I couldn't afford a house and ... because it was cheaper than anywhere else downtown and because ... it's an old building so it had more space" (TO Res. 3). Another owner explained why she chose a condo over a cooperative, which, as noted previously, is considered a viable alternative in New York but not in Toronto: "We had the sense that condos had less rules ... so that was sort of a plus but ... we just wanted the location, the price fit our budget at the time ... the feel of the building, and the apartment itself" (NYC Res. 2).

Investment in condo units as commodities can be consistent with financialization, which may be defined as a process whereby "personal finance becomes ... how life is to be lived" (Martin 2002, 17). More broadly, Walks (2014, 33) argues that financialization "entails monetization of various commodities, processes, and flows and their transformation into liquid tradable financial assets."[2] For investors, condo units are becoming more closely associated with this process, and commodification pertaining to the condo is taken up in more detail in Chapter 3, but here what is discussed is how such investment is considered by resident owners. Many decisions by both resident and non-resident owner types are informed, shaped, and made possible by knowledge provided by real estate agents.

Resident owners, like non-resident owners, also talk about their condo units as investments. While the non-resident owner is principally concerned with a condo building's suitability for investment, some resident owners see their purchase partially as an investment consistent with commodification. The latter notion is nicely captured by this resident owner: "It is the first real estate property we've ever owned, I think that does change your relationship to your home and you think about it differently ... as an investment in addition to a home" (NYC Res. 6). Another related: "It has become an investment. I believe everyone who purchased lived in it initially ... but some have moved out and continued to rent them" (NYC Res. 15). Another New York owner suggested personal reasons combined with the condo as an investment: "Say if you're leaving the country for a few years on a work assignment, I would have been able to rent it out. So it's the convenience. And when I saw the space ... I just loved the layout of it. So that was ... more personal reasons. But I thought it was a good investment" (NYC Res. 3). Another Toronto owner claimed his purchase of a condo unit was plainly an investment, one that would have a value that would "always maintain itself" due to location rather than, for example, anything to do with its governance (which initially tended to be absent from rationales):

> I wanted to make an investment ... a real estate purchase, and I chose this building because first of all it was new and secondly because it backs on to a cemetery so nobody can build behind it so I knew that the value would always maintain itself because it's pretty private and also the location is very desirable. It's close to the subway, close to Yonge Street, major shopping areas, location. (TO Res. 4)

But sometimes investment was not the initial intention of a non-resident owner, which suggests that the distinction between the two types of owners is not always permanent. As one owner recounted: "I haven't actually lived in it, it's an investment. The intention initially when purchased was to move in but things changed so ... it's been rented on a couple of occasions (TO Res. 6). Overall, the resident owner is currently imagined as at least a small-scale investor; but that is not necessarily her or his central motivation for becoming a condo owner. This is not true of the non-resident owner.

Non-Resident Owners

As a brief to Ontario's latest statutory review related: "Owners are ... buying into the condo scene as an investment [and] may become a landlord by leasing the unit and eventually sell[ing] the unit at a profit" (Condo Briefs 2012). One key condo conqueror is the non-resident owner. One board member explained further:

> When condos became huge, developers said: "Whoa, we have a problem here, because we want to sell to everybody. We don't just want to sell to a family. We want to sell to what they call investors." So you can buy a unit, a two-bedroom unit, and put ... different, unrelated people in there. It's rented ... So it opens up the pool of potential buyers. (TO Board 4)

Another board member, who was also a condo architect in Toronto, related:

> That's a bad problem right now because [for] a great number of the units being sold ... the purchasers are investors ... so there is [sic] a lot of investors coming in here ... who have the money [and] want to get their money out

> of their country and this is ... one of the best places in the world to invest. (TO Board 5/Architect)

A resident from New York contrasted sheer investment with the building additionally being a "home":

> I would say: "Is there anyone in this room who thinks that the objectives of the sponsor are the same as the objectives of us? Is there anyone here who thinks they are the same?" An investor wants to make money. He wants to derive a profit from his rents each month. We're here because this is our own. It's our investment also but ... it's our home. So you're messing with my money ... You have undercut the value of my apartment. I know what I could probably sell this for now and if this building wasn't so fucked up, it would be selling for a hundred or two hundred thousand dollars more than I know it can sell for. (NYC Res. 9)

One condo board member, who also writes about the condo industry, explained that there are "different ways of making the condo a business, an investment, rather than a place to live" (TO Board 4).

Absent from media coverage and legislative debate about the condo during its emergence in the 1960s, despite historically low rental unit availability in Toronto (e.g., *Toronto Star* 1967; Wills 1967; Farrell 1966), was this notion of the non-resident owner. Early on no distinction was made between resident and non-resident owners, but gradually a clear division emerged. This division arose via a multiplicity of knowledges, common and expert, from owners and industry representatives. The creation of the renter as the "other" of condo governance is closely related to this development. It is a consequence of what Foucault (1982, 208) aptly calls "dividing practices,"[3] which are intimately linked to knowledges and power relations. This "othering" creates not only the renter but also the non-resident owner as mutually constitutive categories: one relies on the other for its existence at the opposite ends of a spectrum that positions the previously undistinguished resident owner in the middle as both owner and small-scale investor. But the non-resident owner would now reside outside the condo and rent the unit while its value increased, and, over time, the unit's purchase would be covered by renters. One resident remarked on the position of the non-resident: "The problem is ... they don't want to lose out on their investments. So they're not going to live there ... they're going to rent [out their unit] because they're getting their mortgage paid every month" (TO

Res. 7). Further illustrating this tight tether between non-resident owner and renter is the fact that, by the 1980s, in condo market research rented units were deemed equivalent to investor units. The renter served as an indicator (because some condo units are rented out only seasonally – for example, by retired and/or more affluent Torontonians and New Yorkers who spend winters elsewhere, often in warmer climates[4]) of the condo real estate market's strength. The quantity of rented condo units "compared to the total universe is an indicator of investor (versus resident owner) penetration in the market" (Hitchcock 1981, 2). This meant that renter availability was logically necessary for a condo real estate market and its expansion, a point not lost on low-income urban housing advocates who draw attention to the fact that rental and social housing stock in North American cities continues to dwindle due to condo conversions and government funding cutbacks, respectively (see Chapter 8; see Hildebrand 2013).

Yet it was not always the case, particularly in New York, that non-resident owners were the only ones invested in the idea of renting out units. Conversions also led to renting out since these arrangements sometimes generated new non-resident owners, too. A resident owner explained how investors emerged from a conversion and its relationship with renting:

> You get a good price as an insider when a building converts, because they ... need to ... get like two-thirds for a non-eviction conversion. There are eviction conversions and non-eviction conversions, based on the number of people who line up and say, "I want to buy." If not that many people want to buy, then they are allowed to stay as renters, and you have a building that's part renters and part owners. But if you get a large majority you can get what's called an eviction conversion. So I don't know how many people in our building are still there from original, when it converted. A lot ... cashed out or else they converted it into an investment where they don't live there but they rent it out. They got it at such a good price and the value was so high as a rental now that they simply rent it out. (NYC Res. 11)

Some distinguishing between non-resident and resident owners invokes the language of ethnic or racial difference. Thus, for example, one condo architect remarked about non-resident owners:

> For example, the Orientals that are coming in from China, the families that are bringing their kids here to school, rather than ... having to live in

> the dormitory, which they don't like ... they buy a condo for them. Ideal investment for them and it's a place for their kids to live. There are buildings downtown that are entirely occupied by Oriental investors ... Good quality buildings too. Good investment. (TO Board 2/Architect)

Such explicitly racialized discourse was relatively rare, however, compared to the presence of the resident/non-resident owner distinction. This distinction was articulated more often in domestic/foreign rather than in racialized terms. As one board member claimed:[5] "All the condos that they've built and all the foreign investment, because I mean you can make a lot on a property from buying it from plans and then it's built. You can make one hundred grand so we have all these foreign investors buying them and, like I said, renting them out" (TO Board 7). Another Toronto building had a remarkably large proportion of non-resident owned units that were being rented out, which, it was claimed, raised "issues": "When we first moved in it was 90 percent. So there's a lot of investors, which makes sense. But people are buying, they're moving in and living there, and that is great because a really high rental population brings issues with people coming and going" (TO Board 6). However, when problems arose, while inevitably part of the same phenomenon, non-resident owners sometimes received a free pass relative to renters. For example, one board member remarked upon the two owner types but blamed the renter for any problems:

> It can be very difficult to deal with tenants. Lots of people buy condos as investments, they rent them out, and the board, as a corporation, we have to deal with the owner. And the problem isn't the owner, the problem is with the tenant because they're not following the rules, being too noisy – whatever. So we have to go through the owner, and if the tenant starts something that causes a problem the owner is on the hook for that. So I think there needs to be more direct ways for the board to deal directly with the people who are living there. (TO Board 6)

Another resident owner similarly commented about non-resident owners: "So they don't want investors ... and I don't mean that in a bad sense, but they don't want a lot of transients as far as people moving in moving out" (NYC Res. 9). This negative characterization of renters as transient (instead of, for example, "mobile") is a common thread throughout this book (especially in

Chapter 4 on condo governance and renters, and in Chapter 6 on policing nuisance).

One resident owner succinctly captured a problem concerning governance as it relates to non-resident owners and the basic resident/non-resident owner schism, contrasting "monetary aspects" with "quality of life":

> There's a lot of people in the building that were voicing their opinion ... about the cell tower; concerned about the health issues ... The board ... says ... don't worry about it, and then they just go ahead and do it. They don't even vote and so that to me is somebody who doesn't live in the building, doesn't care about health and is only looking to increase the revenue or the income at the cost of quality of life. So that kind of a person, that's more about the monetary aspects of the building versus the quality of life of ... [the community and its residents], you could say [a] realtor versus [an] in-house regular resident viewpoint. (NYC Res. 10)

For a former board member, the onset of non-resident owners was not immediate but happened over several years:

> Early on we didn't have a lot of non-resident owners. We have more now. So I think when I was on the inaugural board ... I think we had maybe one or two non-resident owners. More people at that time were taking an opportunity to flip their units, so those folks ... saw an opportunity to make the money, they sold their units and they moved out. So we didn't have a lot of renter non-resident owners then. Now, my second tour we had more. (NYC Res. 15)

Another resident similarly explained that the number of investors grew over time and that, in one instance, because the owner was an investor it meant she could "do whatever she wanted":

> They ... started moving to Florida, but they kept their apartments as an income. So that was the problem. The people were owners of the units and ... there were not really restrictions on the subletting and they have moved out of the city and they were just getting income by subletting their apartment ... We had a neighbour here at the condo that she kind of could do whatever she wanted to because she bought the units as investments ...

> While she was in the building there was the condo board that couldn't do too much to her because she owned her own unit. (NYC Res.12)

More significantly, a condo resident distinguished his "long view" from the non-resident owner's "short view" affecting governance decisions about fees and upkeep:

> There's the people like us that have the long view, like we want this to be our life's home for a long time, and ... there are the short view kind of people that are, "Well it doesn't make any sense to put money into this because I'm out, I'm out, or I didn't spend that much in the first place so why should I pony up any more money or invest in the crumbling outer shell of the building?" (NYC Res. 8)

A condo lawyer, remarking about the Toronto condo context, similarly remarked about a lack of "long-term interest": "We've allowed huge amounts of investors ... So we have buildings with investors who have no long-term interest in a building. They don't care. They're just interested in getting their revenue [from renters] on an ongoing basis" (TO Lawyer 2). A condo real estate agent remarked, in contrast, about the resident owner's view: "If you live there you have an invested interest in making sure it doesn't look like a welfare building because nothing is being fixed and maintenance is at the lower end and nothing is being cleaned ... for an owner-occupier [resident owner]" (TO Real Estate 1). Yet another owner explained the basic difference between the two owner types and problems stemming from non-resident owners:

> People who do live in the building but aren't necessarily interested in trying to change things because there'll be blowback and they're afraid, or they're investor-owners who aren't members of the sponsors' family but they're quite happy to have no repairs done and low fees and [leave] everything just the way it was because they don't mind if the ceiling falls down because they're not living there so ... they really don't care, and they make pretty good market rent on these units and they're not under rent control so they just can throw anybody out who ever complains about the ceiling falling down and they just get a new tenant and get a little Silly Putty and stick everything back together and off they go ... The rental turnover is incredible. There are moving vans coming up and down the street all

> the damn time ... There's no way for us who live here to have any sense of like whose moving in, when are they moving in, how many times. (NYC Res. 8)

One major consequence of the growth of non-resident owners in relation to condo governance concerns maintaining low or unsustainable maintenance fees – the primary source of funds and the lifeblood of the long-term viability of condo buildings. An industry representative and board member similarly pointed to bad board decisions due to the increase in non-resident owners: "The Yonge Street corridor where they've been built the last ten years ... [has] a large percentage of investor-owned units. I'd say in those cases the condo corporation, what they've kept on doing was trying to keep the fees as low as possible [when they should have been] put into the reserve fund and saved" (TO Board 5). A resident of another building recounted a similar view of non-resident owners' aims: "We have very high condo fees. So I think for an investor, that's a tough pill to swallow. It's tough to sell something when you have ... quite high condo fees every month" (TO Res. 8). Investors seek to avoid increasing fees not only because they cannot gain access to the services they allow but also because the higher rents required to recover higher fees are thought to discourage renters from leasing before the investor is ready to sell for profit.

Another important result of the emergence of the non-resident owner in greater numbers, albeit this is not common in Toronto and New York, is the prospect of the forcible dissolution of condo corporations (see Harris and Gilewicz 2015). This has occurred in Chicago (Rodkin 2017) as well as in Florida and Singapore. Dissolution is often an effort to seize the valuable land upon which a condo building is constructed for redevelopment (Harris and Gilewicz 2015, 265; but see Rodkin 2017) and, in practice, is associated with older buildings. Non-resident owners sometimes effectively dissolve the condo corporation despite the wishes of resident owners wanting to reside in the building. This is accomplished when non-resident owners can secure enough units, and therefore votes, to satisfy the requirement for dissolution in the condo statute (e.g., 80 percent of unit holders) of the particular jurisdiction in question (Harris and Gilewicz 2015).[6] Thus, in these cases, investors do not merely influence condo governance but effectively end it. They also stop something else that is increasingly difficult to create through the condo: "The dissolution of [a] condominium dismantles the mechanism for collective governance and destroys the public or communal life of title holders within the legal form" (Harris and Gilewicz 2015, 288). But it is necessary to mention two related points regarding governance. This first is that dissolution, if it were to increase in Toronto and New York and elsewhere in North America, does not mean that the condoization trend would be reversed; indeed, redevelopment following dissolution could easily mean substantially taller new-build condo high-rises or otherwise larger, more profitable condo complexes being constructed on the same land or combining with existing land to build larger and/or more higher-end condo buildings horizontally. The other point is that non-resident owners could also, in principle at least, use the possibility of "dissolution" as a club to dominate the remaining minority resident owners or other investors on the board to secure the governing decisions they desire (e.g., using condo corporation funds to improve aesthetics rather than maintaining systems for greater profits from their unit sales, or keeping fees unrealistically low to ensure profit from renters).

Another significant consequence of the division of owners into two types is the solidification of condo property as a commodity. The non-resident owner's emergence shows the study of condo governance is also the study of how private property relations are born and continuously reconstituted. As noted, most resident owners see condo units as investments (at least to some degree) as well as places to live, as homes, but the non-resident owner positions the condo as commodified property rather than valuing it for these or related reasons.[7]

Relatedly, after the first condo complexes emerged in Toronto and New York the practice of hiring property managers proliferated. This development has occurred in lockstep with condo buildings becoming larger and condo governance becoming more complex. Each development is not necessarily causing the other but, rather, mutually supporting it over time. In Toronto in particular, the shift towards more high-rise condo towers in addition to one- or two-level condo townhouses occurred alongside the growth of property management. The high-rise condo's workings and infrastructure are decidedly more multifaceted and typically involve more residents than what is associated with condo townhouses, partially due to the former needing to share costlier common elements to make them viable (high-rise elevators being a key example). Thus, condo governance is increasingly contracted to a property management firm that, in turn, contracts with service providers to assist governing these elements and condo life more broadly. Managers are integral to governing condo affairs since it came to be assumed that they wield an assortment of skills and broker and deploy knowledge that few board members possess.

BOARDS

The condo board is deemed to be a private residential government that presides over condo owners, common elements, and spaces (McKenzie 2011, 13; 2006). All condo statutes in North America stipulate the requirements for a condo corporation or equivalent and, specifically, a governing board. Ontario's 1998 statute, for example, provided for the creation of a declaration (often thought of as a condo corporation's constitution) (section 7a), bylaws (section 56[1]), and rules (section 58[1]) that govern a corporation's powers, responsibilities, and authority. The statute mandates an elected corporate board to represent all owners; to oversee use and maintenance of common elements via specific measures and procedures to ensure unit owners' compliance with the declaration, bylaws, and rules (sections 27–41); and to enforce the collection of common fees from owners (sections 84–88). Condo buildings are formed through a governing corporation ruled by this elected board. Members (called "directors" in Toronto and "managers" in New York consistent with the corresponding statutes, but hereinafter all are called "members") of the board are then typically empowered to serve for a several-year term. Condo statutes place responsibility for a condo building's finances, operating systems, common spaces, and other operations (including arranging and signing contracts) on these boards. The board is charged with governing resident conduct by establishing and enforcing rules. Traditionally, with little or no institutional oversight or training (but see Chapter 8) from municipal, provincial/state, or federal governments, boards are to assume liabilities, make managerial and financial decisions, and police nuisances, often by turning to a seemingly ever-growing range of commodities and related agents claiming to aid these endeavours (see also McKenzie 2011).

Interviews and other sources used for this study provided some insight into boards. They revealed that boards tend to meet only once a month in Toronto and New York. However, being a board member, even when contracting a property manager and other agents' involvement, is still deemed an arduous, time-consuming position. It entails rule-making and decisions about a building's everyday workings and long-term viability and, thus, also setting the all-important mandatory monthly maintenance fee level. The president's role is particularly involved, as a New York board president explained:

> I was the only person ... who wanted to join the board and they needed a new person ... and none of the other people on the board who have been

> on the board for years wanted to be president. So they asked me to be president ... That has made my relations with the other people here that much more involved. Everyone on the board lives here and ... I collaborate with them almost daily via e-mail and certainly in person a lot. And then I get questions from people about, you know, all kinds of things about the building. I speak to the super almost daily about the building ... and on and on. Especially if you are board president you are going to be very involved with the building and your neighbours. (NYC Board 5)

At the same time, owners are not expected to challenge everyday issues or board practices, in part, because they are ignorant of routine board activities. As a long-time condo real estate agent and industry observer remarked, this includes those few owners who seek to become board members:

> Most people don't even know what it means to be a board member. They – the common platform is: "I'll lower your fees. If you elect me, I'll lower your fees." And they don't know ... Totally being in the dark, not knowing a thing, not seeing any financial statement ... they don't know what contracts are being negotiated. So when they do that, of course it creates a problem, because they have to meet their campaign platform. (TO Real Estate 1)

Interviews and other sources revealed that, even though they are part owners of common elements and spaces, most owners are ignorant of board activities (and the legal requirements thereof) regarding those elements and spaces. And owners expressed little to no sense of community duty to rotate in or otherwise become a board member. And boards, because they are only one element of an assemblage, are not as powerful in condo governance as they might first appear or as depicted by some owners and in statute. This is not only because they are hampered by contracts and financial realities, as the above interviewee suggests, but also because of the influence of property managers, myriad legal knowledges, and, for example, processes of risk avoidance, and securitization bearing down upon and shaping their decisions.

A major argument of this book is that the notion that condo boards govern condo relations, conduct, and spaces – condo life – in practice is highly misleading since boards have become increasingly dependent upon an array of other elements, and those elements, in turn, have become dependent upon boards. Nonetheless, it is vital to pay some attention to boards within assemblages if one is to gain insight into condo governance. Thus, boards are best currently conceived as a necessary but not sufficient agent and element of condo governance.

Little is known about the make-up of condo boards in North American cities. Owners cannot necessarily provide much information to researchers about board composition as many are simply unaware of it (as noted in the epigraph at this chapter's outset). But interviews with board members in Toronto and New York revealed that all their boards comprised either five or seven members. According to a long-time Toronto condo property manager, a position often entailing management of a large number of buildings over a career, most boards in Toronto have five members (TO Manager 5).

In both cities, owners had a consistent, common sentiment regarding board participation. As a Toronto board member succinctly put it (albeit with obvious over-statement): "Nobody wants to get on the board" (TO Board 8). This is consistent with the few findings available about condo boards in previous condo governance research in North America (e.g., Barton and Silverman 1994; see also Chen and Webster 2005; and Nelson 2005 regarding homeowner associations). Significantly, the stated reasons for becoming a board member typically concern control and maintaining or increasing property values rather than a sense of civic duty or wanting to create or maintain community:

> The reason I did get on the board is because I wanted a building to look the way I wanted it to look and I have very high standards, and the only way you can control that is if you're on the board ... More than aesthetics. It's the way the building's maintained. It's more maintenance so it kept the value up. That was the idea, to keep the value up. (TO Board 8)

Another Toronto board member similarly explained: "When we bought a condo, right from the start I said I'm going to try to be on the board because this is a major investment and I like to protect my investments" (TO Board 6). A board member from a different Toronto condo complex elaborated:

> The reason I got involved in the condo [board] is because it's my investment, it's to know what's happening. When I first got on, I had just moved in there ... and why don't you just try to get on the board? ... and literally I didn't know nothing. So basically I put my name in and I wasn't successful, but then they had a notice up for the social committee in the building. I thought okay it's a way of getting involved, and getting to know people because I want to get on the board, right? (TO Board 9)

This tendency was echoed in New York. One owner there explained that a common rationale in his building for becoming a board member was that "most people want to protect their investment, and they want to have a say in their building" (NYC Res. 11). Another explained:

> There were activities going on ... [with] the board that I didn't necessarily condone. And I was worried about the investment just in general terms about how things were run. So that's why I was interested in getting on the board ... just trying to bring some ... costs down. Helping them to manage their costs better than how it was being [done]. (NYC Res. 10)

Resident owners, who also saw their units partially as an investment, saw this as the main reason to participate on the board.

Interviews in New York revealed that board members tended to be white men. Almost all were middle aged or older. No boards in the condo buildings studied more closely were found to include persons under forty years old. Many board members were professionals – lawyers, bankers, professors, and engineers. In one condo building, however, the board mostly comprised businesspersons:

> The board was composed largely of small business owners and now the board is composed largely of people who work in large enterprises and are used to more regimented kind of black letter rules. They don't make individual exceptions. They understand things like setting a precedent ... they are a little bit more sophisticated than they used to be. (NYC Res. 4)

Based on interviews in Toronto, most board members in that city were also white men, though with a greater representation of visible minorities and women than found in New York, and a very few board members were in their thirties rather than all being over forty. Some boards in both cities included non-resident members, with a greater proportion seeming to be present in New York condo boards. Board composition in Toronto was like that in New York as far as including professional members, including teachers, lawyers, engineers, business owners, real estate agents, and professors. Overall, residents tended to prefer professionals and felt that these individuals were the most qualified board members. However, not all boards had members from what are usually deemed to be professional vocations, suggesting that a condo board need not include such persons. One board member described his board as comprising a "retired bookkeeper, retired door salesman, [a] young man that ... calls himself an entrepreneur, and then there is a retired woman from airport security" (TO Board 24). If there was one occupation that appeared especially often on Toronto and New York condo boards it was real estate agent.

The split in owner types mattered when it came to electing board members. According to one resident:

> If you want to make it an income property building it's going to be an income property building, but most of us live here, we want to live here and we shouldn't elect board members that are more geared toward minimizing the costs ... to maximize their own short-term profit as opposed to people that want to keep this as a long-term investment and a place to live. (NYC Res. 13)

A condo real estate agent and former condo property manager similarly remarked upon reasons owners seek to become board members:

> It's a lot of hidden agendas that are driving their reasons to be on the board. Of course, as an investor they say "keep the fees low," but not "always remember that I'm here because I was elected to represent my community and every decision that I make or that I'm voting on is for the betterment of the community." (TO Real Estate 1)

When non-resident owners become board members of a condo corporation, they are presumed to make decisions exclusively to secure their investment rather than to ensure long-term residential "community" betterment, although the focus on investment is evident among resident owners too.

OWNER-BOARD RELATIONS

The study of condo governance in Toronto and New York revealed much owner-board distrust and conflict. Although this is evident in other housing forms, such as social housing (McCormack 2009), for condo buildings it tends to be related to the cleavage of owners into main types and how this plays out at the board level. For present purposes it makes sense to provide an idea of the range of owner-board relations. Interviews showed that, for some buildings, the common view of condo governance as conflict-ridden is warranted. Though not elaborated below, it is significant that there are few owners who show awareness of the influence of a wider assemblage of agents beyond boards in their relations and conflicts. In other words, there is limited owner recognition that various agents intimately influence condo governance among those owners who distrust, or whose views or practices conflict with, the board. Yet the innumerable examples from interviews and the other data sources used in this study indicate that not all owner-board relations are mired in distrust and conflict. Several examples from Toronto and New York provide the flavour of these relations, which ranged from trust to legal conflict.

Many owners could not recall the names of their board members or, if they could, they tended to be unsure where (or whether) they lived in their building. Regardless of how well they knew the board members, however, sometimes owners plainly had the full trust of their boards. For example, according to this Toronto owner: "They seem to be very good at planning, and they seem to be very concerned about maintaining the legislation I understand does require a certain level of reserves, and they seem to be quite conscientious about making sure that we have more than enough in the reserve" (TO Res. 46). But other owners were suspicious of boards and their decisions:

> She's going to every board meeting or AGM and she said, "How do you know what's going on or where your money's going?" I'm like, "I trust people," but she's going, "Yeah but you never know. You could have some type of shady board members who take your money or they're not spending money or they're spending too much money." Because she has a friend that was on a board and she's an accountant, so she saw a lot of mishandling of monies. And since she's been on the board she's been able to save everyone, so they haven't had increases in their condo fees in a few years. So that's why she goes to her board meetings to ensure that everything is transparent. (TO Res. 43)

A recently elected board member sought to form an owners' group to investigate problems with the previous board: "We're forming a group to find out what's happening in our building, we've been so complacent, so trusting, so ignorant for the past six years and we trusted the board of directors to do right by us" (TO Board 35). In another Toronto building the board refused to provide the new board with financial statements after being "voted out":

> We've asked them for our financials, we've asked them for an AGM, I mean it's the law, ... but they don't do it and they've got away with it for so long

> until a bunch of us owners got together, we hired a lawyer, we had to take them to court, and it's after a year of going to court and fighting them we actually got that AGM and we voted them out finally and now they won't hand over all the documents to the new board. (TO Res. 59)

A New York owner explained what he thought would happen if board elections and decisions were challenged: "In some [condo] buildings ... if they challenge it they become ... a trouble maker, and they might get very bad service and are never going to get an okay for a renovation" (NYC Res. 11). Such fear is, of course, not conducive to a notion of a condo community. Based upon numerous owner accounts from various condo buildings and industry representatives as well as analyses of numerous condo-specific documents in condo buildings in Toronto and New York, there tends to be limited contact among owners. A New York resident owner said that the main concern about her condo building and its governance was

> the lack of quote, unquote "neighbourhood feel." Maybe that's something that I, that should be pushed forward. Maybe I should be the one that should actively go out of my way to ... meet more people because I had noticed a general feeling of everybody keeps to themselves. And I think it's getting worse in the building. I think now that there is [sic] more tenants moving in. (NYC Res. 6)

Owners reported that their AGMs tend to be poorly attended. This was a major concern reported by condo owners to Ontario's statutory review, and it was linked to the growth of non-resident owners: "The high number of absentee owners in many condominium buildings has made it difficult to achieve quorum at annual general meetings impeding the ability to make fundamental changes to corporation by-laws" (Ontario 2012, 50). Regarding her building's AGM, one Toronto owner related: "we get less than 50 percent actually in attendance" (TO Res. 62). In another building, in responding to being asked whether there was "a lot of attendance at the AGM," a Toronto board member replied: "No. We get a quorum because most of them are by proxies. Let's say we get about eighty proxies ... and the people ... numbered about [only] twenty-five" (TO Board 11). A New York condo owner similarly remarked: "They have ... an annual meeting and you know attendance is always spotty. A lot of people won't really – either can't come or some people just don't bother" (NYC Res. 23). In one response to whether the AGM was well attended a board member from another Toronto condo building said "no." She contrasted the AGM with an arguably less important meeting for the building's long-term well-being: "Not as good as it should be. No. They allow proxies ... about 60, 70 suites represented out of 152. But when we had the voting for the new lobby ... for which carpet they wanted and ... for the furniture, we had 107 suites that came down to vote. That's more than what they get at the AGM" (TO Board 27). In a minority of condo buildings there was slightly more than 50 percent attendance for some AGMs, according to owners and board members, but typically only if there was a contentious issue to be discussed.

ORGANIZED OWNER PRESSURE FOR STATUTORY REFORM

Partially because of occasional serious conflicts, but also due to recognition of major fraud perpetrated by boards or property managers in condo buildings, over several years pressure from some owners has been gradually increasing for provincial and state governments in North America to improve government oversight of condo governance and boards as well as, to a much lesser degree, over property managers and developers through statutory reform. This is evinced in the emergence of organized condo owner associations that raise awareness of issues and push for statutory changes that would benefit members. Examples in Ontario include the Canadian Alliance for Condo Owners Rights (CAFCOR 2016) and the Condo Owners Association (COA 2016), both emerging in the mid-2000s, and in New York the Alliance of Condo and Co-op Owners (ACCO 2016) and the Council of New York Cooperatives and Condominiums (CNYC 2016), which first took form in the 1970s and reflected the presence of the longer-standing cooperative. In Ontario it is only recently that greater government oversight of board practices has again become possible due to the introduction of a new condo authority via the passage of the latest round of condo statute reforms (a similar Condo Office was made possible in the 1978 statutory reforms but never implemented). A similar bill (A6941) for a condo "ombudsman," lobbied for by ACCO (Prevost 2011), was advanced in the New York State Senate beginning in 2011.[8] As one New York condo owner advocate explained to an owner looking for a way to respond to suspected criminal acts committed by his board and property management firm:

> Once the sponsor is no longer in control, the only legal way is through the court system. This is expensive and time consuming. I am working with

> several groups to get an "Ombudsman Bill" passed, which would give co-op and condo owners a government agency [that had] the ability to hear non-sponsor major complaints. We need owners to get on board by discussing this bill and putting pressure on your state elected officials to back this most important bill. It was introduced in the Senate by Liz Krueger. The more owners we get to push this the more likely we can get it passed. We need everyone to make this a priority if there is any hope of getting the state to help us. (New York Board Talk, 2012)

This bill, which would create the Office of the Cooperative and Condominium Ombudsman for New York State, remains with the Senate Finance Committee and Assembly Housing Committees as of mid-2018 and has yet to be voted upon by either legislative body.

Though condo owner pressure for statutory reform may increase from time to time, including more recently, it is easy to forget that, since the 1960s, such reform has been perpetually promised. And, perhaps not unrelatedly, organized owner calls for statutory reform are closely watched by other assembled agents of the condo industry. These agents are now part of more resourceful national or regional industry organizations set to shape and influence any statutory law reform and corresponding policy whenever it should be deemed necessary. This seems to be common across North American jurisdictions. As McKenzie (2011, 20) writes: "The professionals who service CIDs [including condo complexes] are well organized to protect their interests in the policy arena, while owner interests are not so well represented." In most Canadian provinces, for example, there are chapters of the Canadian Condominium Institute (CCI), including one representing Toronto, that comprise primarily insurance, law, and property management representatives as well as a few owners. Property managers and developers in Ontario are similarly represented by the Association of Condo Managers of Ontario (ACMO) and the Ontario Home Builders Association, respectively.

CONCLUSION

Understanding condo governance requires paying attention to owners and the boards on which they volunteer. These are key governing agents. Condo owners have undergone division and are now understood to be of two distinct types, the resident owner and the non-resident owner. The latter type also helps constitute the category of the condo renter. The resident owner is concerned to some degree with investment and thus shares intentions with the non-resident owner. This binary classification is not an end-state, as suggested by much research identifying reasons people purchase condo units; rather, it is fluid and shifts over time depending on the multiple processes, agents, knowledges, and other elements that become assembled and disassembled in the condo world. This suggests the potential for the further segmentation of owner types consistent with the growing markets of commercial firms benefiting from and specializing in condo buying, selling, renting, securing, insuring, and governing. The dividing up of condo owners represents the classification of governed populations par excellence, a practice about which Foucault (1977) wrote in some detail.

Closer study of condo governance reveals an assemblage of agents and elements that makes governance possible beyond owners and boards. Nonetheless, relations between owners and boards still matter when it comes to understanding condo governance. These relations currently range from trust, to distrust, to outright conflict, which, at times, leads to legal and other means of governance and resolution, occasionally only after owners organize among themselves within or, more rarely, across buildings. But within these conflicts, except for property managers, there is little recognition of the influence of agents other than boards. The next chapter looks at these various other agents and elements and identifies key processes comprising condoization.

3

Assembling the Condo
Processes, Agents, and Knowledges

> This is all you scratch my back and I'll scratch yours.
>
> – *TO BOARD 32*

> We see a lot too of insurance issues because condo insurance is very complicated and a lot of even the property managers don't quite understand how to apply the law in that case.
>
> – *TO LAWYER 3*

Boards govern condo buildings, but they do so through an array of knowledges and technologies and in relation to agents assembled via various processes. This is common to condo governance across North America. This chapter first examines condo governance's relation to development and developers; however, to fully understand condoization and condo governance, other neglected processes, agents, and knowledges also need to be discerned and examined. Here several institutional processes informing and shaping condoization and condo governance – commodification, juridification, risk avoidance, and securitization – are explored. Each is associated with key agents and corresponding organizations: lawyers, real estate agents, property managers, insurance brokers/assessors, and security personnel. These agents are arguably among the most deeply implicated in condoization and condo governance aside from developers and municipal and provincial/state governments.[1] Informal interactions and the related generation and exchange of common knowledge among condo residents may also partially shape condo life and how it is governed daily, although these interactions are not necessarily independent of the elements discussed here and may well be becoming supplanted or smothered by commercial forms.

The remainder of this chapter draws on accounts of condo owners, board members, and industry representatives and unfolds in three sections. The first section illustrates the nexus between condo development and governance by providing several examples of overlap. The second section looks at how institutional processes are indispensable to condoization and condo governance as well as the influence of their associated agents and knowledges. The third section discusses some ways in which these multiple processes, agents, and knowledges are mutually reinforcing and constitutive – how they are assembled. The chapter concludes by underscoring several implications of the foregoing for understanding condoization and condo governance.

CONDO DEVELOPMENT AND GOVERNANCE

Condo (property) development is said to be occurring alongside profound global changes in urban governance. Critical scholars in urban studies often term these changes the rolling out of urban neoliberalization (e.g., Lin et al. 2015; Peck, Theodore, and Brenner 2010; Brenner, Peck, and Theodore 2009; Brenner and Theodore 2002; Peck and Tickell 2002), including in relation to Toronto (Keil 2009) and New York (Brash 2011), the primary and secondary urban contexts upon which this book focuses. Other cogent analyses are to be lauded for exploring the spread of the condo as a distinctive property form in its own right, paying close attention to the role of developers as powerful agents who build, redevelop, and reshape the city (Kern 2007, 2010a; Rosen and Walks 2013; Rosen 2016, 2017); to the influence of government policies that encourage this development (Lehrer and Wieditz 2009); and/or demonstrating the effects of enabling condo statutes on urban development patterns (Harris 2011). Some critical scholarship on the condo specifically attends to its development in relation to gentrification and urban neoliberalism (e.g., Lehrer and Wieditz 2009; Kern 2010a). It is vital to acknowledge the fact that developers and neoliberal governmental policies encourage condo growth. Yet condoization in Toronto, New York, and beyond is not only about developer manoeuvres and capital influx due to neoliberal planning policies. As discussed in the introduction, although condo development and condo governance are usually examined separately in urban geography and socio-legal studies (see, for example, McKenzie 2011; Blandy, Dixon, and Dupuis 2006) respectively, they overlap considerably. Below are several examples that illustrate this overlap.

A first example of overlap stems from a formal legal process stipulated in Ontario's condo statute (typically known as "turnover" in condo statutes in North America and elsewhere) under the heading "Transfer of Control by Declarant" and described in sections 42 and 43 of Ontario's Condominium Act (hereafter Condo Act), 1998. This is initiated when a condo developer sells enough units to allow a building to be registered as a condo corporation.[2] This process necessitates the formation of a board of owners to assume governance of common property from the developer. Yet this transition is structured so as to ensure the developer's influence on condo governance during and – equally important – *after* formal transition. Developers may wish to continue to have this influence, to maintain profits from renting out adjoined commercial space (usually as storefront units), or to ensure that they are not found responsible should the construction be substandard. As the developer registers the condo corporation's governing documents (the declaration, bylaws, and rules), her or his influence is experienced long after ceding formal control of the condo corporation's affairs to the board. In one New York building with many developer-owned units, one owner explained:

> The sponsor [the legal term for the person arranging the condo conversion or new build in New York City/State; "developer" is the term used in Toronto/Ontario] owns a lot of units and he has all those stores down there. Besides owning the stores ... he owns twenty-nine out of the seventy-eight residential units. It gives him an enormous amount of voting power. And I'm sure you heard this before ... We don't feel as though we are controlling our own destiny, that we are running the building. We feel as though the sponsor handpicks through the power of his vote who he wants to be on the board ... and the bylaws say that he should give up control (NYC Res. 9).

A new board has great difficulty amending the declaration, partially due to the absence of protocols encouraging owner participation in condo governance (see below) as well as to the high threshold of votes required by law (e.g., section 107 of Ontario's Condo Act, 1998, requires 80 or 90 percent of owners, depending on the issue, to agree to amend the declaration). Attaining the necessary quorum and votes to overturn bylaws is also onerous. As one owner explained: "Getting quorum in a large building ... is difficult so it's hard to get anything passed even if the board supports it ... I understand why you have to have a certain percentage, but I wish that it was lower ... for a change in the bylaws in particular" (TO Res. 52). A unit owner in another Toronto building echoed these concerns but, when remarking on AGM attendance, implied a less congenial relationship between the board and owners: "The problem is that the AGMs are attended by those people that are already aware of these issues but it's not enough to make a difference because the majority of the AGM attendees are by proxy. That's how you get the quorum and that's the way that the board controls it" (TO Res. 53). In this case, the quorum to ensure the AGM could happen was achieved via proxies from owners unable or unwilling to attend, a tendency prevalent in the many of the buildings studied and one that concentrates voting power and contributes to sustained influence, albeit not always or only on the part of developers. In this owner's experience, this unwillingness to attend the AGM to vote occurred because "people who choose to live in condos have the mentality that everything is fine, everything is going to be taken care of for them and that they don't want to get involved in the politics. And unfortunately that's where a lot of problems stem from. You will never get enough people" (TO Res. 53).

A second example of overlap between development and governance pertains to relations between developers and property management companies. In Toronto, property management companies that dominate the condo market are often arms of major condo development corporations. For example, Tridel, perhaps the best-known Toronto condo developer, and Del Property Management both operate under the parent corporation, Tridel Group of Companies (Tridel 2018). Moreover, interviews revealed that developer-linked property management firms are often retained by the first condo board following transition to owner governance. One owner stated: "so [Tri]del has all sorts of buildings around the city so the property management comes in through them. That's a good thing because we don't have to worry" (TO Res. 54). While seemingly innocuous, other interviews revealed there may be reason to "worry" since contracting with such a firm can have long-lasting implications for building governance. This arrangement allows developer influence to continue long after formal transition to owner control. A common concern expressed among owners and board members had to do with developer-owned (or selected) property management companies that ignore "developer's construction deficiencies" (Hyman 2006, 5) during the first year, when, in Ontario, new condo buildings are still under a mandated building warranty. A long-time condo property manager explained:

> Here's the problem: a lot of times the developer, before they even register the condo, hires a management company ... more interested in keeping control for the developer then he is in ensuring the board and the owners are serviced properly because he's more interested in getting [the contract for] the next building ... okay? And he doesn't have to argue about the price ... In subsequent years it becomes an issue but [especially] if you're in for the one year you can prevent lots of damage to the developer by ignoring things and then in the end the owners have to pay that bill because it didn't come in the first year [warranty period] audit and ... there is no repercussion, nor recourse. Once it's done, it's done, and that's why it's critical that in the first year you don't have the crony of the builder managing the building ... there to be buddies with the developer. He's not going to push any buttons so the developer is getting off scot-free: wallpapers' falling off, the systems are broken, and the garage door is hanging funny and nobody gives a flying fuck and so a few years down the road ... the corporation has to replace everything and then the owners pay the bill. (TO Manager 6)

This "problem" is exacerbated by the fact that some owners and board members reported that property management companies can become difficult to remove when their practices are deemed of poor quality, corrupt, or otherwise detrimental to the condo building.

A third example of overlap comes from a condo building in which a "special assessment" (see Chapter 5) had recently been levied on owners.[3] As explained in Chapter 1, typically a board deploys this exceptional measure to overcome large deficits in the "reserve fund," which is supposed to cover replacement costs and repairs of major common elements such as roofs and boilers. These are unique to the condo world, are supposed to be an exceptional last resort, and can have serious consequences for lower-income condo owners in particular:

> If you buy a condo ... your building may look great today and great tomorrow, but you could be asked to come up with $5,000 and demanded to pay it immediately or within thirty days or you get liened and you could

> ultimately lose your unit. That understanding doesn't exist with respect to affordability of condos. If you don't want to fix your roof in your house, fine, you can live with the leak ... or live without heat, fine. But that doesn't work in ... condos, and that's something that people don't understand when they live in a condo. (TO Real Estate 1)

Reserve fund deficits often emerge when monthly maintenance fees are kept too low over time or when there is faulty construction. As a result, special assessments often bridge the divide between development and governance. In this instance, the special assessment was directly linked to further development:

> We got a notice from property management that the garage is going to be repaired ... and they plastered on us a special assessment of almost $8,000 per parking spot. When we bought this unit the garage structure ... [was] already like that but nothing has been done to maintain it. The philosophy of the developer is: Why spend money now when he wants to build a phase two on that? In the meantime, ... because of the damage [over] six years ... we were faced with a $5 million restoration cost ... But our problem is that he sold the air space and another developer is building a new condo there and as a requirement the city said, "in order for you to build that you have to make sure that this garage structure is sound to support that new condo ..." [But] why are we paying? ... In the [condo] bylaw it says that owners have to vote for any major repair or restoration but none of that's [been] done. (TO Board 35)

Similarly, at another building a profitable telecommunications tower was affixed to the condo edifice, with some units still owned by the developer after turnover. But the residential condo owners unknowingly paid for most of the tower, which perhaps eventually led to a special assessment or a substantial increase in monthly fees. A real estate agent explained:

> Owners are going ... to be hugely shocked in year number two. For example, the developers retain storefront units in a mixed-use site ... [with] a telecommunications tower that they own and that's unitized, but they have no common element fees. In the schedule it's 0.0001, the smallest proportion possible, so they pay no common element fees and that tower is beside the most expensive unit in the building, the penthouse unit. And

> I would not want my client to live there. The health hazard is unknown, and at the same time they're subsidizing that developer-owned unit ... I call it the razzamatazz that is the way of the market. It's complete fraud ... it's so glossed over, candy-coated, and omitted of facts [sic] that would directly affect the [condo unit] purchaser's decision. (TO Real Estate 1)

Some condo complexes in Toronto were discovered to be developed in phases and as multiple buildings. Thus, one phase is developed and governed, and its governance lays the foundation for the next developmental phase, which, in turn, is governed in ways that provide for the third phase and so on. Rather than being separate processes, governance and development are intimately intertwined, along with other agents and elements, in a complex assemblage. Governance and development are therefore not easily distinguished over time. In some instances, the physical connection between development and governance stems from shared facilities between phases. One respondent from a two-phase complex remarked upon the difficulties created for property maintenance by being governed by three boards:[4] "If you're [the shared facilities board] approving a $5,000 or $10,000 upgrade ... how do you know your tower is going to agree to that? You have to come back and discuss" (TO Board 9). In this instance, further improvements to the condo complex were complicated by the governmental structure initially set by the developer.

What is remarkable is that several of these kinds of overlap are longstanding in Ontario and elsewhere in North America. Thus, in 1978, in analyzing Ontario's condo statutory deficiencies, the legal scholar B. McLellan identified "developer self-dealing or 'sweetheart contracts.'" He explained:

> Prior to the taking over of the condominium corporation by the unit owners, developers would enter into long-term contracts with a management company *which they owned or had an interest in.* Often these contracts had escalation clauses as well. The condominium corporation thus inherited lengthy contracts which were more costly and which often provided for lower quality service than could be acquired elsewhere. Developers sometimes constructed recreational facilities on land which they owned and which was adjacent to the condominium and leased the facilities to the corporation at exorbitant rates. (McLellan 1978, 48; emphasis added)

The influence of developers on governance during the transition from developer to owner control is also found in the Australian context, which is one of the few in which this process has been recently studied. It sees similar conflicts of interest stemming from the relationship between developer and the first contracted property management firm, the first bylaws that favour developer interests after owners take control, and controlling proxy votes (see Easthope et al. 2014, 295–96). Why these and other arrangements have been permitted to continue or expand as condoization has flourished reflects how condo governance has become assembled. However, the main point is that condo development rarely recedes into the past for any given building; legislative requirements have not prevented the developer's influence from lingering in condo governance relations long after the transition to unit owner control. Development's endpoint is not the legally mandated transition to unit owners' governance of the condo building and formation of a board of owners.

A fourth example of overlap between development and governance is that current condo developer marketing materials systematically avoid mention of condo governance arrangements and the importance of owner participation therein. Analysis of ten Toronto and ten New York condo developers' online marketing materials revealed only one that mentioned governance and related board participation or remarked upon them as a civic opportunity or an opportunity to build/sustain community. The single exception was Toronto's PlazaCorp, which at least noted board participation as an opportunity (albeit this was largely hidden at the bottom of a section entitled "Why choose condominium living"), indicating that the board allowed owners to help make decisions about upkeep and daily operations and that it "serves to build a sense of community among owners" (www.pureplaza.com/condo-living). Nor was it mentioned in any developers' marketing that board participation and AGM attendance are opportunities to learn how governance and the board work in a condo building. The more typical webpage for would-be condo purchasers, that of Concord Adex, developer of one of the largest condo complexes in Toronto to date, City Place, incredulously reads:

> An investment in a new condo is an investment in the future. New condo units appreciate in value significantly. In fact, the annual average sold index price rose above 8 percent in 2012. Many owners sold their condominium investments to realize returns well above inflation. In a three to four year time period, that's a 24–32 percent capital appreciation when you resell your unit ... New condominiums are just that – bright, shiny and new! Initial maintenance and repairs will be minimal as everything from the carpets to the appliances and paint on the walls is new. *New condominiums*

are also taken care of by a condo management board that will deal with any maintenance that may develop over time – hence saving you the hassle.[5]

The simple fact that the "management" board requires owner participation is not presented to prospective condo owners. Plainly, the condo unit here is, almost exclusively, an investment commodity and, accordingly, comes with "minimal" worry or "hassle" – all is "taken care of." In the analysis of developer websites, typical was the suggestion that a condo unit in a building offers "direct access 24/7 to everything you need in life" (Centre Court Developments 2014). In promoting the notion "of your care free home" (www.pureplaza.com/condo-living), developers influence condo governance, future board composition, and residents' lives. Avoidance of involvement in condo governance (see Barton and Silverman 1994) on the part of owners and the related lack of community that accompanies this avoidance likely commences from point of purchase, at least partially due to developer marketing influence or wilful neglect. The near complete lack of attention to governance or community engagement in developer marketing materials for new owners may be problematic and expensive for the latter down the line.

A fifth example of overlap, and related to the above, is the way developers market condo fees. Among new-build condo complexes, the developer is found to influence governance by selling units with low, unsustainable monthly fees to attract buyers, but these fees increase significantly after the first year of ownership (e.g., Fleming 2011). As one Toronto board member stated:

> To sell units in a building when they tell you they charge so much a square foot for maintenance fees is a big fat lie. They're selling it based on that maintenance fee and it's always too low and as soon as the board goes in they have to raise the fees because it's not enough to cover the costs. (TO Board 7)

This practice is apparently also prevalent among condo developers beyond New York and Toronto. For example, regarding Australian condo (and other multi-title) developments, Easthope et al. (2014, 295) remark that, among developers, "there appears to be a widespread underestimation of initial levy [or fee] contributions." This practice has several effects. As this board member stated, these include making the initial board implement a policy "to raise fees to ensure sustainability of the building and the reserve" (TO Board 7), and this, in turn, affects their possible re-election since raising fees tends to be extremely unpopular, especially among new condo owners (TO Real Estate 1). Another board member related: "People in condos seem to think they shouldn't pay much for some strange reason. Even if they've owned a house, they think they should pay very low fees" (TO Board 8). A long-time Toronto condo real estate agent and industry observer further explained the consequence of low fees and how they are linked to myriad governance issues:

> If ... maintenance fees have been kept unreasonably low, [the] reserve fund is underfunded, [and] major repairs to common elements and replacements are being deferred ... it touches on governance directly. I'm talking about TSSA [Technical Standards and Safety Authority, which regulates elevators], fire code, roof anchors ... health and safety compliance for their staff and any contractors doing work. That's what I mean by ... governance. If they're circumventing these things and not doing the generator testing and all those things that are required, of course fees will go down. And it won't be necessarily visible to the owner until it's too late ... Three years later there's a special assessment and the owner can't afford it. (TO Real Estate 1)

This same observer described how the low fees were part of a larger number of developer "tricks" in Toronto, all of which shape governance (see also Canada's Public Policy Forum 2013c, 16, 20):

> The goal of the developer is to sell ... the units as fast as possible at the highest price, and to give you the illusion – because it is an illusion – of warranty coverage and quality living, which is not the true life of condo living, and thirdly, low common element fees. Because all of those things unravel in year two – all of them, or earlier, depending on the warranty coverage issues that carry on ... There are a lot of tricks that you might have heard about that the developers are playing – there's the deferred maintenance cost, deferred expenses to year number two, whether it's a mortgage purchase or a leasing cost that only start in year number two ... The owners get a 30 to 40 percent hit in the second year, and they all wonder why. (TO Real Estate 1)

This situation is long-standing too, despite previous statutory reforms. McLellan (1978, 48) earlier identified the situation in which "a developer underestimates the monthly fee to be paid for maintenance of the common elements and other building expenses. The purchaser thus discovers his fee doubling or tripling a year after he has bought his unit." The lack of owner attention to expectations to pay for regular maintenance can lead to the deterioration of the common elements, reserve fund deficits, and myriad other governance issues. Though entailing a slightly different arrangement, in a converted condo building in New York, one owner remarked upon the effect of the developer retaining control:

> The sponsor never sold the appropriate amount of units that you're supposed to sell ... to make the condo a viable condo ... I think they're supposed to sell it all off so that the ... condo[s] are run by the owners. But he, himself, still owns a ton of units and it's family members and other generations of his family [who] own a tremendous amount of the units, so really they still treat the building like a rental property. And ... many of us ... who live here ... sincerely want our building to be properly maintained and to be a good investment. [But] we just kind of like supplement his expenses, and we don't really get the appropriate services or planned maintenance. So, as a result, the building is not in good condition, there's no strategic plan to address it. (NYC Res. 6)

In one instance of transition from developer to owner control, the declaration specified that owners need not occupy their units. This had a dramatic effect on governance because it encouraged unit purchases by investors who were not planning to reside in the condo building (i.e., non-resident owners): "So the resident owner ... would ... have a higher stake in making sure the maintenance is done and the fees go up and ... and obviously their equity continues to rise, as opposed to the investor who is more interested in the cash flow to make sure that they can ... maximize their net profit" (TO Real Estate 1). This divide between non-resident and resident owners is significant in many buildings partially because non-resident owners rent their units to renters whom resident owners tend to perceive as apathetic about, or even antithetical to, a building's long-term integrity. As one condo owner explained:

> If I live here and I've bought, I'm very invested in the rules and how they're enforced, whereas the person next to me renting couldn't give a shit and neither could the offshore owner and so if you've got a building full of people like that ... the building's going down the toilet because stuff's not being enforced or maintained. (TO Res. 9)

These are only several among many possible examples of overlap between condo governance and development and some of their consequences.

CONDOIZATION'S OTHER PROCESSES, AGENTS, AND KNOWLEDGES

Now that we have discussed development, this section elaborates the roles of law, insurance, property management, and security agents or firms in condo governance, thus revealing it as a complex assemblage that entails knowledge flows. Each agent is closely associated with an identifiable process that helps comprise condoization. Thus, law firms advocate, and benefit directly from, the further juridification (or legalization) of social life. They market themselves as being exclusively positioned to mitigate and work through the uncertain effects of this process, and they sell their services and specialized knowledge accordingly. Similarly, private insurance benefits from increased reliance on privatized (rather than state or public) forms of risk avoidance. The more that risks can be identified in relation to condo life and packaged as commodities that will enable their avoidance, the more this institution profits. Property management is closely associated with the process of commodification more generally. Security firms provide specialized personnel ("concierges") to ensure that condo private property is secured and that it is increasingly governed through the implantation of security measures. These various firms provide expertise to manage numerous problems (including, but not limited to, those identified as risks) that arise in living on privately governed property – expertise that is increasingly purchased by boards and property managers. Here, each institutional agent, knowledge, and process is discussed in relation to the condo.

Property Management Firms and Commodification of Governance

Condoization entails the commodification of condo governance and expert knowledge. Of course, real estate and law firms also provide commodified knowledge for condo governance, but it is property management that is perhaps most exemplary of this process. As noted previously, at the birth of condo statutes in Ontario, New York State, and elsewhere in North America, there was little mention of property management firm involvement in condo governance. The New York statute of 1964 (section 339v-a) outlined minimal parameters for bylaws that refer to a board regarding election, removal, powers, and "whether or not the board may engage the services of a manager or managing agent or both," but this plainly meant that it was imagined that condo complexes would operate without these agents too. The original Ontario statute omits mention of property management on the behalf of boards. In the original condo concept from the 1960s in North America these activities were primarily conceived as owners' duties that were arranged through their boards. However, the property management industry has since grown rapidly both in North America and globally. The fact that the emergence and growth of condo property management firms has emerged concomitantly with the rise of non-resident owners should not be overlooked. Both approach the condo as property interests in need of protection – not necessarily as a community, a residence, or a necessity– exclusively. As a property manager who manages two condo high-rises in Toronto and who was interviewed for a trade magazine article on condo security remarked: "Our ultimate goal is to provide them a sense of peace of mind for their investment and maintain high property values" (Brown 2010, 17).

The argument for condo property management is premised on a "free rider problem," which is that unit owners are notoriously reluctant to participate on condo boards in North America, preferring to let others govern condo life on their behalf. Early in the condo's North American emergence, scholars noted: "In large projects, therefore, owners would be less willing to participate in management because the benefits of significant time and personal efforts are spread over many units. Given this condition the owner of units, even if they have appropriate skills, may incline toward being 'free riders'" (Mittelbach and Ebin 1975, 178–79). Interviews revealed owner reluctance to participate on boards or volunteer services to their own buildings, preferring instead to let others organize and oversee it. Property management's entry into the condo world presumes this problem – again, largely unanticipated in original condo statutes – which assumed that all owners would reside in (rather than occupy *or* invest in/rent units) and willingly manage the affairs of the condo building. By 1972, when writing about the condo, Rosenberg (1972) had begun to note that property management firms were moving into condo governance arrangements. And, as this occurred, self-managed condo buildings gradually began to decrease. Rarely stated publicly, the daily provision of condo governance has been increasingly commodified ever since.

Property management is not merely a tool of a condo board, as a bureaucracy is to a political representative; rather, it is often the board's profit-driven "overseer": "And we're the ones that are going to advise [the board of] the laws like this. Boards are more apt to follow our direction in terms of the law for fear that they're going to be exposed. Self-management doesn't have any body overseeing them" (TO Manager 7). Condo lawyers dispense legal knowledge and encourage its flow into condo buildings, but property managers are expected to apply it:

> We're there as a liaison to the board ... we're versed in the legislation and we want them to understand this is how it should run through the law. So we're there as their advisors if you will, to make sure they understand how the law works and that they're in compliance with the law ... That said, we also do enforce their declaration, their bylaw, their rules ... We act as the bad cop ... on behalf of the corporation to ensure that the rules are obliged by. (TO Manager 8)

One property manager explained that how the law is applied distinguishes property-managed condo practices from self-managed condo practices:

> Example: self-managed group, the [board] president did not like a neighbour's cat, so he went to the door, and he told them, if he sees that cat outside, he's going to trap that cat and kill that cat ... But ... we wouldn't do that. We wouldn't say "we're going to kill your cat." But they did ... That's the difference ... There's no neighbour relationship, there's no biases, we don't dislike you because this or because that. We just do our job ... So that would be the difference ... Self-managed has the tendency to not always follow ... the law. (TO Manager 6)

Despite proliferation, the nature of condo property management has become a central concern for some condo owners. This is due in no small part to the lack of state regulation. Until recently, in Ontario, as in many other jurisdictions, there have been no minimum requirements for establishing a property management firm or becoming a condo property manager (Canada's Public Policy Forum 2013a). In New York State there is no specific condo property management licensing other than what applies if a condo property manager lists condo properties, collects rent, or otherwise performs activities related to the role of a real estate broker (New York State 2017).[6] Ontario's reformed condo statute's regulations promise to address this via new licensing, although how it will be administered and enforced raises doubts about its likely veracity. This limited regulation has undoubtedly contributed to the rapid growth of the industry. Although property managers' knowledge is sold to condo boards and owners, unlike lawyers and real estate agents, the key agents of this process tend to receive less financial reward relative to the firms themselves. This partially reflects their questionable expert status. One Toronto area property manager with thirty years' experience stated that, typically, property management company arrangements involve low salaries for managers (reflecting a lack of industry regulation) but large profits for the firms:

> Many companies won't pay their top managers more than $60,000 a year now. For that they expect you to manage three, four, five buildings, each pulling in $200,000 a year in management fees. Okay, so you make $60,000 but you're going to be bringing in $800,000 and they're going to work you like a dog and then when they wear you out they ... get somebody else. (TO Manager 3)

Regardless of their expert or professional status, property managers are best understood as knowledge brokers. They acquire and relay legal and other knowledge among owners, renters, and boards and often decide or influence the companies and individuals (including lawyers) with which boards contract for services and materials. Boards often defer to property managers regarding these vital governance decisions:

> Q: Part of the property manager's job in condos is for repairs to get the bids ... Do you ever veto the property manager's opinion?
>
> A: Well basically we might get three bids on something and he'll make a recommendation and I'd say 99 percent of the time it's right. (TO Board 38)

Of course, how a board determines whether a recommendation is "right" is unclear: the metrics used to gauge property manager performance are far from uniform (Canada's Public Policy Forum 2013c, 33). Since regulation within the industry has been informal or industry-led, education of property managers is handled by vested interests; ACMO provides educational information for property managers and there is a voluntary code of conduct called "ACMO 2000." Notwithstanding the impending, uncertain licensing permitted by the new statute in Ontario, the lack of defined, standardized skills means condo boards cannot be guaranteed a consistent standard of service from property management firms and managers. Therefore, whether a property manager's recommendations are "right" is difficult for board members and other owners to discern. But it is vital to also note that, currently, boards sometimes request that property managers flout the law, and the contractual relationship prevents any recourse. For example, one former property manager explained a property manager's current options when, under a regime that is not licensed, a board will not defer to the property manager's view and requests her/him to engage in unlawful conduct or legal avoidance. Under current arrangements the manager cannot easily refuse to comply by telling the board that she or he might lose her/his licence:

> Choice one says, "No, I can't do that." The board says, "That's very nice, here's your termination notice." Or the manager can say, "No, I'm not going to do it, here's my resignation if you're insisting," or, which is very common, "I will do it and I will put it in writing that I object to doing it." So some of those options will be gone [after proper licensing for property managers] ... The only option that is correct is that you resign because if it's found out, [it] doesn't matter that you object[ed]. The fact that you're doing it because your client [the board] is telling you, that's not following lawful instructions ... If it's unlawful, you shouldn't be following it, and that's extremely common. Of course, they don't want to lose a contract ... there's nothing to stop them from saying "no" to an instruction like that, whether it be to fire someone improperly or not doing the regulatory requirements on health and safety or dealing with all the other requirements that you have ... I hope [we] will at least have a very firm line a manager cannot cross anymore. They can't get away with doing something wrong because they said their client [the board] insisted. (TO Real Estate 1)

Despite limited regulation and licensing, property management firms are nonetheless actively engaged in problematizing and, thereby, commodifying the minutiae of condo life and property through contracts. And condo governance is nothing if not preoccupied with minutiae. One contract between a property management company and a condo board that described the manager's duties comprised twenty-four standard typed pages (Property Management Contract 2014). Etching a task in a contract transforms it from the owners' governing responsibility to a purchased commodity. A key section (11) states that the property manager is to

11(r.) make arrangements for, and provide minimum and essential building operations, including but not limited to:

i. carbon monoxide monitoring and certificate;
ii. drainage;
iii. electricity;
iv. elevators;
v. filtering for odours and air cleanliness;
vi. fire, safety, security ... communications systems and certificates;
vii. flood and leak cleanup, correction and repair;
viii. fuel, including generator;
ix. garage doors, ramps and gate arms (4);
x. garbage organization, disposal and prompt pickup;
xi. generator and certificate;
xii. hazards removal;
xiii. heating;
xiv. hollow metal doors, fittings, closer, frames and magnetic locks;
xv. lighting throughout the property, interior and exterior;
xvi. pest and rodent prevention and eradication;
xvii. plumbing and leak prevention or correction;
xviii. signage is clear and consistent (every single door ... properly labelled);
xix. snow and ice removal;
xx. telephone and internet services for the offices, security, the rooftop, the pool and elevators;
xxi. ventilation and make-up air;
xxii. water supply; and
xxiii. other mandatory minimum building services as may be required.

11(s.) inspect, repair and maintain all assets of the Corporation in excellent functional condition and in premium appearance ...

i. all grounds, fences, landscaped and rooftop areas;
ii. garages, arms, barriers, cages, corridors and stairs;
iii. major machinery and equipment;
iv. service, utility and storage rooms;

v. all common elements and recreational facilities ...
vi. repair and patching of all floors, all drop and stucco ceilings, walls and throughways ...
xii. Any other components of the common elements.

(Property Management Contract 2014, 14–15)

Because of such arrangements one property manager related that she is "driven by what is most urgent rather than the most important ... respond to their phone calls and e-mails ... running the elevators, running the hot water in the building, running the mechanical systems, the roof ... health, fire and safety" (TO Manager 5).

As noted earlier, among the most significant requirements for property managers is that they know condo law and an array of other legal knowledges pertaining to all manner of conduct and things encountered in condo arrangements: "Be knowledgeable about all municipal, provincial and federal guidelines and standards related to high-rise multi-unit residential buildings and notify the Board of any significant changes in same" (Property Management Contract 2014, 19).

Related manager responsibilities include maintaining records of Toronto Public Health enquiries, security incidents, and board meeting agendas. Of course, none of these tasks *must* be commodified through a legal agreement like this. Indeed, in a minority of condo buildings studied in Toronto and New York, some tasks were (still) found to be conducted by board members. Sometimes these duties are de-commodified – that is, taken from property manager control and returned to the purview of owner or board member volunteers – but more often the opposite occurs.

The volume of knowledge entering and exiting a property manager's purview is significant and is aided by new commodities and sophisticated technologies, including software to manage the knowledge flow generated by security personnel. One such technology increasingly deployed and endorsed by Ontario condo industry organizations CCI and ACMO is software – aptly named Condo Control Central (2017) – that helps digitally bind agents of an assemblage. It is thus both a reflection and a tool of an assemblage. Residents, security personnel, service providers, board members, and, of course, property managers have varying channels to transfer knowledge in and to receive knowledge in the form of reports, including who entered the building and when, which resident has asked for the most parking permits, who made noise complaints (and how many were received last week), who has a package awaiting pickup from the concierge, and which elevator will be down for maintenance and when. As noted previously regarding classification of condo populations, these, too, are quintessential classification practices that were addressed by Foucault. In famously discussing emergent forms of knowledge (or "disciplines"), Foucault (1977, 205) might have been describing condo assemblages in that they, too, "bring into play the power relations ... inside the very texture of the multiplicity, as discreetly as possible ... [and] to this correspond anonymous instruments of power, coextensive with the multiplicity that they regiment, such as hierarchical surveillance, continuous registration, perpetual assessment and classification."

Relatedly, with the emergence of such software and systematic financial, maintenance, and security information collection pertaining to condo buildings and boards, this information becomes available remotely to property managers. When monitored this way (which is a form of surveillance) by property managers, who are typically assigned to several condo buildings in Toronto and New York via contracts, this further extends the notion of condo governance working from far beyond a condo building's walls. Not unlike how the scientists of Latour's studies work, the property management firm's generated reports become "inscription devices" that represent and permit intervention into these condo arrangements from a distant central location, thus permitting "government at a distance" (Rose and Miller 1992; see also Lippert 2007; Haggerty 2001, 83). Put simply, they permit the condo world – the elements, spaces, and conduct comprising it – to be inscribed. Condo buildings and the board members supposedly governing them are especially resistant to being moved or collected in one place or watched over time, but representing the building as numbers, maintenance schedules, security incidents, and overdue fee payments in instantly produced digitized reports is decidedly easier to manipulate, scrutinize, and govern. Condo Control Central indeed.

The more important point here is that the detailed practices of property managers underscore that, once developed, the condo does not simply exist as property; rather, its materiality and internal spaces are continuously reconstituted through specialized property manager knowledge and inscription practices and assembled via other agents and knowledges. Thus, there is a sense in which condo development and the related constitution of property never ceases, and the commodification of condo governance and spaces moves with it, lockstep, into the future. This is not to suggest, however, that the arrangements that sustain the condo as commodity cannot one day collapse.

Real Estate Firms, Aestheticization, and Commodification

Commodification in relation to condo owners is evident in an increasing preoccupation with investment and property values,[7] sometimes to the extent of defining owners' identities. The notion of the condo as commodity (as well as its link to juridification) is captured nicely in the reflections of one New York condo owner:

> The main thing about having ... a condo ... is owning your own real estate. As I said this is a very, well, large part of most people's net worth. Now ... I have seen [*New York*] *Times* articles where it's the majority of people's retirement ... so I look at it more as a financial transaction ... of renting versus buying, you know, where is the tipping point? ... I look at the financial equation and ... the point of view of an investment. You might lose somewhere and after four years you get back all the money that you paid because of the appreciation in it, after you pay lawyers to buy and pay lawyers to sell. (NYC Res. 11)

In another New York condo building more educated owners encouraged other owners to see units as investments:

> Several of us were educated folks and we want to help people in the building who were ... working class and maybe not as educated to understand ... what the potential opportunity could be for them because ... several of them had been in the building for several years so they stood to gain a lot ... if they thought of this as an investment. Some of them were two-bedroom apartments that they could get a ... sweet deal on. (NYC Res. 15)

An owner who was also a New York real estate agent from a different complex revealed the influence of real estate knowledge on his board's governance decisions:

> I'm really pissed off because people's resale value has been going down. The real estate market all over the city has been going up, but especially in this neighbourhood ... I know, I work in the business. And ours is flat or going down. It's flat. Because people can't get mortgages. When they take a look at the numbers or their attorney of a buyer, he's going to see these numbers and say, "Uh this building is not financially in good shape." And these people, the board, has messed around with my investment. They

are messing with my money, my investment, and I love my house ... it feels very comfortable, but we should be determining our financial structure of how we run the building. (NYC Res. 9)

This resident went on to explain:

> I don't think the sponsor is looking to sell them because it's a catch 22. They put themselves in a position where ... their values have gone down just like the rest of our values are going down because they're here and banks won't loan in the building when they see the high percentage of sponsor units. It's not a[n] ... approved building ... so the big lenders ... wouldn't touch this building ... You can't get a thirty-year fixed mortgage in this building right now ... So they don't want to sell now because the values are down, but the values are down because they're here. It's a little screwy ... before the 2008 housing bubble, they were giving mortgages to anyone who had a pulse. (NYC Res. 9)

As noted in Chapter 2, resident owners in Toronto and New York see their condo units as investments to some degree and correspondingly acquire knowledge about property value trends. One owner explained: "People are very interested in like, 'Isn't it crazy that an apartment that sold two years ago for however much, is now selling this year for like 50 percent more?' ... like the steep increase in prices people are interested in" (NYC Res. 1). Another explained:

> From an investment perspective I would never in my wildest fantasy have expected it to appreciate the way that it has. Especially considering when I bought it everybody's like, "You're going to take a bath on this." So no. It has definitely appreciated in value. There's no question. The neighbourhood's improved. Not that it was bad before. But it's done nothing but get better. (NYC Res. 4)

One owner connected the presence of renters to knowledge of lower property values in the building:

> So about 40 percent ... of 190 [units] are rented out to tenants, and they are not owners living in them, which most people know, in condos, that causes a problem because they don't have the same sort of feeling of

keeping the place, you know, looking nice and safe as owners, [who] have more vested interest in keeping it nice. So property [values] are lower because of that. (TO Res. 11)

Though some knowledge about property values comes from tax assessments, knowledge from real estate firms and agents also contributes to experiencing condo units as commodities with rising and falling prices. In another instance, an owner decided to buy her unit, as opposed to a "cooperative" or detached dwelling, by drawing on real estate knowledge:

> And what's interesting is I did decide to buy there because I could tell ... real estate was going up in price really fast. For example, when I started renting there it was about ... $1,100 a month for a one bedroom. And by the time I left the average was $2,000 a month for a one bedroom. Over about six years ... you know it was a really shocking change, but at the same time that's right when the housing market was in the pit. So I kind of got lucky on other peoples' bad luck because a couple who had lived in the neighbourhood for over twenty years and owned the apartment, they lost their jobs and moved out of the city. So they sold their apartment for really low value ... $370,000. And now the average apartment on that block ... for a one bedroom is over $600,000. So I kind of saw that that was happening and specifically said this block, the architecture is going to stay really nice ... it's always going to be a kind of civic centre. So I wanted to live right on that block ... but a real estate [agent said] ... owning something there might be a good idea. So I made sure to get a condo. I mean that was a specific decision I made to not go for a co-op. (NYC Res. 28)

A Toronto owner explained the hesitance to question or resist the board regarding decisions thought to affect property values: "A lot of people ... said ... frankly we really don't want to do this [to the] board because it may affect the value of our condo so therefore we'll hide our hands, put our heads under the carpet. They're all terrified of their condo values going down if they blow the whistle" (TO Res. 15). A board member from Toronto, who was also a real estate agent, explained how special assessments in relation to property values were dreaded:

> Regarding the special assessment, we had it for two years. It started right after I purchased my place here. Actually, there are a lot of new home

> buyers that are so scared about those special assessments they say that if the place has special assessments they run away from it, they don't buy it ... I was one of the people that was in that position before when I bought it. But then I said ... better to pay special assessment for one or two years or better increase the maintenance of the property which remains like that, you cannot lower it anymore. So increasing a maintenance [fee] of a condo is something that makes people buy or not buy. Because if our maintenance is much higher than the other condos around us then this place will go down in value. This is a normal thing that we discuss in real estate and everything. Special assessment was put at the time because the reserve fund was not enough to cover the expenses for this year's repairs so each family on top of the maintenance ... paid an extra 175 to two hundred dollars. (TO Board 17)

The following accounts also suggest that, in the condo world, commodification is contingently linked with a sub-process of "aestheticization" in seeking to preserve the property values of buildings and units. Aestheticization means governing through aesthetics (see Pow 2009; Walby and Lippert 2011). From the condo's outset, it has been marked by myriad enforceable house rules concerning any colour, decoration (including US flags), and related alterations of individual units that could affect the building's aesthetic and, ultimately, its value in the marketplace. These two processes – aestheticization and commodification – are reflected in condo owners' motivations for board participation. Many board directors indicated their initiative was to ensure control over the condo qua investment in their buildings' appearance. Board decisions regarding renovations are also linked to real estate knowledge.

A Toronto owner related how a real estate agent on the board convinced other owners to renovate: "In 2008 he made a huge, huge renovation in the lobby completely ... from up to down. Different style now. It is more modern ... He tried to convince the people ... this change of style would increase the value of the property which ... is not the case because that is very subjective" (TO Res. 10). In another instance the failure to spend on renovations became an issue: "The value of the unit has not gone up and the running of the board is terrible ... it's doing them harm because the value of our units is not going up, everyone around us is going up and it's not spending money that eventually we're going to have to pay for" (TO Board 15). Another Toronto condo board member explained the influence of acquired real estate knowledge on renovation decisions:

> This takes us back to this major renovation project which started with the statement saying that property values here are inconsistent with others in the neighbourhood and we have to do this renovation work, we're falling behind the times, then it went on to say that realtors accept this as fact. We couldn't get them to name one realtor that they said was the source of that, we couldn't get them to unveil any statement, any factual basis for saying the values were inconsistent. Far from it. We spoke to realtors and we examined building values, "we" being the people opposing the renovations, and went back citing, saying to them that we've had realtors that say that's nonsense and we can find no evidence whatsoever of inconsistencies in property values so there is no massive pressing need to launch into this huge renovation scheme. (TO Board 14)

Thus, aesthetics was often thought to be related to property values:

> There was a mission and a vision statement that we could follow which said we wanted to keep up with standards that are sort of applicable to our level of luxury building, but it is high, high-end luxury buildings and you sort of know where your rank is in that space so you want to maintain it at that level, you don't ever want to let it go below because people spent good money to own something and so it's important to keep up with the aesthetics and the property, the details ... No, this one hasn't gone up in pricing because of the management of the previous board, so actually we are under a hundred thousand dollars in the market. (TO Board 16)

A New York owner remarked upon how aesthetic changes to the condo building related to property value: "The general consensus about modernizing space and making it a little more friendly for kids and updating some equipment, is it's a good thing that kind of enhances the value" (NYC Res. 27). Another owner similarly remarked about renovations to her Toronto building:

> There's just been a lot of stuff that he has done ... and it should make our property values go up, which is stuff that everybody appreciates, maybe not in everyone's taste and it may not always be done to the highest whatever calibre of workmanship, but he seems to be managing the money very well, and so you may not like what he's done, [but] they're small changes that everybody benefits from. (TO Res. 13)

In yet another instance in Toronto, a real estate agent influenced spending decisions through attention to property aesthetics rather than to critical infrastructure, such as boilers or water pipes:

> My [board president] predecessor Brenda is a real estate agent. So of course Brenda would be far more interested in rehabilitating the lobby ... for the ridiculous amount of $80,000 because she hired a consultant who was a good friend of hers and I think she got paid $10,000 for ... some stupid designs ... But when she became president four years ago ... I said, "Brenda, check ... the hot water lines in the building." (TO Board 32)

Commodification entails the pursuit and acquisition of knowledge from real estate agents about property value. Not surprisingly "empty nesters" (who, with first-time residential buyers, are among the most common condo purchasers) often suggest that real estate agents influenced their decision to sell a detached home and to purchase their condo for "financial advantage":

> I lived in my bungalow ... I was told by a real estate agent that when that woman [on the corner] was prepared to sell, I should sell ... It was to my financial advantage because of the way builders are always after two properties ... So when she was ready to go into a nursing home we put our places up for sale together ... It was a good financial move. (TO Res. 17)

This is but one of numerous possible examples of the close connection between real estate knowledge and ongoing commodification. Thus, in a New York complex:

> Q: Was there any talk at all about ... the impact on the value of your property?
>
> A: That was part ... of the pitch ..., you have to spend ... twelve hundred bucks because I think the first year too ... my payment is only like twenty-five dollars a month, so it couldn't have been that much. That's what I pay for the assessment, $25.88 a month. There was a ... presentation ... we brought in a realtor and they talked about – it may have been a separate meeting, the realtor told us that now, if the building was renovated, that having that curb appeal, having the "aha" for people when they first walked into the lobby, adds potentially X dollars to your building's value, your unit's value. I don't

remember the number. So that was part of the information session that we had early on as well. There was a realtor ... that was brought in. (NYC Res. 15)

However, the vital point here is that real estate agents and firms may influence condo governance in less apparent ways via knowledge transfer. In the four decades following Ontario's passage of condo legislation and subsequent creation of the province's first condo buildings, real estate agents did not declare themselves condo specialists. Now some do. For example, would-be owners in Toronto can now enlist the services of real estate "condo experts" (https://www.facebook.com/yourcondoexperts) or the "condo kings" (http://www.thecondokings.com). In addition to motivating and shaping a condo purchase, real estate expertise can also affect condo governance in that some owners see real estate qualifications as ideal for board membership:

Q: So what do you think of the people on the board?

A: ... often they're people who do have some qualifications, so they ... have real estate backgrounds. (TO Res. 5)

One board member related that knowledge provided by a real estate agent led to the identification of a governance issue requiring immediate action:

> I know everything that is going on in this building with regards to lawsuits ... I know which units are up for sale, the condition of the units, how much they're being sold for ... I found out ... some asshole in this building was trying to sell his unit with fucking great holes in the bathroom ... and there was no toilet ... Well if there's a gaping hole of course I'm going to be concerned about it if it's not capped, and it wasn't capped, and how did I find this out? From the real estate agents! Because a friend of mine wanted to buy a one-bedroom unit and was taken in there by her agent. She said, "Jason, there's no toilet in here, there's just a hole in the floor." Well shit hit the fan over that one because ... we could have one hell of a sewage flood! (TO Board 32)

Intensive concern about property values has a direct bearing on how condo governing priorities are set. This translates into gleaning knowledge from real estate agents as property value experts. A Toronto board member, who was also an architect, related how his board conducted a study of real estate information and engaged real estate agents to gather knowledge for a board decision on building improvements:

> [W]e actually do [sic] a study ... we had some units that were for sale and the common comment that we hear is that the condo fees are a bit on the high side but we looked at other buildings too ... and we're at the average of our size and age and ... basically I just looked around at all the various listings around Toronto and ...they'll provide you with all the facts and figures ... we actually had some extra money yet to play with and we're trying to figure out, we actually did kind of talk to ... some realtors and got their opinion on if you were to improve the building or if you're looking to spend what do you think buyers would be looking at? (TO Board 5/Architect)

This underscores how development and governance overlap as it shows that the real estate industry's influence on condo governance does not end with selling all the units following condo conversion or construction; instead, many units "turn over" or circulate in and out of the market, and real estate agents' knowledge influences how this circulation occurs.

Consistent with the influence of real estate knowledge, it was common to find boards that included one or even two real estate agents as members. Some owners tended to think that these individuals were self-interested and made board decisions to their own benefit. For example, in a New York condo building one resident said: "We've got people on the board that ... are realtors ... who want to do real estate in our building, and the way they do it is by getting on the board and making [condo building] rules such that they work to their benefit" (NYC Res. 10). But, in a Toronto condo building, a board member explained that he declared his role in real estate, as well as its likely influence, upon being elected to the board:

> They were aware. I did declare I am working in real estate. I was telling them I would try to increase the value of the property here and also try to keep the maintenance down as much as possible. I was voted in, and sure there are people that say, "Oh, this guy is in real estate and maybe he wants to sell and buy here," but it is up to the people to vote. (TO Board 18/Real Estate)

Some buildings become rumoured, via knowledge from real estate agents, to be on a "black list" of properties (associated with poor board management of reserve funds) held by federal government mortgage agencies. This could prevent would-be buyers from obtaining mortgage insurance, thereby fostering condo owner fear brought on by the dramatically decreased likelihood that their unit would be purchased at market price. For example, a property manager explained that real estate agents were aware of a black list of devalued condo buildings:

> They will tell you, "Oh, we don't have a blacklist." It's a pile of crap. 'Cause I got it clear from an inside man in the thing ... However, they will never admit it's a blacklist. But basically, they've told every bank: "Don't ever bring a deal to me from this address." Won't touch it. Now what do you think they just did? They completely devalued the property. (TO Manager 1)

When owners learn of this, consistent with commodification, they typically become concerned. Similar angst centred on the suggestion that a "self-managed" condo, as opposed to a condo that contracted with a property management firm, would lower property values and scare away buyers due to real estate agent rumour mongering. An owner explained:

> A lot of them think ... it's going to be self-managed ... I don't know where their heads are, that should not be allowed ..., it's not managed ... they won't sign the cheques now to pay the bills, they're going to go right down the tubes ... There was a rumour going around that CMHC [Canada Mortgage and Housing Corporation] wasn't giving mortgages on these buildings and I called CMHC and [it] ... said that's not true ... It made me so angry because ... the real estate agent has no right to say that, but the guy I talked to said it's lazy, the market's good now ... they're not going to go in your building ... So they blow people off and it's not true. (TO Board 3)

Such reliance on real estate agent knowledge works in conjunction with other processes,[8] such as juridification.

Law Firms and Juridification

One of Ontario's first condo developers, Burton Winberg of the Rockport Group, was quoted in the fortieth anniversary *Toronto Star* article about the first Ontario condo built in Toronto under the inaugural 1967 condo statute:

"It sounded like a good opportunity and I'd seen condos in California and was interested in them" (Hanes 2008). That law firms and juridification are key components of condoization is evident from this point onward. Winberg remarked about Ontario's first condo complex: "The problem was no one could pronounce condominium, let alone understand the concept of joint ownership of elements." He continued: "It took a real sales job. Buyers were scared and the legal profession didn't understand the concept. It took a lot of training on our part to *get the legal profession to convince owners* it was okay to buy" (emphasis added). The growth of law firms claiming specialization in condo law has mirrored the condo's proliferation. These firms are central to juridification – the role of legal knowledge in constituting the condo. Born of a legislative initiative (Risk 1968), the condo has always been juridical, but the argument here is that juridical reasoning about condo issues is increasing, as is seen in the growth of court cases and legal decisions concerning condo governance in Ontario and other jurisdictions. The reliance on lawyers and courts to resolve governance issues is growing, and the role of the legal profession is expanding with it (see especially Chapters 4 and 5).

As noted in Chapter 1, the first Ontario Condo Act, 1967, was brief and entailed twenty-seven sections available in regular type on eighteen standard pages, while the first New York State condo statute was about sixteen pages. Condo statutes have since grown in size and complexity, entailing numerous minor amendments and major reforms since their inception in most US states (McKenzie 2011) and Canadian provinces. For example, the next Ontario Condo Act, 1978, expanded to sixty-three sections. The Condo Act, 1998, includes 188 sections on seventy-one standard pages (Gardiner 2001). As a property manager remarked about the 1998 Ontario condo statute that came into force in 2001: "It's more expressive ... it's not like a one liner and you're like, 'Well, it could mean this, it could mean that,' it goes on and it expands, even into the regulations, it expands" (TO Manager 9). The latest Ontario revised statute has expanded yet further. Statutes like Ontario's are present in other North American jurisdictions too. Though perhaps the extent or length of legal texts is a rough measure, it nonetheless signifies the growing juridification of condo life.

Though other knowledges are relevant to condo governance, the main ways of dealing with the many problems encountered in condo buildings continue to involve legal knowledge. Because there is typically little government oversight of condo governance in North America (Lippert and Williams 2012), though this may be changing (albeit not necessarily to owner and renter benefit), resolution of condo governance conflict is partially dependent on the courts. Indeed, condo governance in the US is known for a high degree of litigiousness among boards and owners (see Kress 1995; McKenzie 1994). And there is some evidence that "litigation among co-owners is rising" in the US (Lasner 2012, 280). In condo buildings in Canada there is a similar but lesser-known litigious environment. For example, one case involving condo governance, pertaining to the right of Orthodox Jews to construct succahs on condo balconies (*Syndicat Northcrest v. Amselem*, 2004), reached Canada's Supreme Court. Perhaps more significant are numerous other condo governance cases, some involving nuisances, that have reached provincial supreme or superior courts, such as in British Columbia (e.g., Luymes 2014). And in several provinces the increase of condo governance-related cases and resulting costs over the past two decades, including in Ontario, has led to the introduction of a requirement to pursue mediation or alternative dispute resolution in statutes before seeking resolutions in the courts (Beazley 2013). This was a move that, at least in Ontario, owners widely agreed had failed to resolve disputes (Canada's Public Policy Forum 2013b). But this has not prevented condo mediators from seeking to influence the latest round of reforms.

Even by 2008 a major Toronto newspaper article commenced by reporting: "Fights involving condo owners and condo boards are one of the most rapidly growing areas of law in Canada" (Rusk 2008). As an additional, albeit rough, measure of this juridification, based on the "Canlit" database of Canadian legal decisions, there were 223 cases referring to "condominium" decided in the Superior Court of Justice in Ontario from 30 April 2016 to 30 April 2017 alone, while between 2003 and 2004 there were only 81 cases. For all Canadian courts from the same period between 2000 and 2001 there were 337 decisions, and from 2016 to 2017 there were 948 decisions. More difficult to quantify is the written threat to take an owner, board, or service provider to court, which is also a large part of juridification – for example, when lawyers threaten to sue owners on behalf of boards via letters and the owners relent without it entering the courts, or if the dispute enters the courts and then the case is dismissed (e.g., Silverstein 2002). As condo governance has become increasingly juridified, however, law firms have typically catered more to boards, which have much deeper pockets than owners, in Ontario and New York (see also McKenzie 2011). Typical was one owner's remark that "suing boards is possible ... but hard because very few law firms will take up the fight" (TO Res. 57). In many cases this has had deleterious effects on the ability of owners to contribute to condo governance or to rectify actual or perceived board, property management, and other condo service provider misconduct or incompetence. A particularly knowledgeable condo owner remarked:

> The owners pay the condo fees [and] have a corporation lawyer to protect themselves from legal issues ... but ... that lawyer is there to protect the board. He is there working for the board, not for anyone else. So when you take the board to court for something it's your own lawyer. The condo lawyer is defending the board against you. (TO Res. 58)

There is also general deference to lawyers among owners who, in interviews, reported hesitance or failure to acquire a working knowledge of the condo statute or potential legal avenues for recourse. This lack of knowledge of condo arrangements also contributes to owners' confusion about their potential role in governance. Both owners and board members routinely defer to legal expertise. One board member stated he found it unnecessary to learn the bylaws and rules of his corporation, reasoning that "if there's an issue in most cases [we] either go through our accountant or our lawyer if it's contentious" (TO Board 34). This lack of knowledge among many owners is consistent with the legal profession further inserting itself into board practices. In some buildings the involvement of lawyers was significant:

> The Condo Act ... is of absolutely no assistance to me whatsoever. If you have a problem and you want to get something resolved quickly you can't, and you have to hire a lawyer and that costs a hell of a lot of money. Our annual legal fees in this building are totally out of whack with what we should be paying ... We pay over $70,000 a year in legal fees to our solicitor. (TO Board 32)

A Toronto condo lawyer remarked upon one condo board reacting to an owner (who apparently had been able to secure legal counsel) who had "spent well over $250,000 fighting him and all his lawsuits and no one will buy a unit in the building" (TO Lawyer 2).

Traditionally, chairing the condo's AGM has been undertaken by the board president. However, interviews revealed that, in deference to their legal knowledge, some boards have begun paying lawyers to lead AGMs. As a board member in one such condo building remarked: "The issue was raised at the last AGM. How could homeowners be involved in the decision making? The board, by law, has to make the decisions, okay? But my question was to the lawyer, our lawyer who chairs the meeting: How could we get involved and ... have input?" (TO Board 29). In another Toronto complex, a board member stated that this deference to lawyers at the AGM was partially due to members' reticence to consult or quote the condo statute "immediately, in front of a very large audience" (TO Board 16). The legal profession has acquired a privileged standing in condo governance as it is intimately positioned with regard to the execution of governing obligations, sometimes to the detriment of individual owner interests. In a different Toronto complex, an owner expressed dismay at the lawyer's role during board meetings, indicating that board members

> make sure that there's a counsel in the meeting when the objections or even questions that they don't fancy [are raised] ... They make sure the lawyer ... steps in and intervenes and stops the conversation, stops the questioning, and says, "This is not the place for this discussion." [Question: So where would be the place for the discussion?] A ... pre-meeting before the board meeting to voice the issues, but that's basically all there is – you voice your issues. There's nothing after that. (TO Res. 48)

An emergency court-appointed administrator for condo buildings – whose role is to place the condo corporation and building back on a financially viable footing – elaborated further upon the influence of condo lawyers on condo governance and the need to challenge it:

> And because I challenged management and the lawyers, it bit me ... because they don't like being challenged ... they don't like to be told that: "No, I don't agree with you and I want to minimize your billings as a lawyer. I don't want you at every meeting; I don't want your input in my report, it's my report, not yours. I don't need you to come ... to every AGM or owners' meeting, what's the point of that?" It intimidates the owners and will cost them an unnecessary expense. (TO Administrator 1)

Thus, lawyers are – perhaps not surprisingly – key agents of the juridification of condo governance.

Legal knowledges are themselves commodified to a significant degree in the condo world. Commodification is evident in for-profit training in classrooms or via manuals regarding the condo statute and myriad other forms of legal knowledge for property managers and board members.[9] Of course, the very existence of condo-specific legal training and law firms that serve the condo industry demonstrates the notion that specialized legal knowledge as it pertains to the condo is available for purchase.

One condo law firm sells legal knowledge to boards that adhere to the condo statute in the form of generic condo bylaws for CDN$3,500 (TO Board 22). Most Toronto condo law firms now sell model or generic general bylaws to existing condo corporations. For example, the website of the major Toronto condo law firm Gardiner, Miller and Arnold (GMA) reads:

> Does your condominium have by-laws that take full advantage of the *Condominium Act's* range of by-law powers? Under the Act, there are numerous powers that a corporation can have so long as they are contained in a by-law. This can include granting a telecommunication access license, creating a standard unit and establishing a mediation/arbitration process. It is amazing how many corporations fail to take full advantage of these powers. (GMA 2015a)

The comprehensive general bylaw and the standard unit bylaw are offered for CDN$2,500. This excludes the standard unit bylaw, which is an additional CDN$1,280 plus tax:

> Comprehensive General By-law (CGBL) – We recommend adoption of our CGBL, incorporating typical general by-law provisions, plus applicable Condo Act provisions and over 200 practical by-law improvements (including each of the separate by-laws and forms ... below). The applicable directors' resolution, By-law Procedures, Notice to Owners, explanatory article and other documents are included in the Package ($2,500 + HST, with [an] hourly rate for optional services and for drafting and processing times spent in excess of 3 hours). (GMA 2015a)

Generic rule packages for condo high-rises or townhouses are available for additional fees. The choice of generic rules for CDN$1,280 plus tax is the "recommended choice," as opposed to hiring lawyers to examine existing rules and revise them accordingly. This condo law firm will: "Prepare GMA's Comprehensive (High-rise Townhouse) Rules and provide a 28 page menu of rules for the board's selection to suit the circumstances ($1,280 + disbursements [approx. $30.00] and HST, with hourly rate for revisions response time spent in excess of 3 hours)" (GMA 2015b). These are only some of the listed legal services for purchase by condo boards and property managers. More generally, legal knowledge is to be provided by lawyers to purchasers regarding how the condo building has been managed to that point:

> The attorney for the buyer [is] supposed to read the [board meeting] minutes. I assume that all the minutes are available because they were available with the old management when I was on the board ... And so I think that either the buyer or the attorney of the buyer never read the minutes ... That's important because I know that the value of my apartment could be lower because of this [missed] liability. (NYC Res. 12)

Legal knowledge is regularly purchased when property management's efforts to enforce a house rule violation fail. A Toronto condo lawyer explained what he did for the property management company to confront rule violations in a specific building and how that building became juridified, with the end result being an expensive bill paid by owners:

> So if a unit holder or tenant does not comply with the condo documents usually the management company will send them a letter. And then they will send them a second letter and then they will call us and then we will do a letter and then if they don't apply we start court action. And it's expensive. (TO Lawyer 3)

Another Toronto condo complex permitted three instead of two chances for compliance. Here a board member remarked about an alteration contrary to a rule enacted to ensure the building remained aesthetically pleasing:

> So the rule is we send them three notification letters. So ... one of the owners put [up] an awning without asking permission from the board. So then we sent them a letter saying that this is against the declaration and the rules, you have to remove it. One time, two times, three times within a month and a half then every two weeks. If it's not removed a letter from the lawyers saying you have to remove it and then you have to pay for this letter, which might be two to three hundred dollars. Then if he doesn't remove it then we send people to remove it, then we charge back the amount to his unit. (TO Board 10)

These are some of many possible examples of juridification.

Insurance Firms and Risk Avoidance

Much has been written in recent years about the profound but largely unrecognized influence of private insurance on the governance of everyday life (Baker 2010; O'Malley 2004; Ericson, Doyle, and Barry 2003; Defert 1991), including on municipal urban governance (e.g., Walby and Lippert 2015, 80–98). While a board of resident owners was originally assigned legal responsibility for governing condo conduct and spaces, as shown above, governance is now provided as much, if not more, through external agents with specific designs on outcomes. And here it is vital to note that the condo was born of financial risk aversion when, in the late 1960s, American and Canadian federal governments decided to backstop condo mortgages. However, state and provincial governments' condo statutes did not immediately require the insurance of common elements. For example, in Ontario, the extensive statutory review in 1977, despite devoting a chapter to condo insurance, avoided recommending it as a requirement, and the subsequent 1978 act based upon the review did not mandate it. However, twenty years later, mandatory property insurance for the corporation and common elements and units caused by "major perils" (section 99) and liability insurance for board members (section 102) was made a requirement in Ontario's Condo Act, 1998. While some building declarations had previously required that condo corporations have insurance (Ontario 1977), by 2001, when the 1998 act came into force, private insurance was uniformly and legally required, by statute, to have a place in condo life and has been spreading ever since. Similarly, New York's current condo statute and its section 339b requires the condo board to purchase insurance if the declaration or bylaws require it – a situation found, without exception, in the New York condo buildings studied – or if it is a "qualified leasehold condominium" (where the condo corporation does not own the land beneath the building), thus having the same consequence.

Insurance compliance and claims often involve actual or threatened legal action and, in this way, encourage the involvement of lawyers in condo governance. One Toronto condo lawyer noted that her firm, in addition to working for hundreds of condo boards, also engaged in related "defence work for insurance companies" (TO Lawyer 2). Private insurance has since carved out new markets, several of which directly depend on legal knowledge (see Chapter 4).

The condo segment of the private insurance industry has grown with the condo's rapid proliferation since the 1960s, and it is profitable. "Generally, property insurance per se is more profitable than other lines ... [and] condo insurance on its own is generally fairly profitable from a property standpoint" (TO Insurance 1). The presence of private insurance in the condo is intensifying as new insurance markets are carved out. An insurance representative explained that a condo corporation

> is required to carry insurance mandated by the Condominium Act ... in way of protection for the benefit of all unit owners within the corporation ...There's six areas of coverages [sic] that we have to provide: property, general liability, directors and officers' liability, fidelity coverage for the loss of money to the corporation, human rights protection and board of mechanical coverage. (TO Insurance 2)

It is noteworthy that three (i.e., half) of these six types of coverage pertain directly to a form of legal liability (general liability, director liability, and human rights law), and all are therefore highly dependent on the volume and nature of the flow of legal knowledge through the condo. For these types, insurance firms must be in ongoing receipt of risk knowledge regarding lawsuit trends in relation to condo buildings to adjust premiums – one traditional means of risk sharing – in ways that secure profits. In these instances, legal knowledge and risk knowledge become one and the same. Although never stated publicly, nor necessarily purposely orchestrated in specific instances of governance, insurance depends on legal knowledge *not* arriving in a form easily and completely drawn into board members' or property managers' governing efforts so as to reduce legal liability below the threshold that guarantees insurance profits (generated through legal liability insurance policies).[10] Such legal liability is evident, for example, in relation to elevators. Put differently, as translation of legal knowledge into members' and managers' efforts to govern condo life approaches comprehensiveness, risk stemming from legal liability approaches zero. If it were achieved, there would be nothing to insure, thus closing off a profitable market niche for legal liability insurance. However, it has happened that some insurance providers have cut off condo boards in Toronto from liability insurance because they determined they had not completed reserve fund studies, which have been required since the 1998 Ontario statute, and therefore were in contravention of the law (TO Condo Umbrella Organization 1). For these reasons, private insurance depends on legal knowledge flowing through narrow channels and widespread "excerpting" (see Chapter 4), which virtually guarantees this narrowness. There is a sense in which condo statutes, by requiring that insurance be purchased, and condo lawyers, by delving into details of governing, construct this insurance market. At the same time, as Ericson, Doyle, and Barry (2003, 6) explain more broadly, "Insurance objectifies risk by making it subject to contract and adjudication ... [and] helps the law to assign liability to the party most able to distribute the loss through insurance" (see also Priest 1990). Externally provided risk knowledge and legal knowledge work together in the condo world. Neither is given at the outset: they and their corresponding processes become assembled as condoization.

Security Firms and Securitization

Developing with these other processes is securitization. Like suburban gated communities (Low 2013), condo developers promise owners physical security in their urban complexes (Kern 2010b). And, as a result, security is increasingly equated with condo living. As one condo manager interviewed for a security trade magazine remarked: "The boards are very concerned with security. Most residents really pay detailed attention to security services because once they choose to live in a condo they want security" (Brown 2010, 18). One aspect of increasing the physical security of condo buildings involves contracting private security personnel to conduct various duties. The securitization of access and egress is also evident in New York, in the form of traditional "doormen" (see Bearman 2005). In Toronto, these personnel were usually labelled "concierges," a term common to the hotel industry and one that, rather than evoking security, implies the leisure and pampering consistent with a "carefree" condo lifestyle.

One such concierge in a Toronto building explained his extensive contractual duties and those of the security guards under his supervision. He was also clear on the distinction between these roles:

> The concierge's main duty is to be the first interaction in access control. With procedures established by management, the concierge either grants or denies access, plus gives direction to assist. The concierge also directs the patrol guards as needed. The patrol guard duties are to check designated locations, open/close amenities, and monitor equipment as directed by management. Furthermore, the patrol guard is to remain available to respond to the direction of the concierge (if one is on-site) as the patrol guard is the arms and legs of the concierge. Concierge is like a monitoring

> dispatcher, patrol guard is inspector and response. Both duties are required to observe, report and respond. All actions [are] documented in log books. (TO Security 1)

In condo buildings security guards commonly engage in "inspections, escorts, watch, emergency response, enforcement of client rules and regulations ... and all other manner of criminal and nuisance activity" (TO Security 1). Such policing of "nuisance activity" by these contracted security agents and others, as part of condo governance, is discussed in Chapter 6.

Consistent with an assemblage, condo security agents work closely with contracted property managers. If the latter's trade is primarily brokering various knowledges, the former's trade is collecting, storing, and relating security knowledge. Accordingly, these security agents not only follow procedures "by management," they are in near constant contact with managers, transferring security knowledge shortly after it is produced. Consistent with being only one element of a governing assemblage rather than the foremost agent of daily condo governance, the board was contacted only once a month: "As the site supervisor I debrief with the property manager at least twice in an eight-hour shift. Debriefs regard all concerns that took place after hours, upcoming events, direction, and duty reviews. The board as a body is debriefed monthly as required regarding all issues concerning security. Board debriefs are general overviews" (TO Security 1). A security firm's contract, not only that of a specific concierge/security guard, is subject to review, termination, and replacement based in part upon these debriefings. In this case, the board is to make the decision, as this same "concierge" explained: "At the end of a contract the company is up for review. If the review is positive, the contract is renewed for another term [and is] determined by the condo's Board of Directors. A negative review results in another bid competition with the previous company omitted from participating" (TO Security 1).

Security is used for marketing new-build condo complexes and, due to increased costs for developers, is not without a downside. As one condo architect working for developers put it, security is

> a delicate issue because [for] a developer, it may [be] a good selling point for him where he has security all over in the corridors, in the common areas, and he has that security for the building. But it's expensive for him. He's not going to gain anything from it except a marketing point of view, selling the unit, saying, "Your building is secure," where someone else's

building [is] with no security, do I want to buy a unit in *that* building? (TO Board 2/Architect)

Security provision is a prominent selling point among developers seeking to capitalize on and create a sense of insecurity linked to tropes about criminal opportunists lurking in cities. An analysis of twenty condo developer marketing websites from both Toronto and New York revealed much attention to security. For example, the website for the new-build "Picasso" condo building in Toronto features a stunning array of security arrangements that accompany a unit's purchase, both human "concierge" and technological (e.g., "Enterphone system and cameras"). These are listed under "general features" and "foyer" and then under a "security" category:

Peace of Mind

- Security cameras linked to concierge for surveillance monitoring
- One uniformed 24 hour, 7 day a week concierge
- Personally encoded in-suite speaker intrusion alarm and key pad with digital display, featuring suite to concierge digital display communication monitored by concierge
- Remote control access to resident underground parking garage
- Electronic access control system to recreation amenities, parking garage, and other common areas
- Underground security system complete with security key device. Two-way communication system from underground to concierge
- Key fob access to main entrance
- All exterior doors from common areas and amenities monitored at concierge desk via security cameras
- Property management office on site
- Secure, well-lit and painted underground parking garage ...
- Key fob access from underground parking to elevator lobby
- Enterphone system and cameras located in lobby of main entrance complete with in-suite Monitoring facility and operates with suite land line phone or mobile phone, allowing residents to view visitors through dedicated television channel.[11]

The "Milan" in Manhattan similarly advertises "building features" with security:

- Attended Lobby
- Concierge
- Full-time Doorman ...
- Around-the-clock doorman, concierge
- All units feature custom climate control and electronic security.[12]

The marketing continues after the private security provider has been selected by the board. As one property manager interviewed for a somewhat partial security trade magazine article entitled "Condo Culture" remarked: "While G4S [a transnational security guard provider] is a little bit on the high side cost-wise ... as soon as I announced who was chosen as security provider the board said, 'Put a notice out that we have leaders providing security in our building'" (Brown 2010, 18).

Surveillance is a growing part of securitization and takes several forms (see Chapters 5 and 6). Here physical security is what is chiefly at issue. As condo complexes have grown, so too has securitization: "For large condo properties the security budget is generally one of the main items of the operating budget. It depends on the size of the site ... but can be as much as $250,000 CDN per site" (Brown 2010, 17). One transnational security guard corporation, G4S, now has an entire, separate "condominium division" (Brown 2010, 17) securing Toronto condo complexes.

Despite the marketing and actual arrangements of developers, security provision is part of condo governance too and not merely of development. Often boards initiate further security enhancements – and thus securitization. One board member recalled: "We had somebody sneak in through the parking door garage ... and break into a car, so after that happened there was an effort to just reinvest a little bit of money and upgrade the video systems and there's a heightened awareness amongst the security guards" (TO Res. 62). In a larger condo complex in Toronto a board member related: "The property manager got some quotes and diagrams about the cameras of all the levels and we added five new ones, so we are really well covered ... There was some debate because it was really expensive" (TO Board 36). There was a greater frequency of vandalism in a different building, and the board member explained the response: "We have other cameras we added for security. We increased the number of cameras that the builder had installed in the garage. In fact, we changed them to higher quality cameras and we put one in ... this hallway leading to this party room" (TO Board 26). Finally, one property manager lamented poorly secured entry points, alleging it made the building vulnerable:

We had eighteen break-ins because the developer put a bunch of cheap locks on the doors, but basically a screwdriver ... pops the door open. So the corporation is paying $100,000 in lock replacements. Now we have high security, high-end security, medical locks, not copy-able, not bump-able, you can't thread into it. In other words, you can't cut a thing ... When they felt unsafe then they were willing to spend the money. (TO Manager 4)

With obligations to uphold security standards, condo boards become big security consumers as they allocate large proportions of annual budgets to acquire controls, alarms, surveillance systems, and security personnel. This makes condo high-rises resemble vertically arranged gated communities (see also Rosen and Walks 2015b), although, curiously, the horizontal kind has received far more attention in urban studies and socio-legal literatures (e.g., Levi 2009; Grant 2005; Low 2003), especially in the US. Indeed, the limited access to condo complexes that prevails, even within buildings, renders it difficult to distinguish the two. Intensifying security measures is often explicitly aimed at fortifying premises, sometimes due to owner demands. As one board member explained: "Some people will complain about security, they want like instant response, virtually a real police force here, 'cause we have had ... over the years a number of instances of cars being stolen from the underground garage ... We had a real raft of thefts there, we've had some drug dealing" (TO Board 30). Yet, despite the developer's and then the boards' efforts to securitize common property via purchased security, these measures were far from secure. As one board member recollected:

There was [an] incident where someone got through the front door and went directly to the basement and selectively began to break into cars and, in the case of convertibles, he had a pocket knife and so he cut the soft top all for the sake of small change that was left in the console ... The security guard at that time was apparently resting his eyes not watching the cameras, so that firm was let go. (TO Board 39)

Another board member similarly recalled an incident involving vandalism and theft:

We had a lot of tire slashing ... we had people vandalizing cars and taking the GPS out of them ... And they broke in and damaged quite a few cars

... The security gatehouse, where they have cameras everywhere ... didn't see these people. And I think that sometimes they fall asleep. I think a couple of the guards were fired over that. (TO Board 27)

In some cases, owners mobilized their security personnel to address crime beyond the condo's boundaries. In one incident an owner witnessed illicit drug sales close to the condo building: "We have some little basketball courts and we have kids who are dealing with dope in our little park across the street so I kind of worked with the concierges to kind of stop that ... It's not good to have people dealing like that in the neighbourhood" (NYC Res. 14). The foregoing examples demonstrate that condo residents rely heavily on security providers to nullify feelings of insecurity. Because condo owners are encouraged to have high expectations for security, and because criminal activity can tarnish a condo building's reputation and property value, condo property managers typically respond rapidly to property crimes. This often involves intensification of security measures and further securitization.

MUTUALLY REINFORCING ASSEMBLED PROCESSES, AGENTS, AND KNOWLEDGES[13]

The identified key elements of condoization – the various processes, agents, and knowledges described in the foregoing – are closely related and often mutually reinforcing and constitutive, consistent with the notion of an assemblage. Owners revealed numerous ways in which these processes and their associated actors assembled in the administration of condo life.

One real estate agent explained how he transfers knowledge to potential owners, thus showing how real estate agents, property managers (i.e., commodification), and potential owners become linked in governance as well as revealing how, in this instance, boards are not involved:

> Because of my knowledge of condos, I can find out who's managing it, and ... I will try to get a hold of the manager and say: "Look, I've got a client potentially buying here. I'm potentially listing. Anything I should know about?" ... The listings themselves are covered by the real estate boards that you're using ... But because ... real estate transactions in the province happen here [Toronto], it's interesting to know that many of the fields that you would expect to be required to [actually] be optional,

> such as a management company and ... the maintenance fee ... it's not checked ... If there are ten listings in a building, there might be three management companies listed ... And my point back to governance is, if your board is concerned that your property is well represented, and properly represented, wouldn't it behoove them to make sure the listing says the right manager so that's clear where the status certificate is supposed to come from? The buyer can check and do some due diligence or the agents representing the buyer can do some due diligence. (TO Real Estate 1)

In another case a real estate agent told an owner that it was not necessary to know the condo statute:

> Q: Do you ever refer to the Condo Act, do you have to know it? Is that a responsibility of yours?
>
> A: No ... because I have a lot of friends that are real estate agents and they tell me that the Condo Act is a pretty difficult piece of paper to read and to fully understand so I don't even bother. (TO Res. 47)

A property manager explained how insurance supported the property management industry in its risk avoidance preferences: "Insurance companies are getting less likely to insure a self-managed board over a professionally managed board. They haven't really gone forward with that yet. But they're talking about pulling insurance away, a lot of the companies are concerned that self-management could be [a] self-destructive entity ... from an insurance point of view" (TO Manager 5). This essentially means, in this instance, that, if mandatory insurance becomes more difficult or more expensive due to higher policy premiums and deductibles, condo unit owners will find it potentially *more* rather than *less* costly to continue to self-manage (or switch to self-management of their condo building) rather than to contract with a property management firm.

In another instance, property management and condo law firms (i.e., commodification and juridification) are seen to work closely together:

> The manager had a very close relationship with the lawyer, so she hired his law firm to send out letters to residents every time she had a complaint ... So if someone's music is too loud next thing they know they get a letter from the lawyer, a threatening letter. And the corporation would be slapped

> with three hundred bucks to pay for this frickin' letter. So that was just going on and on and it should not be that kind of relationship ... You can't just send a threatening letter to everybody who says something you don't like. (TO Res. 56)

The convergence of several processes is further reflected in the following board member's account of a condo building with governance issues:

> There is a condo board ... in Toronto ... They were telling an owner, "You ever tell anybody about our problems with this building, we will sue you with defamation of title, you are bringing down our property values" ... And they will come out and say it without realizing what they're saying. They're saying: "We want to cheat the people coming into our building. The present buyers want to cheat the future buyers." And our board is going to help us and our lawyer is going to help us. And our manager is going to help us. So sucker, we are going suck you in and when you get in, thank us. (TO Board 4)

Property management also entails and contributes to juridification as managers are expected to administer not only the condo statute but also a wide array of legal regulations ranging from workplace harassment to elevator maintenance. One property manager related that there "are all these crazy new rules ... none of us can keep on top of these things, nobody tells us about these things, they [state or private regulators] just come and say 'here's your ticket, you're being charged ... you didn't do this'" (TO Manager 4). In responding to a question about whether a property manager would typically know specific rules of a building, a condo lawyer working for a Toronto-based firm representing more than six hundred condo corporations further indicated the mutual support that exists between lawyers and property managers:

> Depends on how good the manager is. But what's important is that they pick up the phone when they don't know and they call the lawyer. So if they don't know they should be able ... to determine whether they're giving the right answer to somebody. So you know what also happens in the industry is you tend to work with a particular management company. Okay? So I work with several management companies with whom I have a really good relationship. They send me clients and I send them clients because we like the way we work. (TO Lawyer 2)

Lawyers are intimately involved in real estate purchases, but condo unit purchases in particular are claimed to be a hidden minefield that only a condo lawyer could navigate:

> You should always find a lawyer who is a condo lawyer because it's an entirely different ballgame than buying a house ... Your lawyer should sit down with you and go over the status certificate ... of the building, which should contain information as to future special assessments, anything that's wrong ... and also go over the bylaws and the rules with you. (TO Board 17)

A contracted security guard explained how rule enforcement worked in his condo building, again showing how key agents (property managers, security personnel, insurance personnel, and lawyers) and processes are interdependent when it comes to daily condo governance:

> For deliberate violations and those that believe they are entitled to break the rules, we issue a three-copy violation slip with direction of compliance. Each copy goes to the applicable person (offender, security, and management). If direction of compliance is not met enforcement is directed by management, normally resulting in suspension from use of amenities, fines, lawsuit, or even criminal charges. An example rule, residents only may use the gymnasium facility under insurance protocols. Resident and guest use gym equipment ... security cautions rules (guest not allowed) ... directs parties to stop ... parties stop ... no notice given, but report made ... next day same resident and guest repeat violation ... security ignored by parties ... issues violation by mail ... security generated report to management ... management directs electronic key access denied to resident until reinstated by management ... security disables resident's electronic access to the gym. (TO Security 1)

Unlike the property manager and security personnel relations noted earlier, other accompanying agents of governance are assembled and lurking in the temporal shadows. Thus, in the past, the "insurance protocol" that led to the creation and enforcement of this house rule was written by insurance personnel as part of the policies purchased by the condo corporation (insuring corporation assets and against legal liability). This is a purchase now required by condo statute in Ontario, as noted earlier, and if it were decided to file a "lawsuit" to ensure compliance in this instance, a condo lawyer would soon be contacted to initiate this procedure. This arrangement is also a matter of knowledges making governance possible, with this single infraction being variously transferred through the assemblage and translated from risk knowledge (risk of guests being harmed or damaging common elements, the gym equipment, or space) to security knowledge (guests rendering the gym space insecure) to property management knowledge (the perpetrator affecting the property has ignored security and has to be dealt with) to legal knowledge (the perpetrator must be threatened with a lawsuit and, if necessary, taken to court) according to the various agents that become enlisted. The incident will also take on a different appearance depending on the agent and type of knowledge and, accordingly, become instantiated in differing formats following translation (an insurance claim or policy violation report, security report, management report, legal filing, and [later] juridical decision). But with each transfer the ties among the agents and processes are reinforced, in a sense creating an assemblage and the condo anew.

There is a subtler but perhaps no less consequential way that these various elements are mutually reinforcing. Juridical decisions (such as those discussed in relation to policing nuisance) from the courts recognize security and property managers as legitimate agents operating in the condo world; they recognize their role in responding to nuisance complaints and, in so doing, further conjoin relations among them. Thus, a Supreme Court of Justice of Ontario decision discussed in Chapter 6 documents the role of security and property management in responding to noise nuisance in *Italiano v. Toronto Standard Condominium Corporation No. 1507*.

Securitization and commodification broadly overlap since security is obviously also a commodity purchased by the condo corporation as "concierges" and roaming guards rather than, or in addition to, something achieved via reliance on public police and resident volunteers. But they also assemble in instances such as when contracted security personnel and property managers are deemed to have a common client – the condo corporation – to whom they dispense knowledge at monthly meetings. Thus, the district manager of the condo division of G4S noted regarding working with property management firms at particular condo buildings: "We try and ... partner with our clients. We have a mutual client and that's that condo corporation, so I want to make sure our direct report [to the board] is not getting blasted [by the property manager] because the security is too tough or too lenient" (Brown 2010, 18).

This is not to suggest that mutual support among elements of an assemblage is seamless and that one agent type does not occasionally deem another type inadequate in some way, including regarding knowledge transfer. Thus, the following comments of an insurance broker who provides condo insurance in Ontario reveal two things: (1) that their work in this instance is intimately connected to actions of condo lawyers and real estate agents characteristic of an assemblage and (2) that their corresponding knowledges have not always arrived to the satisfaction of private insurance:

> It was found that ... a very large percentage, I think it was as high as 40 percent of unit owners, weren't carrying insurance and at that time the question was why? Why are the unit owners not carrying insurance? Most of the times the people responded that they didn't know they had to. And that's a failure on the part of ... the legal community, people that are closing the deals for the unit owners that are purchasing. I think the lawyer hasn't brought it to the attention of the unit owner that they need to carry it, they also think that the corporation's policy solves all. Well certainly it will solve the mortgage requirements, it will solve the physical buildings as far as livable standards, but it is not going to protect its contents, personal liability, and a lot of things that are important to a unit owner that can cause a severe financial loss, should they get caught in a situation. The other thing is I think the real estate people, that when the units are being sold or resold, and especially to first-time buyers of condominiums, again the real estate people aren't bringing it to the attention of the unit owner that it [the condo] is a different insurance world and there are certain obligations that are totally different from a homeowner's situation, that need to be addressed, and that's where the problem exists for unit owners. And there is nothing that mandates you have it, so unless the lawyer tells them, the real estate [agent] tells them, or they have [an] insurance agent that understands it, then they can be left high and dry. (TO Insurance 3)

Finally, a seasoned condo property manager discussed relationships among court-appointed administrators (who, in exceptional circumstances consistent with "counter-law," take over boards deemed to be dysfunctional, completely self-interested, or incompetent), property managers, and lawyers, thereby showing even more explicit mutual support initiated by legal knowledge:

> By virtue of this unregulated area, [for] both management and the [court-appointed] administrator, what seems to happen is it's a tag-team approach. "I scratch you on the back, I'll reciprocate." So, "I'll get an appointment; you'll get the management contract." So how can that possibly work if you're working for the owners? ... In fact sometimes [it is] a triad because the lawyer says, "Oh ... I'll do you a favour; let's get you an appointment and you keep me in and maximize my billings," which also happens. So they make good money and maximize ... Everyone is benefitting financially, except they forget what their job is: to help that building that doesn't have any money, and everyone is feeding off it like the jackals ... And on top of it, the judges have seen an advantage in the administrator being ... an owner of a management company, which makes no sense, because every trade that they have a relationship with ... the lawyer and the landscaper and the security guard company and everybody ... is potentially going to benefit ... You're supposed to be thinking what's best for the building. And ... there's case law about this ... I can give you some condo case records and you can check the documentation leading up to the appointment. On what basis has the judge made the decision? And the [condo] corporation who, the lawyer who's said, "Oh, so-and-so would be a good administrator and he's manager or owner of a management company" is promoted because he has all these contacts. ... And again the judges don't have the sensitivity to understand that you're creating a conflict of interest, right? "You helped me in my building, what benefit? Can you help me and my portfolio? Or my Christmas party? Can you fund it for me?" or "We're doing a BBQ this summer, how much are you going ... to contribute?" That all happens, by the way, all of it. (TO Manager 8)

This mutual support and convergence helps form an assemblage.

Each of the key processes and agents discussed above performs a unique role. Issues relating to building governance or infrastructural management are typically directed towards the property manager who may, in turn, direct them towards a condo's lawyer. Building mismanagement and associated owner discontent may lead, as one board member stated, to receiving "a terrible reputation in Condo Land" (TO Board 32) that can be spread by real estate agents and others. This board member's use of "Condo Land," also found in media accounts about Toronto condo buildings (see also Lippert and Walby 2013), is useful for thinking about the interconnected assemblage of lawyers, property management firms, real estate agents, and security personnel. Each of these actors furthers the associated processes of juridification, risk avoidance, commodification, and securitization that constitute the condo and the conquest of Condo Land.

CONCLUSION

Chapter 1 suggests that previous scholarship has perhaps focused too much on condo development to the neglect of vital features of condo governance. Condo development and governance are seen to overlap in the complex process of condoization. One upshot of this overlap, besides suggesting that disparate literatures focusing upon these two aspects have much to share, is that condo development may well be as dependent on governance (and thus its various assembled elements) as governance is on development. This is meant to suggest that the assembled but previously neglected knowledges and agents of condo governance have helped shape and make condo development possible. Furthermore, it may well be that, for example, the emergence of condo-specific property management and security personnel in Toronto are less an effect and more a condition of the possibility of the growth of large condo towers with many floors, hundreds of units and owners, and massive common elements and spaces demanding governance.

In this chapter condoization begins to be seen primarily as a means of governing the urban that enlists multiple other processes, knowledges, and agents that flourish in the condo world. While condo legislation assigns responsibility to a board, nominally external agents such as lawyers, property managers, real estate agents, security personnel, and private insurance representatives are also shown to be intimately implicated in condo governance. Condo governance now heavily relies upon these external agents and is shaped by these related processes. The various governing agents and knowledges are bound, despite heterogenic forms and aims, into an assemblage. This chapter begins to discern ways in which these processes and corresponding agents and related knowledges can be mutually reinforcing (e.g., when requirements for insurance are placed in condo statutes). In the next chapter, this is further illuminated via a closer look at assembled agents and knowledges pertaining to renters in condo complexes.

This chapter also reveals a peculiar tension between neoliberal logic's expectation that condo residents actively govern themselves as individuals –

something about which governmentality and related scholars have written at length (e.g., Rose 1999; Brady and Lippert 2016) – and residents' increasingly passive reliance not only on formal governance mechanisms but also on external agents and knowledges about which they seem only vaguely aware. This suggests that neoliberalism has less purchase within actual arrangements of condo governance than has been implied in critical urban studies (a point to which I return in the conclusion).

This book's focus on how the condo is constituted reveals that condo governance operates through an assemblage of legal and non-legal processes, strategies, and knowledges. The resulting condo is a legal, social, and spatial relationship among many assembled constituents and elements rather than only a physical edifice at the apparent end point of condo development (consistent with urban neoliberalism or gentrification). And the broader process of condoization cannot be reduced to any one of its rudiments. The fuller picture of this assemblage remains unrecognized by many owners, boards, statutory reformers, and scholars alike.

4

Governing Condo Renters

> They don't have the same sense of ownership and caring about things because they're renting, they don't own.
>
> – *TO BOARD 6*

> I think that our property values are more in jeopardy because ... there's too many renters in the building.
>
> – *NYC RES. 3*

If there were any doubts about the importance of legal knowledge to condo governance, consider a recent annual condo industry conference held in Canada's largest city. For at least the past four years, the two-day Toronto-based conference has concluded with a spectacle unabashedly titled "The Last and Authoritative Word." Near the conference's end contractors' display booths are dismantled and replaced with banquet tables in the hotel's expansive conference room. Condo property management, insurance and law firm representatives, and other private service providers gather for the dinner finale. By the time dessert is served, prominent condo lawyers from across Canada have appeared on a raised stage in armchairs in a semicircle facing one another and the dining audience. For the next hour nuggets of legal wisdom expertly unearthed from the muddy case law of the past year are exhibited for the assembled agents of condo governance who look on with outward deference and inner satiation. A brave few – usually property managers who are expected to apply condo law – step up during the brief "open-mic" session to direct queries to the stage about all manner of condo governance challenges and literally receive "the last and authoritative word" from law's sages, thereby completing a circuit of legal knowledge. This channel for the flow of legal knowledge represents only one trickle of its movement in and out of the condo world, but it is emblematic in bringing representatives of these profit-driven firms together while excluding a decidedly weaker constituent common to all North American jurisdictions – the renter. As discussed in Chapter 8, this arrangement is mirrored in legislative oral hearings over condo statute reform in Ontario, whereby legal knowledge flows from the condo world to the legislature rather than the reverse. Regardless, conference proceedings such as these raise vital questions about condo governance and the flow of legal knowledge. How does legal knowledge flow into the expanding condo world, through what means, and for what purposes? How does this legal governance work? What closely aligned and converging institutional processes does this knowledge shape and make possible? Who is expected to use this knowledge and whom does it target? Even with the condo's growing pervasiveness in North America and globally, little research has explored the knowledges and external agents increasingly implicated in its governance.

The importance of legal governance to the condo therefore lies well beyond the passage or reform of condo statutes. It involves a continual flow of legal knowledge into condo buildings – knowledge that centres on how and whether subsequent court decisions and condo declarations, bylaws, and rules are enforced or ignored. This chapter elaborates how legal governance and external agents' strategies of governance constitute and are brought to bear on the condo's "other" – the renter, a resident who, for the long term, leases from an owner a unit in a condo building. However, the latter part of this chapter also discusses the practice of short-term "hotel" stayers as these persons, despite typically being targeted by separate legal knowledges and agents, are sometimes placed in the same category as long-term renters in condo governance.

Today legal knowledge flows into the condo world through communication channels that include industry conference spectacles, law firm-produced newsletters, legal advice newspaper columns, internet discussion boards, and social networking websites (e.g., Facebook). These channels allow and complement knowledge transfer. Previous research has paid only limited attention to knowledge in relation to governance, including communication "formats" (see Moore and Valverde 2000; Ericson and Haggerty 1997) and practices shaping how knowledge moves through and helps form assemblages (see Lippert 2007; Wilkinson and Lippert 2012). The condo offers an opportunity to focus on this as well. Identifying and examining these taken-for-granted channels of knowledge flow is vital to understanding how (and whether) legal knowledge enters and exits condo realms, mostly to the benefit of commercial firms, and how this knowledge comes to define and target categories of governance within these domains.

Thus, this chapter seeks to demonstrate the importance of the presence of the renter in the condo world as well as how renters are governed and constituted. It then specifically illuminates the role of legal knowledge and of several profit-driven agents – law, private insurance, and property management firms – in shaping condo life by focusing on their targeting of the renter. This analysis reveals how legal channels and practices beyond the courts, and how several external commercial agents identified as operating beyond condo boards, have become implicated and converge in condo governance in relation to the renter. Legal knowledge to deal with the renter is seen flowing into the condo world through communication channels that include – beyond conference spectacles – law firm-produced newsletters, legal advice newspaper columns, and internet discussion boards. Hitherto neglected in socio-legal research, these channels allow and complement knowledge transfer practices such as "excerpting," a significant and widely used form of legal text reduction.

While paramount, condo governance of the renter is not accomplished by legal knowledge wielded by statute-mandated condo boards alone. Increasingly, such governance is also dependent upon private insurance and property management. Private insurance governs the renter by deploying risk surcharges to spread risk through special thresholds that distinguish condo buildings from rental complexes and – when these fail – through direct legal action. More intimately governing the renter and enlisted to apply legal knowledge for this purpose, however, is property management. This industry is expanding rapidly as condo life and – more specifically – solutions to governance problems are more and more commodified. Despite their heterogenic forms and aims, these commercial firms and related processes become bound together, with the renter category emerging as one point of their convergence. By focusing on the renter, this chapter further reveals condo governance as a heterogeneous assemblage of legal and non-legal processes, strategies, and (legal) knowledge flows and also shows how these elements are mutually supportive.

CONDO GOVERNANCE AND THE RENTER

The urban geographer Nicholas Blomley (2005, 126) cogently remarks about renters in relation to private property: "We are suspicious of renters not only because they are poorer, in general, than owners, but also because they rent. As such they are incomplete owners." A condo property manager already quoted in Chapter 2, while suggesting renters were not an issue, nonetheless implied this dominant understanding in the condo world:

> Downtown [Toronto] is high rental ... Is that an issue? It sometimes is on the wear and tear of the building, the maintenance, when you have renters, but I've seen just as bad owners as I have renters. I don't like to make them second class citizens. We like refer to everybody as residents equally as opposed to resident owners because it is really just about educating. There are a lot of good people out there who rent and really respect their homes too, so it shouldn't be a problem, but again it's ... area and the type of owner. (TO Manager 6)

Many owners blamed renters for causing myriad problems for resident owners. In New York a condo owner recounted the effects of a business-owned unit being rented out: "There used to be a couple [of] businesses that owned [a unit] there ... One of them ... was forced to sell because they had too many people coming and going constantly in their apartment which caused an issue with ... the residential neighbours on that floor ... But there's no restriction on renting out" (NYC Res. 25). A resident in a Toronto condo complex suggested that boards should watch the level of rented units in the building due to a downward effect on property values, apparently unaware that subsequent "amendments" were contrary to Canadian case law (as discussed later in this chapter):

> Every board should know because it's kind of at that point when you get saturation of rental units, the property value decreases, so the board should actually be watching that number, and if it's becoming a problem, some amendments and policies should be brought down to curb that. Like [for] the people who put money in there, to keep us safe, our properties safe. (TO Res. 8)

As shown in Chapter 2, already by the 1970s condo owners in North American cities were renting out rather than living in units. By 1980, 40 percent of condo units were renter-occupied (Eilbott 1985). US census data for 2009 reveal roughly the same proportion – one rented unit for every two owner-occupied condo units (or 33 percent of condo units rented) (United States Department of Housing and Urban Development 2011). Canadian census data from the 2016 census reveal a near identical situation, with 33 percent of condo units rented (Statistics Canada 2017b).

Renting a condo unit is easier in Canada than in the US as renting cannot be restricted by condo boards in Ontario and several other provinces (British Columbia permits some restrictions); whereas in cooperatives, which are prevalent in New York, it is more difficult to rent units, thus also making cooperatives "less desirable for persons who wish to purchase the units as investments" (Schill et al. 2007, 284). In New York the number of rented units is sometimes capped in a building through the use of a condo bylaw. The condo thus encourages the growth of investors (and therefore renters too) more than cooperatives, a point returned to below. The extent of renter-occupied condo units is rarely documented in the US and Canada, and it is therefore vital to do so here (see Tables 4.1 and 4.2). Both New York (44 percent) and Toronto (23 percent) have high percentages of condo units occupied by renters,

TABLE 4.1 Owner- and renter-occupied condo units in selected US cities

US city	Owner-occupied condo units	Renter-occupied condo units
Chicago	287.5 (69%)	128.2 (31%)
Houston	27.2 (31%)	60.1 (69%)
Miami	325.3 (56%)	260.6 (44%)
New York	150.8 (56%)	120.1 (44%)
Seattle	72.8 (55%)	59.0 (45%)

Note: Alphabetical order by city. Numbers in thousands.
Source: US Census Bureau (2013a).

TABLE 4.2 Owner- and renter-occupied condo units in selected Canadian cities

Canadian city	Owner-occupied condo units	Renter-occupied condo units
Calgary	64.6 (68.3%)	30.0 (31.7%)
Montreal	151.4 (71.1%)	61.5 (28.9%)
Ottawa	47.6 (73.2%)	17.4 (26.8%)
Toronto	287.4 (77.3%)	84.4 (22.7%)
Vancouver	204.9 (73.3%)	74.6 (26.7%)

Note: Alphabetical order by city. Numbers in thousands.
Source: Statistics Canada (2011).

although these are not the highest proportions compared to other American and Canadian cities with significant condo concentrations.

Surveys of condo owners and anecdotal evidence from board members and unit owners indicate that, regarding condo units, the renter-to-resident owner proportion varies by neighbourhood.[1] It has been known to reach a one-to-two ratio in some markets, as in 1995 in Toronto (and even higher in specific condo buildings like Toronto's City Place condos), and as low as a one-to-four ratio in 2004 in Toronto (Canada Mortgage and Housing Corporation 2007). Most strategies to govern renters discussed below presume an entire unit is rented out by a non-resident owner.

In Toronto and other Ontario cities with fast-rising residential real estate values (Steele 2009), available rental units tend to be *mostly* in condo complexes (see also Eilbott 1985); there are few affordable housing alternatives. Renters enter the condo already in a subordinate position with no formal say about the myriad rules imposed upon them. In principle, if a condo building does not set board member requirements in its bylaws beyond what is required in the statute (e.g., Ontario's 1998 condo statute, subsection 29[1], stipulates qualifications for board members, such as being at least eighteen years old) a renter *could* be elected as a board member. But in that case, he or she would have to be elected by owners since it is only at "meetings of owners" (see subsection 51[1]) that rules, bylaws, and elections can be voted upon (unless someone is attending on behalf of an owner to vote by proxy (subsections 52[3] and [4]). There was, however, not a single mention of the election of a renter in interviews and other data pertaining to numerous condo buildings in Toronto and New York or even the possibility that this could happen. The main point here, however, is that the external non-resident owner – by definition – can afford to reside elsewhere, while it is assumed the renter will stay to endure myriad governing strategies as well as the rules of boards and external agencies and, in practice, have no say in their formation or amendment, despite footing some of the condo bill.

By their mere presence renters call into doubt the condo ideal, which is premised on *owners* sharing responsibility and governing common spaces together. Renters are a discursive affront to the possibility of the condo due to their assumed disregard for the nobility of homeownership and lack of care for property. Writing about property, Blomley (2004, 89) asserts that "those who are imagined as non-owners ... are not only incomplete citizens, but partial and deformed subjects. Perhaps this partially explains the *enduring suspicion toward, and devaluation of, renters*" (emphasis added) and their constitution as "other." Resident owners, then, are deemed to have in common precisely what renters are presumed to lack. In the condo world these dividing practices that constitute this "other" are not unitary; rather, they are discovered to stem from various elements of the assemblage. This imagining of the renter as problematic is evident in interviews and numerous documents. For example, in 1984 the only "National Condominium Market Study" ever conducted in Canada, funded by the Canada Mortgage and Housing Corporation, discussed the renter issue in the following terms: "An obvious concern to many owners is the possibility that their project may become tenant-occupied" (Skaburskis 1984, 22), and it identified "controlling the rental of condominium units" as one of two areas ripe for legislative reform (ibid., 35). In a special section on rental units in a popular condo management guide, the author (a condo lawyer) advises board members: "Do not assume that because someone does not own their unit, that they do not take pride in where they live" (Lincoln 1999, 183), thus reaffirming that a lack of pride among renters is a common perception. By the 1990s the renter had become a category thought to demand intensive governance in the condo world and one that condo statutes had plainly not anticipated. For these reasons the renter category is especially fertile ground from which to unearth and scrutinize the elements of condo governance.

CHANNELS OF LEGAL KNOWLEDGE, EXCERPTING, AND THE RENTER

The legal knowledge to deal with renters continuously flows into the condo via various channels, including the annual condo conference's spectacle and flesh-and-blood lawyers' appearances at board meetings. However, according to interviews with board members and lawyers, most condo boards only enlist lawyers' services when deemed necessary. As a condo lawyer remarked:

> And that's one of the problems. Condo corporations don't want to spend any money ... They do not understand the value of professional services ... whether it be lawyers' services, engineering services ... But of all, legal services are the ones they ... understand the least and think they can live without, which is why they get into so much trouble. (TO Lawyer 4)

Thus, legal knowledge tends to flow through more mundane channels, too, the variety of which is significant: the accessible condo manual (e.g., Loeb 2001), the newspaper advice column, the trade magazine article, the internet discussion board, the "condo law" newsletter, the "condo law blog," and so on. These are the primary means by which legal knowledge is transferred to the agents who govern condo buildings on the ground. These neglected formats allow and complement key practices such as the "excerpting" of legal decisions, which is a form of reduction (Valverde 2005). Excerpting can be seen and explored in relation to a significant legal decision about non-resident owners and renters. In Ontario the trend towards investing and renting out units was supported by a seminal 1974 Ontario Court of Appeal decision (*Peel Condominium Corporation No. 11 v. Caroe et al.*, 1974) that reaffirmed owners' rights to rent their condo unit as property. The court determined that the right to sell or rent one's property is "a fundamental incident of ownership" and that if the Ontario legislature had intended that condo declarations should prevent an owner from leasing a unit, it would have said so "in a clear, unambiguous language." The court held that the statute would only permit the declaration "to provide for single family occupancy, to prohibit the use of a unit as a business premise and the like" (546). This decision meant that a condo unit could now become solely an investment and commodity, not necessarily a residence. A condo law "advice column" in a major Toronto newspaper responds with an excerpt from this 1974 decision to a board member's query about renting:

> Q. The board, of which I am a member, is concerned about the number of units being leased. Can a corporation pass a rule providing that no more than 10 percent of the units may be leased? All existing leases would be grandfathered.
>
> A. A court has held that the right to lease one's unit is *a fundamental incident of ownership*. Limiting leasing to a certain number or percentage of the units would prevent some owners from leasing their units and, therefore, is not permitted. (Hyman 2005a; emphasis added)

At times excerpted legal knowledge competes with that arriving through other channels, for example, directly from a board's lawyer:

> Q. We are a 50-unit self-managed condominium in which 37 units are owner-occupied. A vote was taken at our annual meeting to limit the number of rental units to 25 percent. All of the resident owners in attendance and all but two of the non-resident owners voted in

> favour. *Our lawyer advised that a declaration amendment is necessary, requiring an 80 percent vote of owners.* Is this correct?
>
> A. The Condominium Act provides that a declaration may contain conditions or restrictions with respect to leases of units. An amendment to the declaration ... will require the written consent of owners of 80 percent of all of the units ... *The courts have held, however, that ... the declaration cannot prohibit an owner from leasing a unit.* A provision that limits rentals to 25 percent of the units will prohibit the leasing of any additional units *and will not be enforceable.* (Hyman 2005a; emphases added)

There is also a qualitative aspect to excerpting. An excerpt's content may differ dramatically depending on the institutional purpose for which it is deployed (Valverde 2005); not all tributaries spill into the same reservoirs of knowledge from which governing agents can draw. For example, missing from all channels above is a seemingly gratuitous point made by Judge Galligan near the end of the 1974 decision:

> I think in enacting this legislation the Legislature of Ontario would have known that most mortgagees ... are large corporations. It is of course impossible for such an owner to occupy a unit with its family and guests. I certainly don't think that it was the intention of the Legislature to require that a corporate mortgagee in possession of a unit would be required to let its unit stand alone. (*Peel Condominium Corporation No. 11 v. Caroe et al.*, 1974, 546)

The apparent support of the practice of large corporations renting out condo units en masse for profit because they cannot occupy a unit is rendered invisible by the excerpting that results in Galligan's decision being reduced to "a fundamental incident of ownership." This part of the decision, which justifies the presence of corporate investors rather than individual resident owners regarding condo building ownership, is central because it differs significantly from the original residential condo ideal, which clearly imagined flesh-and-blood resident owners. Inclusion of this nugget about corporate investors in an excerpt in a condo manual or newspaper column would likely be especially unwelcome to boards and resident owners seeking to govern the reviled renter to protect common property or, less likely of late, to establish communities.

One "large corporation" had earlier filed suit against a condo corporation in downtown Toronto for passing rules interfering with its interests (*Apartments International Inc. v. Metropolitan Toronto Condominium Corporation No. 1170,* 2002). In this and a simultaneous case, the courts decided a condo board could pass "rules that prohibited leases where the term was less than 3 months" (Bardai 2003, 216). This legally excluded the particularly transient short-term hotel stayer from entering condo buildings, but, of course, whether this knowledge flows into all condo complexes faced with a similar challenge is far from given. A potential avenue for avoiding this limitation on leases is offered to one owner who asks about renting his unit:

> Q. I own a condo unit that I rent out. I have received a letter from the board stating that it passed a rule requiring that all unit leases be for a minimum of 12 months. Is the rule valid?
>
> A. Courts have upheld rules setting minimum terms for unit leases. The intention of the restriction is to prevent units being rented on a transient or hotel-like basis. The rule will not invalidate a lease entered into before the rule was passed. *Such rules often contain provisions permitting a lease for less than the minimum period by a resident owner who may be away for a number of months on vacation or business.* (Hyman 2005b; emphasis added)

Excerpts flow through channels and tributaries into the condo world, but at times there is spillover. Thus, an excerpt is often at least partially recycled as it can move from text to text. One excerpt, for example, is seen migrating from the courts to a condo handbook to an industry organization's discussion forum. Here, a condo owner adds to the discussion thread under the subject "owner occupied only" in response to a question about how to limit renters:

> From my reading of Gerry Hyman's *Condominium Handbook* (published by the CCI) I don't think it's possible to prevent owners from leasing their units. Mr. Hyman refers to a 1974 court decision that considered whether a declaration could prohibit the leasing of units. The court held: "... that the right to sell or lease one's property is 'a fundamental incident of ownership'" and "... that the Act would only permit the declaration 'to provide for single family occupancy, to prohibit the use of a unit as a business premise and the like.'" (Canadian Condo Organization Discussion Forum, August 22, 2005)

Unimpressed by this tidbit of knowledge, another condo owner in a final entry reaffirms the renter problem facing condo owners but relates a contrary "understanding" of the legality of the floated response to it:

> My corporation would also like to implement a cap on renting/leasing units. We purchased our condos based on investment and feel that the higher a percentage of rent in the building, the less our investment will be ... It has affected ... our building including garbage disposal, pets not being taken care of properly, common carpeting being soiled, and a high number of noise issues with the renter. We will be starting the process and, in my understanding, this requires a by-law to be written with 51 percent of owners agreeing to the new by-law. It is a legal procedure and your corporation's lawyer should be able to help. (Canadian Condo Organization Discussion Forum, August 22, 2005)

Yet here the author of the original query is also referred (back) to a lawyer for "help." This legal knowledge would have to exit the condo building to complete the circuit of knowledge. Not all seeds of knowledge take firm root; some are blown from format to format, into the condo world and out again.

In another discussion thread entitled "restricting condo rentals" the excerpted decision from the courts was "told" to owners and has seemingly taken root:

> Our condo ... used to be a luxury condo, no more. One person bought four units and somebody else three. *These units are rented ... We were told that we can't restrict bying* [sic] *up units for spec[ulation] and rent them.* I think this is wrong. It would be a different matter to restrict the rental of a single unit because the owner wants to go to Florida say! ... . This restriction is not for taking away the landlord owners [sic] *joy of ownership. It would stop these landlords to take away the enjoyment from their owner occupied neighbors* ... How can one try changing these laws? ("Brenda," Canadian Condo Organization Discussion Forum, February 18, 2006, emphases added)

Here, however, the court's decision is deemed unjust and sparks a resident owner's counter-argument for legal change. It is further transformed and reduced from "a fundamental incident of ownership" to "joy of ownership," a rhetorical move to promote this actor's interests. Thus, the resident owner in a once luxury and presumably joyful condo complex can rhetorically broadcast her plight to seek an actionable response to a query about yet another possible solution to the "renter problem": statutory reform.

OTHER LEGAL STRATEGIES TO DEAL WITH THE RENTER

Since the 1974 decision discussed earlier, numerous other strategies to deal with renters have entered the condo world. For example, a condo manual advises managers and board members as follows: "Because of unruly renters some condo corporations have attempted to terminate leasing of units. Others have tried charging a fee to absentee landlords, which is not a legal procedure and should not be followed" (Lincoln 1999, 185). Another strategy focuses on unit occupancy. If there is a disproportionate number of occupants and – typically – renters in one unit, it is often assumed that disproportionate levels of non-excludable resources will be consumed at other owners' expense. In an oral submission preceding passage of Bill 38, the 1998 statute, a condo lawyer representing "homeowner controlled" condo complexes remarked, "*Overcrowding primarily relates to rental units ... it's tied in with the rental of condominium units*. The amendments are good steps in the right direction" (Pacey 1998; emphasis added). Almost from their inception, condo corporations have been compared to municipalities and, therefore, rather than always relying on condo corporation resources and board authority another legal strategy has been to draw on legal knowledge of existing municipal law (see Chapter 5). Since the renter poses a risk of having to increase common fees, a maximum-occupancy standard consistent with a municipal bylaw can be established. As one industry observer explained: "Residential units can have whatever the city bylaws allow" (TO Board 5). The board can then levy an assessment to recoup extra fees:

> Q. The declaration in our townhouse complex states units are to be used only as single-family dwellings. In at least four out of 31 units, basement apartments have been constructed and rented out. The board has refused to take any action and it appears more owners intend to build and rent out basement apartments, increasing the utility costs we all share through our common expenses. What should be done?
>
> A. The board is obligated to enforce the single-family dwelling requirement in the declaration ... The Condominium Act permits a board

> to pass a by-law ... which establishes standards for the occupancy of residential units. The standards must be either those contained in a by-law of the municipality in which the condo is located or ... standards that reflect the maximum occupancy for ... which the building was designed. (Hyman 2001)

This form of occupancy has been used in the courts to respond to the onset of Airbnb-related short-term rentals, as discussed later in this chapter.

The quantitative extent of excerpting is noteworthy here as well. The cleansed and ordered text that represents the actual 1974 court decision found in the standardized "Ontario Reports" format is seen to be excerpted and dramatically reduced in size from approximately fourteen hundred (full decision) to 118 words (decision summary). It is later truncated to thirty (condo manual), then to five words as "a fundamental incident of ownership" (response to a query in an "advice column"), and finally to three words as "joy of ownership." As mundane as it may first appear, this systematic reduction is demanded by narrow channels of legal knowledge flows: newspaper advice columns need to be concise to fit a page; a subject in a law firm's free legal newsletter must be reduced if it hopes to be read while avoiding providing too much legal advice that could be sold to clients for profit; and so on. Conversely, these narrow channels only become viable means for the flow of knowledge if excerpting is possible.

The incompleteness of the legal knowledge stemming from excerpting may ultimately benefit law firms selling legal services (and insurance firms selling director liability or human rights insurance) to condo boards. Examination of the content of these channels reveals that pragmatic legal knowledge allegedly required by boards and property managers to deal with renters (and with myriad other governance issues) will often be partial or only hinted at in answers to selected questions or in a brief article. But these partial accounts are always accompanied by a reminder (e.g., the law firm's name is prominently displayed at the beginning and end of the newsletter, article, or conference session) of how a more complete picture might be viewed. Such knowledge, it is learned, rests with legal sages positioned upstream (or in armchairs on conference stages) out of the fray and closer to law's more majestic wellsprings in the courts and legislatures. But one must apparently complete the circuit to obtain this knowledge. Much legal knowledge entering the condo through these channels is thus "partial" in a second sense. The authors of condo newsletters, blogs, newspaper advice columns, and workshop presentations provided at no or nominal cost to board members or property managers are more than willing to wade downstream to a condo board meeting to share this more sullied legal knowledge through direct channels, albeit for a higher price at owners' and, ironically, renters' expense.

Private Insurance Firms and the Renter

Before property management applies legal knowledge and more intimately screens and confronts renters, private insurance seeks to be the renter's first line of defence – that is, to govern the renter through insurance requirements. Note the attributes assigned by a major broker for Ontario condo insurance firms to the owner-occupied unit in contrast to the rented unit:

> One thing that does come into play ... is the percentage of units that are owner-occupied versus renter-occupied. Because the consensus is, and the actuarial data shows, that a condo corporation that is 100 percent owner-occupied, they generally take better care of the premises of their overall condo corporation. They are more involved in the entire association, the upkeep of the entire building than one that has a large contingent of rented units. Rented units, they don't generally take the same care and duty in the maintenance of their properties and of really limiting the exposures that are present to the overall corporation. (TO Insurance 2)

Typical of the cold, actuarial gaze of private insurance, it is rented units rather than renters that become moral risks. The actuarial data identify the resident owner as less risky than the renter and actively involved in building upkeep and board affairs, as possessing "care and duty" in unit maintenance and, by implication, with regard to the condo corporation's common property (Ericson, Doyle, and Barry 2003). For private insurance, the renter is a risk to property when it comes to insuring common areas of condo buildings. There is a threshold: "The only real factor that does come into play on the building ... [is] the owner-occupied and the renter-occupied, that percentage mix, because once the renter-occupied home units get to a certain percentage, there are a number of companies that will not insure them on that standpoint because of the fear that it becomes a renter complex and not owner-occupied and then ... how much care is put into it?" (TO Insurance 2). This "renter risk" enters considerations of other forms of insurance that target condo governance, specifically condo director liability insurance:

> For insuring [director liability] ... the premium's going to [be] based specifically on the number of officers on the board and size of operating budget or the number of units ... with a potential surcharge for the number of rented units, a little more risk than owner-occupied units. So generally ... it's pretty much been a surcharge of say 10 to 25 percent ... They'll generally get it to a certain percentage of rented units where some companies will say they no longer want to insure because it's more of a rental complex rather than a condo corporation. (TO Insurance 2)

As noted, insurance has a stake in adequate legal knowledge transfers pertaining to the renter question. Consider one transfer from a condo industry organization's discussion thread to a board member to avoid discrimination and therefore legal liability:

> Q. I live in a 250 unit condominium apartment building and 40 percent [of] units are rented out. Can board of directors make a by-law to charge some extra X amount as part of maintenance fees to unit owners who are renting their units, to offset lavish use of utilities by tenants? or any other suggestion?
>
> A. From my reading of the Act, no. That would be discrimination. You cannot discriminate against any particular owner(s), which your idea would be doing. (Canadian Condo Organization Internet Discussion Board, July 23, 2006)

The avoidance of discrimination due to this board member's receipt of this information benefits insurance and ensures profits because it would avoid an expensive claim lodged through either director liability or human rights insurance policies held by the condo corporation. Such a claim would be expected to follow an owner's successful lawsuit against the condo corporation based upon discrimination against owners who rent their units (i.e., non-resident owners). The fewer such lawsuits and related insurance claims, the more private insurance profits.

Setting special premiums to manage "renter risk" at times fails to encourage adequate governance of renters in condo spaces. In these instances, private insurance can become the last defence against renters' presumed risky tendencies in a condo building by enabling filing suit against renters to recover damages resulting from paying out a claim to a condo corporation or unit holder.

Insurance firms must therefore stay aware of precedents, for example, the 1996 decision *Peel Condominium Corporation No. 16 v. Vaughan*, in which the Ontario court determined that the condo statute and the nature of the insurance coverage of the corporation and the unit owner prevented these two actors from suing one another because subrogation rights had been waived (in this case, renters were thought responsible for a fire in the condo building's common area where renters had been repairing a vehicle). This freed the insurance firm holding these policies (as well as insurance firms in similar situations since) to sue the renters for negligence to recover damages as it was determined that, according to the Condo Act, renters were not covered by a corporation's insurance. As with the 1974 seminal case regarding ownership, excerpts of this 1996 case are seen to migrate from the courts to a Toronto condo law firm website then to a condo property manager newsletter, ACMO's *Quarterly Report* (ACMO 2002), since property managers are expected to watch for renters' negligent behaviour in common areas. Private insurance is not the most important external agent shaping condo governance, but its traditional mechanism of premium-setting combines with legal knowledge and other institutional strategies. Also of importance to condo governance are strategies of property management.

Property Management Firms and the Renter

Property managers deal directly with renters. According to one:

> I have one condo that has a high population of tenants, and our biggest ... problem with them is not so much a lot of normal tenant issues or noise and all that, it's more ... a revolving door. This place is just in and out, in and out. So when you have a lot of activity like that, you have a lot of damage. (TO Manager 7)

It is the transitory tendencies of renters, rather than their mere presence, that is commonly deemed to lead to problems; a long-term renter is thought to have a greater stake in the common property, even if this does not create "community." One manual related that such renters can be screened: "Our condominium community over the years has never had any ... unruly renters. This is mainly due to a good screening process" (Lincoln 1999, 185). Similarly, a property manager related that "Downtown Toronto ... is high rental ... Is that an issue? It sometimes is on the wear and tear of the building, the maintenance when you have renters ... Like do they screen who they're renting to?"

(TO Manager 4). In the condo trade magazine *Condo Voice*, a resident owner contemplating becoming an investor receives advice from a property management firm representative in an article aptly entitled, "To Rent or not to Rent?": "In an ideal world, all condominium owners would actually occupy their own unit ... but as we know it only exists in fairy tales. So, if rentals are a fact of life, how do we control them?" The answer to the first question posed by the article's title is "yes," the unit can be rented without risk but only if this firm's services are purchased, in which case answers to the second question become clear:

> The Tenant will be selected and educated about the community prior to making the commitment to move in. Rules and Regulations as well as registration must be completed well in advance. Digital photos are taken of suite and the parking and locker space ... The only way ... is to engage a company who is well versed with the ever-changing laws. Again, property management-based leasing programs are the only solution. (White 2005, 20)

SHORT-TERM STAYERS: AIRBNB AND BEYOND

In Toronto, New York, and other cities, there is a trend towards investing in condo buildings as hotel-like commercial ventures that permit short-term stays and new ways of arranging units for such purposes. While receiving more attention from local media in these and other North American cities like Chicago (Matthews 2012) in recent years and seemingly now more prevalent, short-term stays are a long-standing development. Thus, as Ontario's first condo statute was being passed in 1967, the *New York Times* reported on a large condo-hotel complex being built near Colorado Springs that permitted several units on each floor to be rented for short-term stays and foresaw "transient visitors and permanent residents living side by side"; however, uniquely in this case, profits would be shared by all current owners in the complex rather than units being individually or corporately owned by non-residents and used to "defray maintenance costs" (*New York Times* 1967). Consistent with the preceding section, mention of long-term renters in this or other condo buildings is completely absent from this 1960s story. And, fourteen years ago, in 2003, Bill 78, "An Act to amend the Condominium Act, 1998 to limit the use of condominiums by transient tenants" was introduced and then passed in the Ontario legislature. Its introduction was justified by a 2001 Ontario Superior Court case in which the judge asserted, implying that a community of resident owners is still a condo ideal, that there is a deleterious effect associated with "encountering absolute strangers":

> It is not unreasonable for the owners to say that the recreational facilities are less inviting when they run the risk of encountering absolute strangers. Nor is it unreasonable for them to say that the transient occupants treat the facilities as if they belong to a hotel. They have no interest in the long-term upkeep, maintenance and repair. They do not know the rules and they have no vested interest as do owners and long-term residents in abiding by them. (*Skyline Executive Properties Inc. v. Metropolitan Toronto Condominium Corporation No. 1280*, 2001)

What is new are sharing-economy features highlighted not only by Airbnb but also by other firms in Ontario and far beyond. One industry observer and long-time condo board member explained:

> City Place, you've heard of that? How about a building of 650 units, five hundred renters. And you've also got suite hotels, in and out. If it's [rented] by the corporation, minimum of thirty days. If it's a suite hotel ... you can rent them by the weekend, the week, a day, you can rent them by the hour. And it's legal. In some of the new buildings you got ... the newest bylaws by Tridel and a couple of others. Suite hotels. So Airbnb. And that's where you can rent by the hour. And it's in there where the condo cannot stop it. You are not allowed to. So they can have furnished units ... with a little cart going from floor to floor, servicing their units. (TO Board 5)

Another industry insider explained this development:

> Many builders build and get zoning approval to have short-term rentals allowed ... So they're going to council and saying, "We want to build a four-hundred-unit, a fifty-story building here, but we want you to allow us to embed within the governing documents and zoning that they can offer it as short-term rentals, like hotel suites." That's happened quite a bit in the city; a lot of people don't realize that their properties have that ability, and the only place they can find it is in the declaration ... So you have to really know what to look for and the owner-occupier will likely not be aware of that ... The wear and tear on the building is high, there's

security concerns ... and it draws a population that typically the owner that lives there doesn't want to see. (TO Real Estate 1)

Indeed, the spectre of Airbnb and the arrival of similar website services in the condo world has garnered much media coverage in Toronto, including an article about one "32-storey condominium tower" in which a security guard generates knowledge about his own building – ironically from external websites – to fight back in a "war against Airbnb":

> Inside, the building's security team these days has been dealing with another, more covert invasion: tourists and partiers trying to rent units for the weekend via websites such as Airbnb, in defiance of the condo board's rules. On the front lines ... is the building's friendly security chief ... who greets many of the tower's hundreds of residents ... In this war against Airbnb ... his tactics include scanning the website and others like it for up to three hours a day for illicit listings in his building, questioning anyone who wanders into the lobby dragging luggage behind them and kicking out any short-term renters he finds. (Gray 2016)

Towards the end of this article, anyone reading it learns how legal knowledge produced by condo lawyers is crucial to this war:

> Even when condo boards have the authority to block Airbnb rentals, actually enforcing the rules can be difficult, warns Toronto condo lawyer Denise Lash. Condo managers cannot impose fines, but they can charge offending condo owners the legal costs of the lawyers' letters sent to reprimand them, usually several hundred dollars. Actually stopping a recalcitrant operator can mean eventually going to court. (Gray 2016)

A recent decision in Ontario's Superior Court of Justice (or supreme court), which is in Toronto's legal jurisdiction, ruled in favour of an Ottawa condo board's effort to restrict short-term rentals in the complex once they were discovered. In *Ottawa-Carleton Standard Condominium Corporation No. 961 v. Menzies*, 2016, the judge upheld short-term rental restrictions in the condo declaration and found that the owner renting the unit had breached the declaration. The ruling was based on the notion that the condo declaration required units to have single-family uses:

> "Single family use" cannot be interpreted to include one's operation of a hotel-like business, with units being offered to complete strangers on the internet, on a repeated basis, for durations as short as a single night. Single family use is incompatible with the notions of "check in" and "check out" times, "cancellation policies," "security deposits," "cleaning fees," instructions on what to do with dirty towels/sheets and it does not operate on credit card payments ... Moreover "Single family use" could not have contemplated ... use of a unit to house out-of-town witnesses and experts for trial preparation or the unit being offered on silent auctions for not-for-profit organizations or to hold a law firm's office functions and Christmas parties. What has happened in this case is a commercial use of the unit.

As with security guards' efforts at policing (other) nuisances, so with the efforts to counter Airbnb: market services have emerged to aid in the use of legal knowledge. So while currently there are at least nine websites advertising condo units to short-term stayers, there is also "BNB Shield," which is specially designed to identify (using algorithms and for a price) presumably predatory condo owners using Airbnb (www.bnbshield.com). This knowledge can be coupled with engaging a condo law firm to confront these owners. In other words, it can be transformed into legal knowledge if the situation is to be "escalated to legal counsel [for] effective and timely enforcement (and recovery of all legal fees)" (Lash 2017a). Of course, this may be only the beginning of the legal fees for the condo corporation if other services and Airbnb decide to defend themselves by employing their own lawyers, not only to fight city regulations, as in New York (Benner 2016) and soon in Toronto (Katawazi 2017), but also to help fund individual Airbnb-using owners' legal defences in suits launched against them by condo boards. Such an effort by Airbnb may involve seeking a decision like the one in 1974 for long-term renters – one that could travel across and influence the condo world rather than rely on building-specific declarations that permit short-term rentals.

MUTUALLY REINFORCING LEGAL KNOWLEDGE FLOWS

How three external agents (property management, law, and insurance) and their associated processes (commodification, juridification, and risk avoidance) and related knowledges are implicated in condo governance are explored in this chapter, which expands upon insights regarding how these elements are mutually reinforcing. Commodification of governance (property management) is seen to lead to a new legal requirement (juridification) that a property management firm contracted with condo boards carry "fidelity coverage," which typically protects against forgery, fraud, and theft on the part of a property manager (risk avoidance). Each institution can exploit condo opportunities created by the renter for another to fill. From the perspective of private insurance:

> A property management firm can actually bring in a lot of benefits if the proper controls are in place for the condominium. If the property manager's being insured on a separate coverage ... for property management it is a way to diversify the risk of the corporation ... if there's a proper contract in place and also if proper tenants are brought in or if the normal contracts are not in place properly the condominium corporation itself has to get the property manager. So they've actually ... reduced their risk a lot by employing a separate property manager. (TO Insurance 3)

Insurance companies encourage adherence to the law by threatening to revoke policies if reserve funds are not maintained, and they imply that self-managed condo complexes are inadequate in this regard, thus showing that institutional processes are mutually supportive. There is legal knowledge associated with each development that travels through these and other channels. For example, industry representatives related that insurance and property management firms retain lawyers and seek to adjust their practices depending on identification of litigation trends and legal precedents regarding the conduct of boards and owners in relation to renters and beyond. These are trends that would be elaborated upon at the kind of condo conference described at this chapter's outset.

CONCLUSION

From the condo's birth in North America, resident owners came to be seen as having a propensity to care for property and to maintain and improve common spaces in the community outside their units' walls; renters came to be seen as the condo's chief "other" and were assumed to lack such propensities. The risky and reviled renter is deemed to live off others' noble risk-taking efforts to own property. Yet the renter is logically and historically *necessary* to the way condo governance and legal knowledge flows are currently configured – and to condoization more broadly – and represents benefits accrued by the powerful commercial actors of the condo industry implicated in these arrangements.

Condo governance (whether involving law, insurance, or property management firms) is underscored here as heterogeneous and the renter as variously immoral, risky, unsafe, or transient, depending on a specific type of agent's gaze. Not the only category targeted in the condo world, the renter nonetheless serves as a key junction of governing agencies and legal knowledge. Indeed, renters accomplish much merely by their presence, but, unlike resident owners, they are not consulted on how their fees (i.e., rent) will be spent (e.g., to cover the fees of law, insurance, security, and property management firms) or on the countless controls and rules imposed on their lives. As noted, since governing and constituting happen at once, to explore how the renter is governed is to show how they are constituted and effectively carved out as a category of governance distinct from other entities, especially owners, in condo governance assemblages. Exploring how the condo renter is governed also further reinforces the argument that condo governance is not so much a seamless fabric as a fabric consisting of mutually reinforcing agents and processes loosely stitched together with tiny strings of legal and other knowledges.

It is not self-evident that components of this condo world, including the legal knowledge circulating through it, cannot be altered and recombined to recognize renters' disenfranchised presence and to yield more democratic and inclusive North American urban housing alternatives, which the condo began to displace decades ago. Even within the condo, if housing alternatives are not forthcoming, the notion of somehow including renters in condo governance arrangements and communities as participants rather than as the "other" has all but disappeared. Illustrative of this are Ontario's two statutory reviews, held almost forty years apart. The 1977 review at least contemplated – if only in passing – the idea of renters participating on boards or bringing useful common knowledge as residents to the table to enhance governance where owners were unwilling: "Where a condominium is unable to draw on tenants or tenants are unwilling to participate, it is possible that the resource base for drawing members to the Board of Directors may be small" (Ontario 1977). By 2013, such notions of renters participating in any way are completely absent from reports of the statutory review (e.g., Canada's Public Policy Forum 2013c). While the Ontario statue does not legally prevent renters from volunteering on condo boards – nor does it legally prevent them from participating in a meaningful way in statutory reform – provincial and state governments have nonetheless failed to confront the reality that renters, rather than resident owners alone, are now a major but disenfranchised and (in cities where there is no alternative affordable housing) exploited condo constituency. But in the absence of policies encouraging formation of alternative housing, such as non-profit cooperatives, legislating renters' full inclusion in condo complexes as members of a community may prove difficult due to the fundamental place renters – as a source of revenue – now hold in governance arrangements. The renter has become an "other" that accrues profits for tightly bound, powerful commercial agencies and investing non-residents, both of which manage to escape the "other" designation. It could be a long time before renters are invited to condo conferences.

5

Condo Governance, Legal Knowledges, and Surveillance

RANDY K. LIPPERT with STEFAN TREFFERS

Eyes ... are watching what's happening, and if they notice something they make a note of it and tell you you're breaking a rule.

– *TO BOARD 40*

Someone suggested putting a camera there just for security ... just for a little extra precaution.

– *NYC RES. 19*

They like all the cameras being there and like the manager being able to sit there and see who the bad guys are and what they're doing and who's doing crap in the elevator. The manager loves watching on the weekend ... you see some very interesting things.

– *TO BOARD 24*

Law ... is still accompanied by certain punishments ... but now everything is framed by ... a series of supervisions, checks, inspections, and varied controls.

– *FOUCAULT (2007, 4)*

This chapter takes a closer look at law and surveillance in the expanding condo world. It explores relevant legal knowledges, forms of surveillance, and how the two relate within condoization, issues relevant to condo complexes in Toronto and New York and, undoubtedly, globally. Much recent scholarship has contemplated the complex relationship between law and state surveillance of populations (Lippert 2015) but not in residential urban environs. In what follows the notion that surveillance is enabled by various legal knowledges flowing into the condo world is demonstrated. Some legal knowledges converge with one another, resembling what Valverde (2009, 139) calls "inter-legality," including those stemming not only from civil law, municipal law, and criminal law but also from evolving condo statutes as a type of "counter-law" (Ericson 2007). This counter-law concept clarifies these developments and comes in two forms (I and II) that, consistent with precautionary logic, seek pre-emption of disasters and often presume worst-case scenarios. Counter-law I is about laws that seek to overcome "traditional principles, standards, and procedures" of law (Ericson 2007, 207). In the condo world these are statutory provisions for exceptional "special assessments" suddenly assigned to owners to cover the cost of repairs and replacement to save the integrity of a condo building. According to interviews and documentary data, these assessments are often the result of consecutive boards' poor planning priorities to maintain common elements such as roofs and boilers, and permitting consistently low fees that result in such funding shortfalls. This form of counter-law is also evident when courts ultimately assign an emergency administrator to replace an incompetent or self-interested condo board to manage the building's finances, maintenance, and repairs.

Counter-law II entails surveillant arrangements that go "broader and deeper" to seek out signs of impending disasters and to pre-empt their occurrence (Ericson 2007, 207). These two forms of counter-law tend to emerge hand in hand. While originally referring mostly to criminal law, counter-law has parallels in the condo world. The relation between legal knowledge and surveillance, however, is not restricted to counter-law. This chapter pays attention to instances in which legal knowledge and surveillance seem to converge in documents, to instances in which board members and other owners invoke notions of law and surveillance in interviews about condo life, and to instances of increasing legal knowledges and surveillance in the condo world over time.

These various legal knowledges have arrived in the condo world through numerous channels. They have spawned video surveillance, key fobs, human surveillance, reserve fund studies, financial audits, and safety inspections that, together, form an assemblage, with points of inter-legality binding these elements together. This surveillance is largely focused on boards' and owners' practices in relation to financial viability and property value, which has accompanied the condo becoming foremost an investment rather than a community and place to reside. Where possible, how these forms of legal knowledge and surveillance are understood or invoked by condo residents or board members is illustrated. Finally, this chapter argues that much legal knowledge and surveillance entering the condo world and forming an assemblage has become commodified – that is, marketed and purchased – rather than developed organically and provided internally in the community. This underscores the fact that the condo represents an ever-expanding conduit for the flow of commodified products and services.[1]

As explained in the introduction and shown in the previous chapter, a key element of the sociology of governance framework is attention to legal knowledge, which here means legislation or statutes, court decisions, and numerous "law-like" rules within organizations, which include bylaws and rules in condo buildings established by boards. Also, it was noted that surveillance is part of securitization and should be understood at least partially as such. Surveillance refers to systematic monitoring of living entities, inanimate objects, processes, and spaces (see also Lyon 2007). This is a broad conception of surveillance, and it can refer to targeting not only individual condo board members, owners, renters, and others accessing and egressing condo buildings and spaces directly but also the remnants and residue of their movements and decisions in paper or electronic files and images. This means that files or documents (such as financial statements or a record of fob use to enter the condo building fitness room) are also monitored systematically. Indeed, it is worthwhile recalling that early scholarship on state surveillance focuses upon keeping and analyzing records and files (Rule 1973) more than on direct observation, although now, and as seen in the condo, this is being administered more by private than by government agents. The practices that condo governance demands (such as managing corporation funds, voting about rules, and ongoing consideration of the viability of its physical elements) are increasingly becoming targets and knowledge of them is sought in various ways. Surveillance means generating these knowledges (e.g., accounting, engineering) about myriad persons, things, and practices. The various targets in the condo world are increasingly subjected to what Foucault (1994, 88–89), undoubtedly the most influential theorist of surveillance, aptly calls "the gaze," understood as "the eye that knows and decides, the eye that governs." Multiple types and aims of the gaze, buttressed by and fomenting manifold legal and other knowledges, are discernable. Yet, for all the attention to files and images, here the gaze's primary focus remains individual conduct. The condo world is increasingly enveloped by the accompanying dream of "a gaze which each individual under its weight will end by interiorizing to the point that he is his own overseer, each individual thus exercising this surveillance over, and against, himself" (Foucault 1980, 155). Before this dream can be realized through such assemblages, surveillance first requires space to grow, and it is primarily legal knowledge that forms the cracks into which it can creep. In turn, surveillance burrows further into these crevices, encouraging legal knowledge to fill resulting voids. This chapter suggests that it has become unclear when or whether this "will end," especially if profits can still be drained out of this world.

LEGAL KNOWLEDGES AND SURVEILLANCE

The rising importance of legal knowledge to condo life includes, but moves well beyond, enabling condo statutes. Surveillance of and within the condo has been gradually growing, often imperceptibly, since the condo's legal birth. Currently, forms of condo surveillance include security-operated video surveillance and key fob access arrangements (often recordable and transferable to property managers via specialized software such as Condo Control Central); residents' intelligence-gathering about other residents and board activities in relation to condo rules; engineers' reserve fund studies; annual accounting audits of a corporation's finances; and compliance with municipal codes among others. This section discusses how statutory and other forms of legal knowledge have led to forms of surveillance in condo complexes. This discussion is not exhaustive but, instead, focuses on key forms of legal knowledge. Each form of legal knowledge discussed corresponds to a form of intensive surveillance of condo inhabitants, spaces, and/or practices.

Statutory Legal Knowledge

As noted in Chapter 3, Ontario's condo statute has grown substantially in size and complexity over time. Yet what is palpable in both Ontario and New York is their respective governments' long-standing reluctance to surveill and adjudicate condo affairs and disputes directly via a provincial or state bureaucracy devoted to it and fully funded by general tax revenues (rather than by an independent authority or "ombudsman" to be funded through mandatory condo owner fees). Resonating with neoliberalism, the state seemingly governs "at a distance" (Rose and Miller 1992) by legally enabling non-state actors to assume surveillant roles. The potential resulting juridification of condo life is significant, but for this chapter's purposes its importance lies in fostering new forms of surveillance. Here statutory knowledge as it pertains to the surveillance of board and resident behaviour within an assemblage is interrogated. Condo house rules and "free riders" are taken up first.

Condo House Rules and "Free Riders"

In condo buildings, house rules are distinct from the declaration and bylaws but nevertheless bestow an equivalent duty of enforcement upon the corporation and board. Failure to properly enforce provisions may result in civil legal action and a subsequent court order forcing boards to ensure compliance. Such legal demands on the corporation to essentially police inhabitants serve to redraw acceptable boundaries of law and surveillance in these spaces and further extend these converging assemblages.

The "free rider problem" is often invoked in some form to justify various condo house rules created by boards and enforced by security personnel, property managers, and lawyers. Even if a sense of community is often absent, as part of shared ownership the condo still imagines owners pulling relatively equal weight by paying fees and maintaining property values. One condo real estate agent and former board member succinctly captured the free rider "mentality" in the condo:

> Someone lives on the main floor of the condo building and doesn't have any children anymore. They're a senior and they don't use the amenities, and they don't use the elevator, "So why should I pay for it?" It's an obvious answer but ... people have that mentality that just because I'm not using it, why should I be paying for it? So the parallel I give is: "Well, do you use the library? Do you drive? Do you go to City Hall and ask for services?" You don't use those, but you're still paying taxes whether you use them or not ... Do you have kids in schools? "No." But you're still paying taxes for it. (TO Real Estate 1)

As noted earlier this equal sharing is rare when it comes to board participation and sense of civic duty as boards are often hard-pressed to find willing owners to assume board positions. In addition, where utility costs are pooled into common fees and spread across units, disproportionate consumption of electricity, water, and heating fuel becomes interpreted as free riding, or a "tragedy of the commons" (see Hardin 1968), to be approached with increased law and surveillance. According to Mancur Olson (1965), in his classic work, "noticeability" of free riders relates to a group's size; the free rider becomes more prevalent in larger groups in which individual action or inaction is less noticeable. Renters are thought by resident owners to free ride and to undermine the community-orientation and collective mantra and promise of condo living. This apprehension is outlined in a 2012 submission to the Ontario's Condo Act review: "A disenfranchised minority of the future will be the remaining owner-occupiers [resident owners] who are living in communities of tenants rather than in the condo community environment that the government originally anticipated" (Condo Briefs 2012, 53). Short of excluding renters from condo buildings entirely (they are already excluded in governing practices), those who govern are eager to make them noticeable. This "noticeability" best describes the aim of surveillance. Yet there is an important but never mentioned aspect of this principle in condo governance. As some condo complexes have become immense, often with hundreds of units, there is less "noticeability" of any specific unit and its owner(s); free riders can presumably board, ride, or disembark the train as though invisible. Thus, there is increasing demand for surveillance on the part of boards of condo inhabitants to better discover any "free-riding" conduct.

Boards are implementing a growing number of house rules. Rules from one condo numbered twenty standard pages governing matters such as parking, visitors, garbage disposal, noise, pets, common amenity use, renovations, and fire safety. A recent media account indicated that in some condo complexes these rules "span 70 pages" (McMahon 2014, 37). Many house rules take on a pre-emptive character as risks of litigation, municipal fines, and property devaluation loom over boards and property managers. Common are house rules concerning deviations from established aesthetic standards (Dowling, Atkinson, and McGuirk 2010). Consider, for example, house rules that regulate decorations on front doors, stipulate appropriate drapery colours, prohibit certain fixtures in hallways and on balconies, or dictate proper attire in common areas.

Various kinds of surveillance are being assembled to ensure compliance with these rules informed by Foucault's "police" logic (see Chapter 6). The first kind is video surveillance of common condo spaces. In condo complexes where security personnel were employed, video surveillance was frequently used to address on-the-spot rule violations. Video surveillance was also used to review infractions and identify perpetrators. For example, one resident related: "There was somebody was smoking in the stairwell. But I think they generally see that ... there's a lot of security cameras through our whole building ... they've figured out who it is and then that was taken care of" (NYC Res. 5). Video surveillance's purpose, in some cases, was merely to deter residents against future violations. In one condo building that was less inclined this way, the property manager would mail residents a video image of their rule infraction along with a bill for correcting its result (TO Board 8). This image was coupled with information from their key fob, which revealed their identity. Here there was no formal hearing or appeal mechanism (perhaps other than through the board).

Functions of video surveillance and key fob systems are diverse. Condo boards find value in these surveillance systems regarding "slips and falls" on condo property, and they are extended to govern condo life through the enforcement of rules such as those that dictate proper waste disposal or amenity use. A security guard contracted with a security firm in one condo building explained that video was used "to replay events and serve as evidence for all recorded investigations. It can also be used if one forgets when something happened as all video is time stamped. Video can be saved and transferred to requesting authorities" (TO Security 2). Under these various circumstances, the surveillant gaze tends to fixate upon condo inhabitants rather than upon external criminal or related threats (see Wright, Glasbeek, and van der Meulen 2015). This is a textbook example of surveillance "creep" (Lippert 2009) and warrants reflection on how surveillance initially enters the condo world under the veneer of safety and security only to take on additional functions, some of which increasingly pervade daily condo life and supplant traditional notions of transgressors as "street criminals."

A second kind of surveillance is that mediated by key fob systems that permit the board, property manager, or contracted security guard to determine what doorways have been accessed, when, and by whom. A unique and identifiable key fob is often issued to each resident of a condo building granting entry to different spaces of the condo. Virtually all recently constructed condo buildings in Toronto have front entrances and internal amenities that require entry using a key fob, with some requiring fobs for access to specific floors as well. Integrated security solutions, such as the workstation sold by Condoplex

Monitoring Systems Inc. (Condoplex n.d.), are monitored in real-time by security personnel and log all key fob uses for posterity (see also Condo Control Central 2017). One resident recalled his experience of how video surveillance and key fob logs had been coupled to address a rule infraction:

> I received a call from the concierge who asked if I had improperly disposed of some computer parts earlier in the day. Apparently, he had reviewed the surveillance tapes for the time at which I had been at the recycling area and matched my key fob entry to my particular apartment. Obviously, his question was rhetorical because they had my photo and identifying information all documented in the system. (TO Res. 2)

A third type of surveillance falls into the category of human surveillance. Increasingly in condo buildings, security personnel routinely patrol to enforce rules as part of their contractual responsibilities. One board member explained: "We have a foot patrol at certain hours ... enforcing rules, whatever they see. And then we'll have a security guard, he'll walk the building and do a route so he checks that there's nothing ... physical going wrong" (TO Board 40). This rule enforcement is being commodified and is increasingly advertised as a principal mandate for security personnel employed in condo buildings. This link between surveillance and rule enforcement in buildings is further exemplified by this claim on a private security firm's website: "Through having a security guard on-site, a condo owner can ensure that rules, regulations, and by-laws are being followed. Security personnel are invaluable as not only a presence to protect the premises from intruders but also in ensuring that your property is being treated respectfully" (Swat Protection Services n.d.).

Board members sometimes actively patrol their building or monitor potential rule violations regarding nuisances after a complaint is received. A Toronto owner explained that it was necessary to patrol because the problem was not obviously the person above or below her unit:

> So I'll stroll around just so I know I'm getting the right person, like I am not blaming the guy above me ... Again, I'm pretty lucky with my neighbours in close proximity, they're all pretty good. And at the times that I have kind of zeroed in on someone that obviously, you know, not a neighbour above or below me, but is playing it awful loud for whatever reason then maybe its [sic] other neighbours. (TO Res. 31)

The nexus of condo rules and surveillance attempts to institute a degree of certainty that never quite materializes as some rules are ignored and/or deemed trivial. While there may be condo complexes in Toronto and New York where rules are fully followed, no evidence of this turned up in an analysis of 160 interviews and thousands of documents from numerous buildings – a situation undoubtedly owing to the high volume of house rules to be followed by residents. Therefore, despite myriad condo house rules, enforcement is ceaseless and demands a ubiquitous surveillant gaze. Hunt (2003, 179) cogently notes that rule making is not only to promote security, safety, and welfare but also to show "an attempt has been made to bring the future under control. If accident, injury, or loss occurs, rule makers are able to demonstrate their foresight in identifying potential risks by taking reasonable steps to prevent or minimize harm." Indeed, Ontario's Condo Act, 1998, states that boards must "take reasonable steps" to ensure that residents and staff abide by the act and a particular condo's declaration, bylaws, and rules.

Condo boards and property managers frequently receive complaints about noise, smoke, pets, parking, and other nuisances. Chapter 6 also notes that complaints reflect how policing nuisance relies on "common knowledge" of mostly resident owners and their experiences of condo living. The capacity to retroactively confirm a complaint can now be facilitated by reviewing surveillance footage or observing key fob-mediated entry logs on the time and space of the infraction. In the absence of visual evidence characteristic of cases involving excessive noise, an aggrieved occupant may be asked to monitor and document all disturbances in violation of rules. That said, condo rules not only mobilize those who have a stake in ensuring compliance but also foster mutual surveillance and, at times, suspicion-raising among condo neighbours, which others have noted as being at odds with community building (Blandy and Lister 2005; McKenzie 2011).

The above examples demonstrate the distinct, but often coordinated, modes of surveillance spawned by condo house rules. Surveillance also spawns new condo house rules or refinements when unwanted behaviour or situations are discovered. A recent example, noted in Chapter 4, entails security personnel discovering those seeking to use the condo building as a hotel (short-term stayers) arriving at or exiting the condo building with suitcases and printouts from Airbnb and monitoring websites for advertising such rentals to determine whether a condo bylaw should be passed to prevent this practice. It is apparent that building-specific legal frameworks are not the only prevailing forces that induce condo corporations to watch resident behaviour.

RESERVE FUND STUDIES: WATCHING FOR A ROOF COLLAPSE

This section discusses imagined risk intimately tied to financial governance of the condo corporation. Introduced in condo statutes in the late 1970s, reserve fund studies are mandated assessments of a building's common elements and systems that were not required in earlier condo statutes (Ontario 1977). If surveillance is systematic monitoring, then a reserve fund study is one form of surveillance that must be conducted by experts "periodically," generally interpreted to mean every three years, as per Ontario's Condo Act, 1998, section 94. While seemingly focused more on the physical edifice (garage, balconies, windows, roof, and landscaping) and common systems (HVAC, electrical, and plumbing), the reserve fund study, more importantly, monitors board conduct and management of funds generated by monthly condo fees paid by owners. The study assesses the necessity and expected costs of major future repairs and replacement of common elements, and whether and how condo boards have allocated sufficient reserve funds to sustain these non-routine expenditures over the long term.

Prior to the 1998 condo statute, the statutory annual contribution to a reserve fund was to be no less than 10 percent of a condo corporation's annual operating budget (Herskowitz and Freedman 2001).[2] As critics noted, however, this arbitrary percentage was never meant to serve as the recommended allocation but, rather, as an absolute minimum, for which penalties would accrue if contributions fell below it. Without legal obligation to do so, many condo boards during this period voluntarily authorized reserve fund studies to proactively chart future expenses (LePage 2013). However, those less inclined to relinquish their budgetary planning responsibilities assumed that maintaining low common fees reflected diligent fiscal stewardship. Such a feat could be accomplished by meeting the minimum contribution requirements of the reserve fund. As many learned, large and presumably unforeseen expenditures could not be met with such low contribution thresholds, often forcing boards to issue exceptional special assessments to forcibly raise funds for emergency repairs and replacements (Herskowitz and Freedman 2001).

To attempt to overcome these problems, the Condo Act, 1998, abandoned the 10 percent minimum in exchange for mandated periodic reserve fund studies.[3] As a result, the financial affairs of condo buildings across Ontario would no longer be confined to the walls of the boardroom and AGM. Instead, they would now be exposed to the scrutiny of yet another grouping of external agents and knowledges, some of which would become responsible for ensuring the board fulfilled its fiduciary duties to the corporation. These experts were to be hired to assess the financial status of the reserve fund and, accordingly, develop a recommended funding plan based on an actuarial calculation of the conditions and projected lifecycles of the condo corporation's assets. The act provides a specific list of designated experts (including engineers, architects, quantity surveyors, accredited appraisers, realtors with reserve planner certification, etc.) who may undertake a reserve fund study (see Ontario Condo Act, 1998). Such a broad pool allows for a substantial range of expert knowledges.

Despite efforts to foster greater financial accountability, the Condo Act, 1998, was criticized for leaving considerable room for boards to deviate from reserve fund study recommendations. Herskowitz and Freedman (2001, 346) explain that section 94(8) of the act "gives the board the sole discretion to either accept the reserve fund study, and correspondingly adopt the funding recommendations proposed in it, or ... recommend its own future funding proposal." Thus, the reserve fund study was non-binding since the 1998 act allows for boards to instead implement their own plans whereby they may delay or opt out of an engineer's or expert assessor's suggested repairs or replacements. In addition, given the contractual and commodified nature of the relationship held with reserve fund planners, boards are free to shop for firms that satisfy financial objectives (Laporte 2007). In fact, as one property manager critical of this arrangement elucidated, the engineering firm's aim is ultimately the engineering contract for design and oversight of repairs and replacements outlined in the reserve fund study. This can be easily compromised if board members deem the reserve fund study's estimates to be too high and thus also antithetical to minimizing increases in common fees (TO Manager 1).

Due to these inherent contradictions in the regulatory framework stemming from the condo statute, some condo corporations continue to experience chronically underfunded reserves. Less than prudent spending, pressure to maintain low common fees, and financial malfeasance constituted the most common explanations among board members and owners for inadequate reserve funds. In practice, reserve fund studies are less than the objective expert surveillance the condo statute promises, but the main point here is that legal knowledge flowing from this statute has led to the growth of this surveillance, in which the engineer or similar expert constitutes one link in an assemblage of agents tasked with monitoring board activity.

When boards fail to plan appropriately, owners (and ultimately renters, too, via increased rents) are left to deal with the consequences. One New York owner expressed frustration with the board's decision to maintain low monthly common fees: "What they did here, they tried to pull a fast one. They kept the common charge artificially low, kept bragging about our low common charge, and anytime we needed any work done, we'd have to have a [special] assessment to pay for it. We had no reserve fund" (NYC Res. 9). Here boards routinely inflict the special assessment, traditionally intended for emergency expenditures, on owners in the absence of an operational reserve fund. The capacity for such sudden, exceptional decisions can lead to corruption:

> A lot of times the board of directors ... wants to sell their units and that board knows ... that the decision about a special assessment has to come down, but they want to sell and they can wait for a bit. They may not put through the approval on it until they sell their unit and so they'll just hold it off. So, there was talk about whether or not the minutes of the board identifies that there's a financial problem going on and it should. (TO Board 18)

Not only does this exceptional use of board authority constitute counter-law I, or "law against law," but it also preserves a permanent state of emergency in which special assessments become the norm when boards are unwilling to rectify their risk avoidance practices. Another respondent sheds light on how low reserves can contribute to weakened eligibility for loans and resulting property devaluation:

> People can't get refinances and people who want to buy into the building have a very hard time getting a loan, most of all of our last sales have been cash sales which means the seller has to sell at a lower price because people can't get decent mortgages ..., and we've never been cited by different banks, they say it's because he [the developer] owns too many units and there aren't enough resident owners, and because the building has no reserve fund. (NYC Res. 6)

In the worst cases of mismanagement, where condo corporations teeter on the brink of financial failure, a court-appointed administrator may subsume board duties consistent with statutory provisions. As an emergency appointment, the coinciding suspension of the board's ability to govern, however necessary, constitutes a form of counter-law I when the limits of pre-existing forms of risk avoidance (authority of the board, reserve fund studies, audits, etc.) are exposed. Considering the exceedingly obvious inability of the board to self-govern, further drastic measures are warranted to thwart the worst-case scenario. However, only at near collapse of the corporation do these surface. Current condo statutory reforms (see Canada's Public Policy Forum 2013a, 2013b, 2013c; and Chapter 8) seek to tighten up reserve fund studies, a need exposed in part by yet another form of condo surveillance: the audit.

AUDITS AND AUDITORS: FINANCIAL WATCHDOGS AND CONDO COPS

The financial auditing process is yet another form of surveillance whereby the financial activities and statements of the condo corporation are scrutinized and thus also governed by external agents. Yet it is vital to note that, before 1978, Ontario's condo statutes did not require that the corporation's financial statements be audited (Ontario 1977). The major legislative review that preceded the revised 1978 act lamented this situation: "This is a serious omission which severely restricts the ability of unit owners to obtain a comprehensive evaluation of the financial affairs of the corporation. The auditor ... is, in effect, the financial watchdog over the Board of Directors ... Audited financial statements should be required by statute" (Ontario 1977, 86). Note that the term "watchdog" is used to characterize the auditor, who is thus positioned as a central agent to guard against potential questionable financial decisions by the board. The 1998 act then gave considerable powers to the auditor to watch these financial doings as outlined in section 67(2):

> The auditor has right of access at all times to all records, documents, accounts and other vouchers of the corporation and is entitled to require from the directors, officers and employees of the corporation or from persons under contract to the corporation to manage the property or its assets the information ... necessary ... to make the report. (Ontario Condo Act, 1998)

The auditor is also tasked with ensuring the board completes the reserve fund study and notifies owners of deviations from the financial plan developed by the reserve fund expert. Note that the auditor is to be appointed by the owners at the AGM rather than by the board or property manager and, in principle, undertakes a role that is independent of both. In practice, auditors may not always maintain an allegiance to owners since, like the reserve fund study expert, they are paid by the board. This, too, shows the commodified nature of this relationship and its implications for governance. Although owners are tasked with electing auditors to oversee the board's management of finances, it is common for boards and managers – by vetting candidates, minimizing selection pools, or seizing the selection process altogether – to have the final say about who will examine their books. Under the least egregious circumstances, the auditor provides oversight by producing an opinion on whether the financial statements of the corporation are in order, fairly represented, and meet the accounting industry's standards. A depiction of the auditor as a "condo cop" within an assemblage illustrates the following manager's experience with this form of surveillance (in this instance coupled with the reserve fund study): "I always say there is a condo cop, because if you have to have an audit – any condo over twenty-five units has to have one ... that summary by the auditor basically says: 'They're not in compliance with the reserve fund, per the auditor ...' So in my opinion, an auditor is a condo cop" (TO Manager 7). However, the current auditing process is mostly symbolic, as one board member asserted: "The auditors only look and see if you added these ... numbers correctly ... Auditors only tell you that I have seen the numbers and you complied by the Ontario Accounting Code. What does that mean? Is this condo in good financial health or not in good financial health? They don't commit" (TO Board 41). Scholars have commented on this ambivalence. In articulating features of "Audit Society," Power (1999) asserts that the purpose of any auditor report is not to engage in communication but, rather, to merely provide quality labels of "fit" or "unfit" in the form of what he aptly calls "comfort certificates." He adds: "Where the audit process is defensively legalized there is a risk of relying too heavily on an industry of empty comfort certificates" and "shallow rituals of verification at the expense of other forms of organizational intelligence" (Power 1999, 123). Despite contrasting perceptions of the auditor's contributions to making board conduct transparent, attention is drawn to how legal knowledge encourages surveillance. The regulatory aspects of condo statutes concerning financial governance is revealing of this relationship whereby legal knowledge fosters counter law II, or surveillant assemblages, that identify areas demanding greater regulation and, thus, more law and surveillance.

CIVIL LAW

Condo life is regularly governed by civil law as it is infused with the condo and other statutes, condo bylaws, and house rules. This becomes even more evident regarding nuisance (see Chapter 6). It is within this domain that litigation against the condo corporation – for example, from "slip and falls" on condo property or inadequate enforcement of a condo's governing documents – is seen as a risk that protrudes from various sources of uncertainties and, as a result, must be avoided or eliminated. In relation to civil law, the condo complex is seen as transforming into a highly juridified and surveilled space, becoming one component of what is at once a governing and a *surveillant* assemblage.

In a civil litigation case, a board demanded a unit owner remove a satellite dish in violation of the condo's declaration. Because the board had not enforced this previously, the court found the board's behaviour to be unreasonably prejudicial and was ordered to pay the unit owner's incurred legal fees (*York Condominium Corporation No. 122 v. Sibblis,* 1989). Mindful of risks arising from such legal action, some boards are encouraged to develop innovative methods of gaining resident compliance. One such tool, known as a "chargeback," involves billing residents for costs of enforcement or correction where a breach of rules, bylaws, or the declaration has occurred. These can be for clean-up, repairs, or the paid time of building staff. One resident explained: "You can't have any fines ... so ... you break the rule ... [and] if the management company writes you a letter, they can charge you let's say twenty-five dollars to write the letter. It's not a fine. It's recouping their costs. The third time they get the lawyer to write it, it's five hundred bucks" (TO Board 40). This allows board members to essentially fine residents despite the act's clear prohibitions against issuing financial penalties. The opportunistic use of this tool to pre-empt risk reflects a departure from established legal standards and thus qualifies as another form of counter-law.

Other provincial legislation is woven into this condo assemblage too. For example, under section 26 of the 1998 act, condo corporations adopt the legal obligations of an occupier as outlined in Ontario's Occupiers' Liability Act, 1990, and are responsible for ensuring that premises and common elements are reasonably safe for all users. The convergence of these legal knowledges also leads to more surveillance. Some legal liability for accidents, even though condo corporation liability insurance is typically purchased, remains with the condo corporation. Legal liability is evident in the 2013 Ontario Superior Court case *Green v. York Region Condominium Corporation No. 834*, in which a Toronto condo owner sued the condo corporation and the inspection and maintenance provider for damages under the Occupier's Liability Act when, in 2005, she could not exit a stuck elevator door and injured her shoulder trying to do so. While the condo corporation and the maintenance provider were ultimately found not liable for the plaintiff's injuries, this case nonetheless highlighted the liability risk inherent in elevator operations (see Chapter 7) and the related demand for regular inspections and surveillance by a contracted third party. What is deemed "reasonable" varies in case law and, thus, falls into the category of uncertainty that forms of counter-law seek to pre-empt.

As noted earlier in this chapter, boards and managers increasingly have a preoccupation with emerging legal risks as the steady flow of civil law into the condo expands the legal implications for action and inaction. Here it is helpful to consider Hunt's (2003, 180) assertion that "encounters with problems that are posed as issues of risk, and that elicit concern with safety, lead to ... juridification." This is evident in the condo, where legality is both imposed from without and is emergent within.

MUNICIPAL LAW

Municipal law also seeps or is drawn into condo buildings, spawning forms of surveillance that bleed over municipal sidewalks onto condo property. As noted about house rules described above, municipal law reflects Foucault's "police" and is also used to counter nuisances (see Chapter 6). These forms may emerge as municipal bylaws or codes that regulate issues such as waste disposal, fire safety, and building safety, to name a few. New York's *Local Law 11* (Geberer 2011) is one example that stipulates that condo buildings of six or more stories must comply with safety inspections of exterior facades every five years and make repairs to any deficiencies outlined in the inspector's report. Touted as one of the most stringent and expensive municipal building-safety codes in New York, it ensures that building owners must expend considerable scaffolding and labour costs for multi-year restorations (Geberer 2011). One New York condo resident lamented: "You have so many years to get the work complete ... but by the time you finish with all the inspections, it's ... time for inspection again!" (NYC Res. 18). Another respondent remarked on the apparent certainty of repairs following inspection: "They come around and that's an expense even if they don't find anything. But they never not find anything" (NYC Board 6). Condo buildings deemed to have substantial safety concerns may warrant further inspection from a municipal official from the Department of Buildings. Relevant here is the intensity and unremitting surveillance that is exacted on the upkeep of the condo building and that speaks to the capacity of the board and its staff for diligence in maintenance and repair. At times municipal fire codes also encourage further surveillance in condo buildings:

> Take the stroller, put it in the fire stairs, because there's no place else for it. [But] you can't do that and what happens is the fire marshal comes by on a regular basis and walks the stairs, and if there's anything in the stairs the building gets fined, and the buildings [have] been fined more than once. Now the Super ... patrols so that we're not in violation of any of those fire codes. (NYC Res. 4)

This also shows the convergence of municipal and condo rules. That the former can also initiate "police" practices is taken up in Chapter 6.

Another way municipal law is implicated in condo governance, as noted in Chapter 4 on renters, is through municipal occupancy standards that dictate the number of occupants that can reside in a unit (Toronto Municipal Code, 2013). Commonly castigated as a culturally insensitive housing policy, the municipal regulation of domestic space in this way has been customary in North America for decades (see Pader 1994). A more recent trend has emerged by which condo corporations, under section 57(4) of Ontario's 1998 condo statute, are permitted to enact their own occupancy standards, circumventing the need to rely on municipal authorities for enforcement. Although occupancy standard bylaws established by the corporation must not be more restrictive than existing municipal standards (generally two persons per room), boards have been eager to directly address over-consumption and the disconcerting free rider problem elaborated earlier. This is equally beneficial to municipal governments wishing to relinquish their regulatory duties although it also erodes the power of municipal governments. The relation between occupant limits and the free rider problem is elucidated by a Toronto board member: "The reason ... is to limit the consumption of electricity, water. For us that is crucial because we are one of few buildings in the downtown area where all utilities are rolled into the common element fee, so we really can't have eight people living in a unit designed for two" (TO Board 16).

Where occupancy standards are contravened, condo boards may recoup increased costs of maintenance, repair, or common utility charges from the offending owner. Not only does this specific response to the free rider problem encourage additional law-like rules, it also demands a corresponding degree of surveillance to ensure compliance. In many newer condo buildings in Toronto, security personnel are enlisted in routine efforts to monitor those who traverse the premises, including owners (who are periodically required to have their photos taken and stored in a digital security system) and visitors (who must sign in upon building entry). In response to a question about whether condo corporations are required by law to ensure that common areas are secure for owners, a concierge elaborated: "Yes they are. Common access control is maintained through electronic entry, such as fob or access card, remote entry by security, plus camera monitoring and sometimes security present at the amenity such as a party room rental with greater than twenty guests" (TO Security 1). While building security personnel are cognizant of potential free riders or undesirable elements, the next section addresses the compounded anxieties that surface when suspected free riders are criminalized.

CRIMINAL LAW

Condo boards are required by statute to attend to the safety and security of their condo corporation's spaces and residents. Chapter 6 shows that public police are sometimes called to respond to nuisance. Increasingly, public police representatives also attend condo industry conferences in Ontario, lending their condo-specific risk assessment services to property managers and making them aware of the signs of, for example, illicit "grow-ops" or other drug labs in condo buildings. This is an effort to establish links that will result in regular intelligence (as opposed to relying on periodic calls for service) regarding what condo crimes (see Lippert, Treffers, and Bud 2017) are occurring in these ostensibly difficult-to-penetrate private realms. Public police can also activate managers and owners to patrol for and report criminal activity in their condo complexes. Illegal drug labs, for example, have a special meaning in condo high-rises: they constitute the perfect storm of condo anxieties. To begin with, concerns may surface about hazardous materials, dangerous reconfigurations of electrical lines, fire risks, and/or the infiltration of organized crime groups attempting to cloak a host of other illicit activities under the guise of an inconspicuous resident (e.g., Kane and Bosanac 2012). Financial problems such as damage to property, reduced property values from negative publicity, and excessive consumption of utilities may be additional concerns. Indeed, noticeability of exorbitant utility costs originating from a free riding condo unit may provoke suspicions of misconduct (e.g., breach of occupancy standards bylaw) or unlawful activity and thus mobilize property managers and security personnel to arrange targeted surveillance on the suspected unit. In one Toronto condo, a board member said that her board decided to install a surveillance camera in the hallway ceiling to watch the comings and goings in one unit suspected of housing a grow-op to collect visual evidence to submit to police (TO Board 42).

When tampered utility meters can conceal disproportionate use of resources, noticeability may increase through residents vigilant about odd smells, noises, excess moisture, or other peculiarities emanating from a unit that go beyond nuisance. In one case, a neighbour's initial complaint about a water leak revealed several illegal drug labs in a Toronto condo building (Bull 2012). In another instance, Toronto police seized $2.1 million after a call about suspicious activities in a Toronto condo complex (Shum 2013). Toronto police later held a press conference to showcase the seizures and to encourage other condo inhabitants to watch for and report similar behaviour. A final case involving a superintendent and two security personnel found operating a large grow-op in a Toronto condo's boiler room illustrates that residents are not the only culpable parties capable of running illegal operations in the condo world (Gillis 2010), especially as more and more external governing agents are entering condo buildings due to securitization and commodification.

Although illegal grow-ops tend to be relatively infrequent when compared to other governance issues, they nevertheless illustrate how particular ideas about criminal activity encourage criminal law and surveillance to enter condo buildings. While public police are expected to respond to suspicious activity, much detection and patrol is expected among owners or security personnel, all of whom are implicated in persisting forms of surveillance. The prospect of occupying condo units for the purposes of illicit activities also inspires closer surveillance of power and water consumption to watch for irregular usage since units with grow-ops use a disproportionate amount of these resources compared to other units. The next section explores the commodified nature of legal knowledge and surveillance and how condo corporations are highly dependent on this expert knowledge, which is accessible through the market.

COMMODIFICATION OF LEGAL KNOWLEDGE AND SURVEILLANCE

As with the commodification of condo governance itself and of legal knowledge, the rise of the condo has coincided with a profound growth in the commodification of surveillance. This increasing commodification is due in no small part to demands (legal mandates and liabilities) placed on condo buildings that derive from various legal knowledges (i.e., condo, municipal, civil, and criminal laws) and compel condo corporations to turn to market-oriented solutions in the absence of government oversight. One board member underscored this absence when he opined that the condo statute does not serve

> owners well at all. I think it [the condo statute] lacks clarity and ... there are all sorts of things that the province could do even as first steps ... requiring that the reserve fund study copy be sent to the province, secondly that the audit report be sent to the province, but the province obviously doesn't want to incur the expense of maintaining a staff to receive these documents. (TO Board 39)

Audits, reserve fund studies, and other contracted services are instead bought and paid with corporation funds and thus owners' rising fees and ultimately renters' rising rents. Other commodified forms of surveillance focus on resident conduct, as noted above regarding key fobs, that entail systematic tracking of individual owners and renters entering and exiting the building and its spaces. The previously noted Condo Control Central, which tracks and is integrated with several condo governance agents, ensures that residents comply with house rules. Founded in 2008, this system purports to be "a web-based system that helps condo property managers, board members, security personnel and owners communicate quickly and easily" (Condo Control Central 2017). Security firms that sell these and other security and surveillance products and services, some of which are transnational security corporations, suggest to condo corporations that security is a top priority for owners, boards, and property managers.[4]

In addition, boards can gain access to the market for free rider solutions to purchase less obvious forms of surveillance. Thus, when occupancy standards and related surveillance fail to resolve disproportionate resource consumption among residents, boards may introduce individual sub-metering to transition away from bulk utility bills and exact detailed surveillance of residents' consumption behaviour. Toronto boards may not always promise reduced common fees via sub-metering. As one owner remarked: "In my instance there is as much money being spent per month on administration fees for electrical as ... maintenance fees ... going towards the administration of the building" (TO Res. 60). Yet it appears that boards adamant about curbing the disproportionate consumption of utilities seek products and services from firms willing to supply them for a price. Faced with a host of legal requirements, risk liabilities, and anxieties, condo boards and property managers are increasingly urged to tap into a fast-growing market of legal knowledge and surveillance. The vast industry that has grown to serve these manufactured needs promises to watch for misbehaviour and self-interested residents who defy imagined collective interests. Owners weary of board decisions are supposed to rely on promises of market mechanisms to oversee them. The fact that this commodification is occurring and that there is an expanding market for both condo legal knowledge and surveillance suggests that prospects for curtailing their unfettered entry into the condo world are doubtful in the short term.

CONCLUSION

The foregoing analysis of the condo world has several implications. Previous research has studied surveillance and regulation of social housing occupants (Cowan and McDermont 2006), homeless persons in accommodated housing (Fopp 2002), tenants in rental buildings (Lister 2005), residents of gated communities (Blandy and Lister 2005), and involving "social landlords" who govern private residences and surrounding communities (Flint and Pawson 2009). Together this work shows the influential role of law and surveillance in various housing forms. Yet condoization entails a distinctive proliferation of law and surveillance not evident in these kinds of housing and that is a vital element of condo conquest. Indeed, this distinctiveness is evident in relation to condo elevators and policing condo nuisances relative to other forms, as discussed in the next two chapters.

In the condo, legal knowledge is seen to nourish the spread of surveillance. First, surveillance is seen to burrow further into condo crevices, encouraging legal knowledge in the form of house rule refinements and regular condo law reform that fill expanding voids in Ontario, New York State, and several other American (see McKenzie 2011, 93–106) and Canadian jurisdictions. The occurrence of law and surveillance in the condo world may be spiralling. Second, surveillance is found to at times be fuelled by increasing identification of unruly owners, and especially renters and free riders, as well as by increasing suspicion of pernicious governing authorities that, together, are fast becoming the "malicious demons" (Ericson 2007) of the condo world. Forms of counter-law premised on precautionary logic are also seen to foster these developments. Third, while provincial and state governments craft increasingly detailed statutes that supposedly govern condo corporations and owners, surveillance and oversight are more and more assigned to an assemblage of private agents (arguably even the nascent Condo Authority in Ontario is more private than public, funded by condo owners and immune from direct political oversight as it is). Rather than centralized, the rhizomatic character of condo surveillance is evident. This raises a fourth point: that legal knowledges and surveillance in condo complexes appear in the form of commodities. And, as the condo spreads, institutional supports for surveillance and a dependency on these markets for their distribution are increasingly written into condo statutes, cheered on by advocates invited to legislative committee hearings. When commodified forms of surveillance fail to correct malpractice on the part of those managing the condo building, or when court-appointed administrators are deemed necessary to replace boards, one may glimpse the frailty of the assertion that the condo is "self-governing." The costs of this frailty are initially borne by resident owners and renters. But one can speculate that soon, when more aging or poorly constructed condo buildings begin to physically fail and their corporations financially collapse, as they did following the 2008 real estate crisis in the US (*Miami Herald* 2009), the burden will shift to the public sphere (not unlike the way policing nuisance in condo buildings begins as a private enterprise but ultimately relies on public police and the courts) (see Chapter 6). This occurs alongside specialized counter-law assessments and court-appointed administrators that reveal themselves as only temporary remedies as responsibility for crumbling properties and unsustainable fees shifts to municipal taxpayers with limited finances. It remains unclear that this extension of precautionary logic, through a spiral of law and surveillance, is beneficial to the condo, its residents, and cities more broadly.

What is clear is that the increasing expert knowledge accompanying this spiral is placing a higher and higher financial burden on the condo itself via increased fees to owners (and ultimately renters) to pay for condo lawyers, security and surveillance professionals and technologies, and other expert knowledges. This financial burden extends to other citizens via public enforcement mechanisms and new fees for new enforcement bodies that are being enacted in Ontario and contemplated for New York State. It is uncertain, too, that all this regulation and surveillance accomplishes what it purports to, which is to achieve security and to eliminate uncertainty in condo governance and living. It is unclear that more statutory legal regulations and more surveillance make for better condo governance. Condo governance seeks to snuff out uncertainty fuelled by precautionary logic. But this might instead mean that it is less rather than more likely that resident owners will become board members who cannot make mistakes for fear of reprisal, or even criminalization, under intensifying legal regulation and surveillance. While there is a risk of imposing yet another expert knowledge here, it also remains uncertain whether, if there were less law, surveillance, or both in the condo world,[5] there might be more board participation among resident owners (and a place for renters at the table); a greater sense of inclusive community and opportunities for meeting and the interaction that foments it; more reliance on natural surveillance and following rules out of common interest (which stems from knowing rather than merely suspecting the neighbour down the hall); and increased reliance on common resident knowledge regarding how and whether to formally respond to minor infractions and exposed "problems."

In the condo, the increasing focus on uncertainty on the ground is where the conditions of trust necessary to form vibrant urban communities are being systematically replaced with doubt, suspicion, and fear of unknowable risks. In such arrangements notions of community are jettisoned or never imagined in the first place for fear of free riding phantoms and other self-interested spectres lurking down the hall and on distant floors while myriad external governing agents outside the condo building, operating at owners' expense, watch from afar. Proliferating forms of surveillance, including video surveillance and audits, promise to stand watch for a price and arrive with legal trappings but apparently never quite deliver. Instead, surveillance exposes more issues, mistakes, petty infractions, and free riding not easily forgotten and that accumulate until they pry open new channels for more legal knowledge to flow into the condo world. More broadly, the fear of catastrophe and the embrace of precaution as a governing logic may result not in more financial and physical security in urban housing but, rather, in a situation in which "civil society unravels [and] ... there is more risk and uncertainty" (Ericson 2007, 218). As precautionary logic and forms of counter-law creep into condo governance, this explains the seemingly insatiable calls for condo law reform in Ontario, New York State, and other North American jurisdictions, a source of legal knowledge that will extend further and further to fill more and more exposed cracks, in the process covering the remains of the original promise, or at least potential, for community in condo life (and, by extension, in urban life).

6

Policing Condo Nuisance

What's a nuisance to me isn't a nuisance to someone else ... and it's not a nuisance when you're driven from your own home. That's far beyond a nuisance to me ... I've been deprived of quiet enjoyment of my home for them to make money.

– TO RES. 16

He was so afraid of second-hand smoke. So there was this little infraction and there was this immense paranoia.

– NYC RES. 14

What police has to govern, its fundamental object, is ... coexistence with each other. It is the fact they live together, reproduce, and that each of them needs a certain amount of food and air to live, to subsist; it is the fact they work alongside each other ... and also that they exist in a space of circulation ... police must take responsibility for all of this kind of sociality.

– FOUCAULT (2007, 326)

One might obtain the sense from condo developer marketing that, once purchased, living in a condo unit in Toronto and New York is free of hassle, brimming with leisurely comfort and security, and approaching utopian urbanity. The "father of condominiums"' allegedly marketed the first condo complex in the US in the early 1960s with a three-word advertisement: "No More Yardwork" (Benson 2012). But inside condo buildings something else is going on entirely. There one encounters the many discomforts of condo living that penetrate units and the sensibilities of residents that defy myriad governing means – those annoying, relentless sounds, smells, and little things left behind to obstruct hallways, elevators, and chutes within or that arrive unannounced on a balcony from without. Such nuisances fill the urban problem space and help define the urban milieu (Lippert and Walby 2014b). Chapter 1 notes that condo governance and condo life are simultaneous and that thus there is a sense in which these nuisances are as much an effect as a target of numerous house rules and enforcement. The study of condo governance reveals its preoccupation with policing these nuisances, which is undoubtedly common to all condo buildings in North America as well as globally. Yet, despite the common phrase "just a nuisance," which implies some distance from gravity, nuisances can pose serious challenges to condo boards as well as to other governing agents in the assemblages (i.e., property managers, security personnel, lawyers, other owners, etc.) confronting them. Indeed, nuisances are sometimes experienced by condo boards and owners as extremely problematic. For example, in New York one board member reflected upon a meeting to deal with regular noise nuisance from residents thus:

> The most contentious meeting we ever had was how to handle the drumming that our neighbours were doing ... from two in the afternoon on a Saturday to two in the morning and so the people on the other side of the building felt ... the people ... affected were being very hard and so it was ... the most contentious meeting that we ever had. (NYC Res. 6)

In Toronto, an ongoing smoke nuisance from a resident was so annoying that one owner, after numerous apparently unsuccessful efforts to resolve it, went so far as to submit a brief to Ontario's latest statutory review in the desperate hope of stopping smoke nuisance: "I tried to complain over 200 times to whomever I can complain to: police, customer care offices, concierges, property management offices. They all told me smokers – my neighbours – can do whatever they wanted inside their units and they were not able to help me" (Condo Briefs 2012).

As condoization proliferates it raises new questions about policing nuisances, including regarding the prevalence and constitution of specific nuisances, through what means and agents they are policed, and how they can become serious, disruptive issues. In an influential socio-legal account, Cooper (2002) argues that policing nuisance can be a means of oppressing particular groups and thus demands paying careful attention to how nuisances are framed and how subjectivity plays an essential role in what is perceived as nuisance behaviour. In what follows, renters – a category that tends to reflect a class position – are unequally blamed for nuisance and/or policed differently compared to resident owners. This alone suggests that nuisance is more revealing of condo governance and condoization than it might first appear and that it deserves more scholarly attention.

One relevant governing logic shaping condo governance is what Foucault (2007) refers to as "police," which is concerned with the minutiae of urban life. "Police" in this sense is typically differentiated from what is understood as the modern "public police." In condo spaces "police" is evinced as coercing residents and targeting myriad aspects of their conduct and environs. Nuisance is not the only target of "police" – aesthetics is another – but it is key among the urban details to which this logic is directed. Insisting they be examined together, this chapter explores "police" and nuisance, as well as how they are experienced in this realm, to reveal the rarely stated fact that both saturate condo life and space.

Policing nuisance consistent with "police" overlaps at times with key processes. Before proceeding, it is necessary to briefly elaborate how policing nuisance relates to such processes and related agents and knowledges of condo governance. Most nuisance comes to light via complaints that reflect how policing nuisance relies on residents' common knowledge and their experiences of condo living, which are then passed to various condo governing agents to seek remedy. Certainly "complaint" and "common" share the Latin prefix "com," meaning "with" or "together." This is not to suggest condo living is not also partially characterized by varying levels (and means) of common tolerance, which is implied and occasionally noted in residents' accounts of condo life. This tolerance is a fundamental element of communal, or at least neighbourly, relations and, among other things, prevents the cost of addressing nuisance complaints from becoming unsustainable. Yet it is possible that such tolerance of nuisance is dwindling in the condo world. If so, it is especially worth noting that policing nuisance can spill into, buttress, and constitute the processes of condoization – risk avoidance, juridification, securitization, and commodification – when deemed prevalent or serious, although the "police" logic shaping it cannot be reduced to any one of these. So, for example, when nuisance reaches a threshold of regularity or gravity of experience and complaint (such as regarding tobacco smoke and resulting fires), it can: trigger hikes in mandatory insurance premiums for the condo corporation, especially if there are more rented units (commonly assumed to be a greater source of nuisance than owner-occupied units) (risk avoidance); lead to paying lawyers to send warning letters to occupants creating the nuisance (juridification); spark increases in security spending for patrols or more visits to units from security personnel where nuisance is suspected (securitization); be thought to reduce property values; and/or lead policing nuisance itself to become marketized as a commodity (commodification). Nuisance itself can best be thought of as condo residue, little sounds, odours, and behaviours constantly shed and left behind by the machinations of the governing assemblage as it shifts and adjusts in contingent ways and as condo property is consumed as a commodity in these urban space-times. This detritus can accumulate in ways that become serious enough to illuminate and activate other processes and related elements; this is the point at which "just a nuisance" translates into something else – for example, where and when "police" becomes precautionary and these two logics merge. Examining policing condo nuisance lends further support to the key argument running through this book, which is that the condo is a set of legal, social, spatial (and occasionally temporal) relationships among numerous actors and things as well as a distinctive arrangement of governance.

This chapter uses interview excerpts selected to exemplify patterns to make three general points. First, olfactory and audio-related nuisances are especially salient in condo buildings. This shows a close fit with Buckley's (1981, 22) remark in his classic work on nuisance court cases: "The majority of nuisance cases concern complaints of discomfort or inconvenience caused by noise or smell" (see also Power 2015). These nuisances challenge condo governance because their verification is often thought to be fleeting, subjective, or impossible. Since policing nuisance includes attention to sounds and smells, this shows that "police" targets more than space and positioning of objects due to aesthetics or other reasons. Second, condo governance informed by "police" when confronting nuisance occasionally borrows from and converges with municipal bylaw, public police, and the public courts. Public police especially tend to be enlisted to confront nuisance when renters rather than owners are deemed its cause, thus reinforcing the notion that the renter is deemed as the "other" and treated as such. This reliance on public means and legal knowledge stemming from, for example, municipal bylaws occurs even though advocates of the condo world often claim it is separate from the public sphere and is self-reliant. These claims are especially salient when it comes to decisions about what services they will cover through condo fees (see Chapter 8 on "double taxation"). This is surprising since "police" practices are being increasingly commodified and the "common knowledge" (Valverde 2003) of residents is being joined or replaced by purchased expert knowledge (and its related trappings) as part of condo conquest.

The third general point this chapter makes is that temporal dimensions of "police" and "nuisance," in conjunction with space, matter when deploying these concepts in the condo world and more broadly. Thus, policing nuisance commences not necessarily when an annoyance stems from a certain space but, instead, when it comes from that space at a certain time, such as after 11:00 p.m. Nuisance comes into being at that particular conjunction of time and space. Overall, this chapter seeks to demonstrate that, given the condoization of North American cities like Toronto and New York, the centrality of "police" and "nuisance" to condo governance and, by extension, to urban life has not previously been fully recognized.

The remainder of this chapter is in three sections. The first further elucidates the concept of "police" as it is discussed in recent sociology of governance literature, which is influenced by Foucault's writings (e.g., Foucault 1991). The second and largest section explores policing nuisance experiences in condo buildings consistent with "police" practices, mostly by drawing on accounts of residents and board members. This section discusses two nuisances dominant in these accounts – noise and smoke. The third section demonstrates that "police"-informed practices confronting nuisance are being joined by mutually reinforcing private agents and expert knowledges beyond resident owners' common knowledge. Thus, "police" is being ever more commodified via services providing expert knowledges with which to confront nuisance.

POLICE LOGIC

"Police" is, as elaborated in Chapter 1, a governing logic. It is often referred to as "the police power" that entails coercive measures to ensure a community's welfare (see Dubber and Valverde 2006; Neocleous 2000; Novak 1996, 70). Leading urban and governance scholars influenced by Foucault, such as Alan Hunt and Nicholas Blomley, have acknowledged and examined "police" in cities (see also Valverde 2011), along with its mundane targets, like vehicle traffic (Hunt 2006) and sidewalk spaces (Blomley 2011). Hunt (2006) examines regulations and automatic signal lights as a form of "police" that confronts proliferating urban traffic. Blomley (2011) explores pedestrianism as a "police" tool. He argues that pedestrianism avoids governing through legal rights and instead elicits "an attention to placement and flow" (Blomley 2011, 4). In their accounts, "police" tends to be tethered to municipal government and local public authorities. Yet contemporary "police" is not necessarily so closely or exclusively tied to municipal government and its agents. These nuanced accounts of "police" do not exhaust the concept's possibilities. Governing arrangements that target behaviour in residential and other urban spaces require further exploration if we are to attain a fuller picture.

Condo governing arrangements, where placement and flow are paramount concerns, can also illuminate "police." In policing nuisance, positioning and flow in relation to space is important, as Blomley (2011) notes, but timing of, for example, noise nuisances has been neglected in previous accounts of "police" (though less so in scholarly discussions of nuisance separate from "police"). It is for this reason these two dimensions of nuisance and how they are policed in the condo world are considered in detail. Exploring "police" in this realm matters because it helps expose the effects of this logic, either on its own or in combination with other logics and processes. Fully understanding condo governance therefore requires close attention to both the logic of "police" and to the logic of nuisance: attention to such governing logics simultaneously lends insight into both.

CONDO NUISANCES

Policing nuisances dominates condo governance, while more serious property crimes, especially those committed by board members and service providers involving embezzlement, bid-rigging, and kickbacks, are, incredulously, often of less concern to owners (see Lippert, Treffers, and Bud 2017). Occasionally policing nuisance merges with other governance issues, including free rider problems and even racial/ethnic conflict, but it cannot be reduced to these. Of course, nuisances are relevant to more traditional rental buildings and detached housing as well, but they are policed differently in the condo context, ostensibly through a board of owners and rules brought to bear on the very persons who own the common elements involved, and who, in principle, approved the rules. The common spaces are at once their own and not their own.

"Police" targets details of daily condo life. Few aspects of the minutiae of condo living escape. Condo house rules foment surveillance as they seek to prevent and control little things. They specify, among other things, whether one can make noise after 11:00 p.m.; the weight or size of pets; clothing to be worn in recreational areas; how long an automobile can be parked in a building's front; how long a guest can stay; whether and how a kitchen can be remodelled; where and how refuse can be placed; and the extent, nature, and timing of alterations to a unit's doors and interiors. As an owner aptly remarked, her board decides rules on the "granular level" that is characteristic of "police": "The board meets monthly ... they tend to discuss issues that are on a pretty granular level. Our board is quite hands-on and if ... in doubt they tend to issue a rule ... [and] be pretty heavy-handed with rules and signs everywhere" (TO Res. 55). House rules are deemed to counter nuisance; the con*do's* and con*don'ts*. During the condo's early years in North America, Mittelbach and Ebin (1975, 176) wrote: "Suffice it to say that one finds in condo housing a wide variety of rules and regulations in effect ... of the 'thou shalt' and 'thou shalt not' type, and essentially express an exercise of the police power, including the institution of penalties." These characterizations befit the widely perceived notion that condo governance entails conflict over the rule-making of boards and enforcement by property managers, security personnel, lawyers, and others. This governance of details, first set in place by developers with boilerplate house rule packages for the first board of a new-build condo building and later (for a price) upheld, refined, or supplemented by boards under the advice of property managers and lawyers, entails close attention to little things that become nuisances when they are out of place (and time) and violate residents' senses. Condo life entails numerous petty rules focused on these seemingly minor things, but these rules and their enforcement often deeply penetrate resident bodies. This is true of common areas as well as of what occurs in units and, especially, among units and common spaces. The inevitable features of conduct due to shared space tend to flow horizontally and vertically. Water leakage, garbage, visitors' access and egress, legal and illicit business enterprises, pets and parties and their relentless residues garner the attention of other owners and are then often reported to property managers, security personnel, board members, and sometimes public police or other public authorities.

Regarding condo governance, one property manager related that there's "a little mantra ... people, parking, and pets ... They're really enforcement issues and ... really affect people on a day-to-day basis" (TO Manager 6). These three "P's" – people, pets, and parking (see also Gardiner Miller Arnold [GMA 2017]; Arabian 1995) – comprise a common set of challenges arising from necessarily sharing condo space (and time). The fact that people are placed on the same plane as pets and parking is fully consonant with "police" logic. This is additionally evident in municipal law, as Blomley shows in relation to a Vancouver municipal bylaw that governs pedestrian flow on sidewalks and targets, not particular kinds of city residents or physical barriers but, instead, a "mashup of people and things" (Blomley 2011, 46; see also Valverde 2012 on the regulation of city street corners).

People are deemed one among several sources of nuisance. A key feature of "police" is that people's intent – the reasons they create a nuisance – is largely irrelevant. Pets – especially dogs – are deemed a nuisance, too. Dogs are assumed to be noise nuisances but are also reviled for what they tend to leave behind. One New York resident explained how this kind of dog product was dealt with in his building: "There used to be incidents where dogs were peeing in the hallways so they implemented a bylaw where if your dog pees in the hallway ... you're going to get fined" (NYC Res. 19). But dogs' behaviour is typically thought to be about residents' behaviour, as a Toronto resident pointed out: "People's dogs pee and poop in various places even in the garage ... and then people don't look after it. So those are issues" (TO Res. 8). Consistent with the increasing commodification of "police," new commercial firms, such as "Poo Prints," are emerging. For a fee, Poo Prints provides registration of owners' dogs' DNA, which can later be compared to dog waste samples discovered in common areas to identify the condo owner-culprit (Bradamore and Spencer 2017). A Toronto-focused article in *Condo Business* magazine (Bradamore and Spencer 2017) explains how boards can implement mandatory registration of dog DNA for all residents in a condo building via a new bylaw or rule to address this type of nuisance (as in the New York condo building mentioned above) but can take this further by tying it to a new technology of surveillance. The article was co-authored by the owner of Poo Prints and a Toronto-based condo lawyer, illustrating a key mutually supportive link among several elements in the assemblage of condo governance.

Dogs were also regularly deemed a source of noise nuisance: "The conflict issues that I hear about between residents are barking dogs ... in our building" (TO Res. 31). In another complex a resident explained that "one unit leaks into another ... one unit complains about a dog's claws being too noisy on the floor" (NYC Res. 22). In a relatively quiet building: "I haven't heard anyone coming to a board meeting complaining about noise except for ... excessively barking dogs ... only because they've left the dog in the apartment by themselves [*sic*] for long periods of time. The dog is lonely and frightened. That's an issue that gets violated" (NYC Res. 15). While there were rules to police pet noise nuisance, this does not necessarily translate into enforcement. For example, in one building, "the rules are specific that you can only have the dog if it's not bugging other people. But, of course, nothing ever seems to be done about it when there is a dog that doesn't shut up" (TO Res. 31).

Parking, and all that is associated with it (parking in front of the building entrance, storing material other than vehicles in parking spaces, owners using visitor parking stalls, and so on), in condo space comprises a large set of issues too complicated to take up here. But all three "P's" are about violating borders of one kind or other and reveal the challenges of condo governance.

Nuisances stemming from people are multiple, but noise and smoke are easily the most common in condo buildings in Toronto and New York. The dominance of these two kinds of nuisance was also reflected in one Toronto condo law firm's online "Tips, Tricks, Knowledge, and Links" webpage, which provides four special downloadable "practical solution" guides to nuisances, not only to pets and short-term stayers but also to noise and smoke (Lash 2017b). Consistent with the manner that legal knowledge flows via "excerpting" into the condo world, these truncated but flashy "guides" end with a picture of this firm's condo lawyers and its contact information, thus suggesting that, for a price, complete legal knowledge is available to confront each type of problem.

Noise emanating from units and smoke from tobacco and marijuana consumption entering common areas and migrating through barriers between these spaces have become a persistent source of nuisance. If inadequately remedied, these nuisances can grow to challenge the very notion of the condo by defying borders between units and common areas. Policing nuisance of this kind is decidedly spatialized. Other nuisances emerge in direct relation to the common spaces of condo living, where spatial positioning and flow are vital, including garbage disposal areas. One resident complained: "People who will leave their bicycles where the trash compactor is, instead of taking it downstairs and putting it away ... Why would you do that? You have an elevator" (NYC Res. 19). A Toronto resident remarked: "Each floor has a garbage chute disposal area; sometimes people leave boxes on the floor when the sign says specifically 'Do not leave boxes on the floor'" (TO Res. 40). Some attention is paid to ensuring flow through common condo space: "Our halls are small because there're only three units on a floor, so we are not to put anything out in the hall. No rugs ... you put it in your unit; you don't put your boots out in the hall; you don't put your strollers in the hall" (NYC Res. 19). The next two sections focus on noise and smoke-related issues, respectively, and they show that there is more to "police" and nuisance than only positioning and flow.

Noise as Nuisance

Policing noise occurs through common knowledge of condo spaces. Thus, noise nuisance tends to become such through residents' complaints to boards, property managers, and security personnel (as opposed to the latter's proactive efforts) and are typically couched in spatial terms: "There was someone complaining about noise from a neighbouring unit above and the answer from the property manager was that ... would be dealt with" (TO Res. 17). "We expect you to maintain a noise level that's compatible with the people around you. That's often an issue in here when the youngsters are staying in the building and they're having a party and it's noisy ... There's always complaints" (TO Board 34). "Like you can't have people partying in the middle of the night and you can't not enforce it ... I think the boys sent warning letters to the people involved in partying next to me" (TO Res. 20). Yet, while many condo house rules focus on positioning and flow in space, temporality in relation to policing noise nuisance is also crucial. The title of Davina Cooper's (2002) insightful revisiting of nuisance in legal and political discourse – "Early Morning Crowing of a Farmyard Cock" – is a reminder that crowing emanating from farmyard space is not enough to render it a nuisance. Indeed, a farmyard is where crowing is expected. Rather, it is when crowing occurs in early morning hours that it becomes a nuisance in urban areas.

Time and Space of Policing Noise

Whereas improper trash disposal can reduce flow through condo space and, for that reason, become a nuisance, the same garbage chute area can become a noise nuisance after a particular time, when it becomes a contravention of a rule: "Some people will use the area after 10:00 p.m. at night when there's a sign there that says 'Don't use the garbage after ten'" (TO Res. 65). Noise nuisance also stems from the renovation of units, an especially common concern in condo complexes. A board member noted: "There are rule infractions ... Some people want to renovate their apartment or improve it and don't follow the rules about when they are going to do ... construction at odd hours ... There's an effort by the management to ... discuss these issues with them and educate them as to ... which hours would be suitable" (TO Board 18). A New York owner identified renovations as the noise source and acknowledged that, while such remodelling may be inevitable – the noise nuisance again described in temporal terms – the nuisance could have been avoided:

> Early on it was a lot around people renovating their apartment and the noise from the construction ... but ... that slowed down and I might be the next one creating noise ... but I think I would be more conscious to let my fellow tenants know that I'm going to be renovating my unit, the people around me, maybe the floors below me, just so they're aware and I would be very mindful of those quiet hours and let the ... construction team ... know when they should be working and ... I don't know that people necessarily do that. (NYC Res. 15)

Noise nuisance can also stem from more mundane activities, such as vacuuming and children playing above – but again at specific times. As a board member recounted: "One of my friends has an ongoing noise complaint from the people up above her vacuuming at midnight, ... you can hear it through the floors down clearly. She complained [but] nothing was done about it ... for over a year" (TO Board 15). Or noise nuisance can stem from using exercise equipment at definite times:

> Really early I hear the bicycle shoes. They have those metal plates. You can hear Cheeka Cheeka, Cheeka in the morning when they're getting their bicycle shoes on. Then you hear Eeoow, Eeoow because they're pumping up the tires, so we know. I'm sure they don't realize that but I know exactly when they're bicycling ... that ... goes straight through the beams which is one reason we're not supposed to have them because it's a really old building and we have all kinds of structural problems, but I don't think the treadmill's going to land in my living room either, so I'm not worried. (NYC Res. 8)

The organization of space within units was deemed related to noise nuisance in adjacent or other units within a complex. In one condo building noise moved horizontally and upward, but at a specific time: "Where noise was high ... people have reported one place that's of issue is the fitness room because apparently the noise travels through the walls to units around it. It's on the ground floor, but if you're on the second floor and somebody drops weights then you can hear it. The fitness room opens at 6:00 a.m." (TO Res. 21). Indeed, many of the above excerpts invoke the timing of sounds and a specific horizontal and vertical arrangement of condo space. Nuisance noise moves "through the floors," "through the beams," and "through the walls," defying spatial boundaries but *only* at specific times. There is a sense in which temporality dissolves condo floors, beams, and walls, permitting sound to penetrate and become a nuisance and demanding policing on the other side. Such sounds are not a nuisance in other instances, when they merely merge with daily condo life. Noise defies private space at precise moments and periods, and this renders it a challenge not only to condo governance but also, more fundamentally, to the condo itself, which is premised on vital demarcation between common and individual space.

Noise nuisance is commonly deemed to emanate from playing music or resident parties and get-togethers: "We have a couple in there that have teenagers and occasionally they'd have a party and we'd have to ... call downstairs to the desk and say 'you've got to tell them to quiet down' ... And they would" (NYC Res. 18). Typically, music and parties become nuisances demanding policing due to their timing. Thus, one New York owner remarked upon a house rule's temporal aspect: "No piano playing if it's after ten o'clock at night, or a radio or a CD player you could hear from another apartment" (NYC Res. 11). In a Toronto complex an owner similarly remarked: "My roommate, she shares a wall with our next-door neighbour and they played very loud music at times so that is a problem. So I guess the rule is you can play music but only until eleven o'clock at night ... we've had to report him several times so that has been ... an annoyance" (TO Res. 22). Elsewhere, even though the rule established an eleven o'clock cut-off, this owner granted some leeway in policing nuisance, but it depended on the day of the week:

> We had a problem very early on in terms of excessive noise from late night parties at the unit below. We ... got that sorted out. There's supposed to be a quiet time after eleven o'clock and most people adhere to it, but at the same

> time on a weekend night when people are having a party we're reasonably flexible. (TO Res. 22)

From her board vantage point, a board member similarly underscored the centrality of timing in policing noise nuisance following a complaint:

> It's not always breaking the rule. Someone will say that the noise is too loud but its twelve noon ... there's nothing we can do. That person isn't really breaking a rule. It's like you hear a noise. You don't like it, but that person has the right to play their music at that time of day ... People think we should be able to do something about it but ... it's not that excessive or outrageous. (NYC Board 2)

The general lack of communication channels and often vertically arranged isolation of residents in high-rises make immediate policing of noise rules difficult, as examples in this section show. Note that many of these examples are also about timing: "So anyone has a problem, you call up the managing agent, you say, 'The person in such and such apartment, they've been playing loud music at two in the morning, something needs to be done.' So they should do something about that, but there's not that line of communication" (NYC Res. 9). Another resident explained how noise nuisance was initially policed through owners but that sometimes this failed:

> Sometimes I think it is just people's noise tolerance levels. Some people operate in a way that says, "Oh, I'm in a community with other people around me. I need to be cognizant of how loud I have my music on after a certain time" ... We have board condo rules and regulations. Some people are aware of them and adhere to them and others have to be reminded ... Like my neighbour, at one point he bought a television. His bedroom and my bedroom buttress each other and I guess he got it with surround sound and he would turn it on and I would just hear all this TV feedback and we had to have several conversations and I had to get the sponsor involved for him to realize. (NYC Res. 15)

Sometimes there was simply no immediate remedy to noise nuisance because no target was present: "They turned the radio ... up really loud. And then they wouldn't turn it off when they left for school and ... so you can't ... get in touch with them and say, 'You cannot leave a radio blaring all day long in your unit'" (TO Res. 27).

In some condo buildings security personnel were activated to police noise nuisance, but again, this was consistent with a definite temporality, occurring not at the cut-off of 11:00 p.m. (a rule in many buildings) but, instead, "beyond" or "well after" it, by "2:00 a.m." or "when they wake me up." "Police" practices dependent upon resident-initiation of common knowledge transfer within buildings can activate security personnel. One resident recounted when security arrived to respond to a complaint late one evening:

> There's a noise complaint going all the time ... I used to invite a lot of friends ... so that wasn't very pleasing to my neighbours and they were complaining and one day the security knocked [on] my door while I was having a party that several neighbours [were] complaining [about] because my noise went beyond eleven or twelve o'clock. It was contrary to the condo rules. (TO Res. 28)

A resident in another building, this time the complainant, similarly explained that some leeway was provided based upon timing: "I have reported my neighbours for loud parties on a Friday night or Saturday night when it's well after 11:00 p.m. so I have reported them. I called the security and said the guy below me is making noise" (TO Res. 29). This leeway is evident in many incidents. In one case the complainant waited until the early morning: "In the summer some girls ... sit in the back until two or three o'clock and they make noise. Then we are to call ... security" (TO Res. 30). In another case, this activation of security was triggered only when the resident was "woken up," again suggesting timing mattered when it came to how noise nuisance was policed: "There have been some pretty loud parties down there. So ... the first thing I do when they wake me up is I call the concierge and they go down there and tell everybody to shut up" (TO Res. 8).

Policing Noise through Legal Knowledges and Surveillance

House rules enacted to police noise nuisance often clearly dictate the internal spatial arrangements of units, a level of intervention unheard of in traditional detached housing. For example, one board member explained that possessions likely to create noise in his condo building were to be positioned in certain ways within the units: "You're supposed to have your pianos and TVs on the outside wall, but some people don't even have one outside wall" (TO Board

36). In many other buildings there were rules about having floor coverings on a certain percentage of floor space. One resident reflected upon this arrangement: "Some folks in our building have made complaints to the board about people being very loud in their apartments and so we've tried to invoke ... 65 to 70 percent of your unit must be covered in carpet and rugs. We've done that. We've written letters" (NYC Res. 20). A Toronto resident noted the effect of this rule's absence: "Whoever bought above me didn't have any floor coverings, so it's all bare floors. I did hear a lot of thumping ... It sounded like a basketball was being bounced on the floor" (TO Res. 16).

In another complex, two owners apparently resorted to threatening a lawsuit due to noise:

> My upstairs neighbour's an architect ... and I sold an apartment on the second floor to this couple who were graphic designers and ... so I said, " ... do not listen to him [the architect]. Get permits for everything you do." So what did they do? ... they got no permits, and they got in a world of trouble with their downstairs neighbours who turned out to be both attorneys and were embittered because the previous owners of that apartment had been two elderly gentlemen in wheelchairs so they made no noise. The couple ... have two little kids so all of the sudden they had all this pounding and dropping of toys. (NYC Res. 23)

In another building an owner explained that policing noise nuisance was related to higher fee levels in his "nicer" building, thus suggesting that noise was not inevitable and that its reduction could be purchased with more expensive, "better" policing:

> There's sometimes noise issues in the building but ... one of the benefits of being in a nicer building – you pay a little bit more maintenance fees and such – is that there's better enforcement of ... rules. So there doesn't seem to be the type of excess noise or complaints that you hear about in many condos. (TO Board 21)

Such an assumption is consonant with the commodification of policing nuisance.

Consistent with the isolation or lack of communication (or community) among residents, municipal bylaws are sometimes invoked to confront noise. One owner related: "I went to him and I said, 'please turn down your stereo ... that's a city bylaw ... Everything has to be quiet after eleven o'clock p.m. ...' There's also another thing that says if it interferes with your living standard conditions, and I said it is" (TO Res. 24). The public police were also used to police nuisance in condo complexes in these circumstances. Thus, despite condo governance often being framed as ostensibly private and outside government influence, some nuisance was dealt with by relying on public police or at least on the threat of calling them. In one instance a board member related how security was called before police:

> The guys who worked for the builder owned places ... and the kids had a wild party ... So the concierge had a difficult time because they had to call the police and they don't want to do that. It has happened, but it got resolved. But ... two in the morning and ... loud music and yelling and screaming and laughing and fighting. (TO Board 19)

Public police were called to another building, partially because security personnel were thought to be of limited effectiveness:

> I had an issue with a neighbour's late night parties and noise and it turned out to be a young kid who would have a party that got out of control so one group of people would get invited and ... the party grew out of control and they were making a lot of noise and a lot of people drunk and rowdy so security can only do so much, the police have to get involved. (TO Res. 25)

Another resident related that public police were ineffective in policing nuisance and that others deemed their use inappropriate due to perceived heavy-handedness:

> We finally left it that this one person would try and negotiate with them, and in fact she asked the people to quit calling the police while that process took place and I think it did stop then, but then nobody called the police after that ... [Question: Was there any real resolution when you called the police?] No, that made them really mad because the police did come twice and shut them down, but they started up again as soon as the police leave. And several of the people in the building said, "Yeah, well we would have done that when we were that age, it's what we would have done, Fuck you."

> … and I did tell them that when I tried personally to talk to them, one of the first times it happened, it was about eleven o'clock at night and … and they thoroughly ignored me. (NYC Res. 6)

At times surveillance of noise nuisances was initiated, including by a former board member who patrolled while listening:

> [When] I was on the board I had that kind of mentality … my nickname was the Building Sheriff because I … try to keep people to the rules … [When] the dog first moved into the building I was trying to figure out where the dog was barking from. I went out of my apartment and I went down and I was listening for the noise, and I saw which apartment it was coming from and … confirmed my suspicions. (NYC Res. 15)

Elsewhere a board member explained that his board's lack of authority led to "monitoring" rather than to immediately calling the public police: "Occasionally there are conflicts between residents related to noise or keeping odd hours that come to the board's attention. We have very little actual authority to resolve stuff like that, but there are other agencies that do, like the police. And we kind of monitor things like that as they percolate" (NYC Board 3). This surveillance of noise nuisance was rarely proactive; usually, it only came after a complaint. One board member explained how noise complaints were handled by creating a file so that, upon further surveillance, it would be possible to discern a pattern: "If we get a noise complaint … we ask for it in writing … it's important that we can follow up not only with [the] person who's making the complaint but also kind of keeping an eye on the unit where the noise is supposed to be coming from, to see if we have more than one complaint" (TO Board 20). This board member elaborated further, saying that, at times, the complainant is watched rather than the alleged source of the noise as this common knowledge begins to flow through the building: "I know when we have noise complaints … if it persists … when the same people are complaining about the noise, we ask them to keep a journal … so that they can check it … and we've actually gone down and we've met with the people who made … the complaint. Sometimes they just want to be heard, so to speak" (TO Board 20).

Since condo statutes formally place responsibility on condo boards to enforce the rules outlined in a corporation's documents, risks emerge from a board's inconsistent or selective policing of noise nuisance and/or surveillance. This can result in significant legal costs to the condo corporation. For example, in the 2013 decision *Dyke v. Metropolitan Toronto Condo. Corp. No. 972,* 2013, the Toronto condo corporation was ordered to pay damages and the legal costs of the resident who had sought an order for the board to enforce its own bylaws and rules about noise. The judge ruled the board's handling of these matters amounted to conduct that unfairly disregarded the interests of the complainant. In practice, there is overlap between the private policing of nuisance with condo buildings and public policing not only in the sense of the police being called but also in the sense that house rules and bylaws are enforced in the public courts. While nuisance conflicts are typically to be resolved through mandatory mediation and then arbitration procedures, these often end up in the public courts or even human rights tribunals to be enforced consistent with juridification. These juridically created rules are brought to bear on residents and boards regarding smoke, noise, and other nuisances. One illustrative example may be found in the decision *Italiano v. Toronto Standard Condominium Corporation No. 1507,* 2008. What began as noise nuisance complaints regarding the resident Italiano's renovations then moved on to calling security several times to visit Italiano's unit (as well as hiring an acoustic expert), then moved on to mediation and arbitration, then eventually entered the Supreme Court of Justice of Ontario. This shows that, even though noise may be deemed "merely" nuisance, policing it can lead to invoking lawyers and juridification and other agents and processes. More broadly, the foregoing examples show that policing noise nuisance features prominently in condo governance. However, rivalling its prevalence is smoke and its closely aligned by-products and residues.

Policing Smoke through Legal Knowledges and Surveillance

How smoke nuisance is policed shows that "police" is about positioning or flow through space but, unlike noise, is rarely about timing. Smoke tends to transgress and render space and time irrelevant; the physical and legal demarcations of collective and individual private space, of which the condo has many, become blurred. Incursions of smoke, sometimes responded to by claims of rights to enjoy private space, compete with smokers' assertions of overzealous regulation of private space (Tippens 2009). Despite emerging demand for smoke-free condo complexes, few boards in North America have managed to institute full smoking bans (Olfene 2013). One former board member in New York related:

> We have had some smoking problems ... When I was on the board we've been asked to deal with somebody that smokes a lot and the smoke would come through the air vents and ... sometimes [we] get it in our apartment and we will complain ... In Manhattan you don't have an option ... and we have to live in a communal space and people do not have the same regard for that. (NYC Res. 18)

Like policing noise, policing smoke nuisance usually commenced with, and was dependent upon, a complaint as common knowledge: "The smoking I would complain [about] because it was an air vent problem so that could be fixed. When we're getting smoke into our bathroom then I know the thing on our roof is not working so I did complain about that" (NYC Res. 18). Another resident noted: "I only report ... cigarette smoking. It's bad. It's common" (NYC Res. 17). Sometimes the source could be identified: "There was smoke coming through from the next-door suite, which was fixed by sealing around some glass panels into the bathroom" (TO Board 25). But other times the source could not be identified and this, as with noise, led to surveillance after a complaint:

> That issue was on the second floor ... We weren't sure where the smoke was coming from and so we were going to individual unit doors and trying to smell if we smelled smoke. So there was that. I've had situations where people leave doors unlocked and I'm trying to figure out who's doing it ... like they leave them propped open so they can get in easy or they ... don't want the door to lock behind them, but if you leave the door open like that it's a security risk. People off the street could just walk into our building. (NYC Res. 15)

In another building, confronting smoke involved levying fines: "There is smoke ... a new rule was put in that the board has the authority to levy fines on homeowners for non-compliance of rules and regulations" (TO Board 29). At times, this movement of smoke across and through units was deemed a problem of building construction quality: "The only thing that ... has affected some people is there are smokers in the building and ... because of the age [of the building] the smoke will try and get up into suites, so that's a bit of annoying" (TO Res. 42). In this instance, it was deemed that little could be done.

But, for some, smoking and its remnants are not merely nuisances: they are a serious fire hazard, a chronic aesthetics issue, or a rights violation. A brief to the most recent statutory reform process in Ontario remarked upon smoke in a condo complex by invoking rights:

> Smoke [was] drifting into other units by way of the pipes in bathrooms mostly but sometimes through electrical outlets and even into the common area halls and stairwells every time the unit door is opened. The board's answer with a great deal of pressure and prodding for several months was to block off these openings, including heavy weather stripping around the front doors. A group has started to work on the possibility of declaring a non-smoking building, but the board is totally not in favour ... Smoking ... causes me a loss of "reasonable enjoyment" of my home. I also believe breathing smoke-free air is a basic human right. (Condo Briefs 2012)

Not unlike the public police with regard to noise, municipal fire officials were called upon to confront smoke nuisance due to its potential gravity:

> This girl was taking her cigarettes; there was a small hole ... in the platform of the stair ... and she was sticking her butts down in it and one day ... a smoke condition appeared in the stairwell and the fire department had to be called and they had to pull down the sheetrock from below that level. She was sticking her cigarettes ... into a floor that was the ceiling of the next level down. And so the fire department pulled the ceiling and just tons of burning cigarette butts fell out. (NYC Res. 27)

Noise or smoke nuisance cases can avoid mediation (usually stipulated in a condo corporation's declaration) and later arbitration via Ontario's Condo Act if it can be demonstrated that they are likely to cause injury, which entails suggesting that fire or ill health are their likely result. In these cases, section 117 of the act could be invoked to send them directly to court, bypassing mediation and arbitration, since the situation violates the act (Deacon 2012). This is also where "police" logic and its focus on details begins to merge with "precautionary" logic, which seeks to avoid the worst-case scenario.

In New York, one building initiated a civil lawsuit to stop smokers, but this was determined to be an "uncertain" remedy:

> The neighbours complain about that all the time because of the second-hand smoke, but we don't really have any power on the board to make her

> not smoke in her apartment. And the laws aren't really on our side because I think the management company tries [to] ... go to court, but they seem like a lot more trouble than it is [worth] for an uncertain outcome ... The city should really do more about that because some of these people are chain-smokers and sit in their apartment smoking. (NYC Res. 26)

In another instance, civil legal action was threatened due to potential harm caused by second-hand smoke:

> The board would send a notice and, in all but one case, they were okay, they were good about it. [But] one would say, "I smoke where I want and shut up." And [we] finally had to send a notice that we would be taking legal action and he would probably have to pay a fair amount of money to his neighbour because second-hand smoke had been proven to be dangerous. (TO Board 24)

At times boards merely threatened to use civil law and related legal knowledge, typically as a last resort. But one time a resident promised such action after special provisions had failed to re-establish the physical boundaries between a unit and common area:

> On our floor there's one ... who lives there who is a smoker. So for years ... he would go in the stairwell and smoke and then he'd just kind of take the cigarette butts and stomp them out. But on the far side of the building on the same floor there's a guy who worked for the Environment Protection Agency and he would actually do special things with the doors and windows on the other side of the building because he was so afraid of second-hand smoke. So there was this little infraction and there was this immense paranoia. And then he said he would sue. (NYC Res. 14)

Civil lawsuits were also threatened by the board in a New York building in an attempt to police marijuana smoke:

> There is also a concern that some people in the building are heavy marijuana smokers and that tends to impact others. In two cases sponsor-owned [rented] units apparently were occupied by heavy marijuana smokers, and we were pressured to threaten to sue them and evict them if they didn't curtail that habit. So we actually sent out letters saying that there had been

> complaints and ... if you don't change we are going to have to start a lawsuit. (NYC Board 1)

More broadly, the failure of boards to attempt to resolve smoking nuisance has resulted in condo corporations being held legally liable for breach of covenant and warranty of habitability at the expense of common funds devoted to legal representation (Klein 2000). As with noise, these examples show how smoke nuisance can carve a channel for the flow of legal knowledge within and beyond a condo building. Additionally, they show an ultimate reliance on the public courts to confront nuisance.

Balconies and Butts: Interstitial Spaces and Exemplary Condo Nuisance

Remedies for smoke nuisance turned not on a conjunction of space and time but on whether it was common or individual condo space being policed. One board member explained the border between these spaces and what the board sought to do when smoke transgressed it:

> The bigger issue ... is what the divide is between what's condo property and what's [individual] private property. There's no smoking in common areas or around the entrance to the condo, but if you're in your unit and you're smoking, that's your business. So people don't understand sometimes that there is a divide between condo property or common area versus owner's property. So if the smells of smoke ... escape into the corridors, or the people smell it, we try to have our air balanced. (TO Board 22)

But the nature of the common elements was also sometimes problematized when it came to policing smoke nuisance:

> There was a bunch of discussion about smoking in the common areas. So nobody smoking in the hallway or the lobby, but there is a huge rooftop terrace and the board put this little plastic [notice] that smoking is not allowed. And I noted some people challenged that, saying that they cannot enforce non-smoking on that kind of common element. (TO Res. 36)

Balconies were more commonly problematized in relation to smoke nuisance. A resident explained why they complained about smoking being permitted on balconies: "You could see literally the smoke doing this underneath the balcony and it would come in my apartment and they'd keep me up all night. I complained ... and I kept going after them" (TO Res. 24). But, unlike units and common hallways and rooftops, balconies are interstitial condo spaces, neither fully individually owned nor commonly used. One resident explained their resistance to its assignment as a common element since it is "exclusive": "A balcony is considered a common element, but it's [an] exclusive common element. And I know that some tenants put complaints about their neighbours smoking on the balconies and the smoke goes to their balcony or their unit ... and the board was ... to make a decision about banning smoking on the balconies or not" (TO Res. 36).

Why smoking should be permitted on balconies was also remarked upon:

> Everybody has a balcony of some sort, and you can't smoke anywhere on the premises like outside, inside the common areas, nowhere. The only place you can smoke is in your unit or on the balcony. Now ... when I have people over, I want them to be able to smoke on my balcony. That was a big deal for me. When I have a party or whatever, if you smoke, I should be able to invite you, you shouldn't have to go outside on the road to have a cigarette. And there are some people who are trying to prohibit that. (TO Res. 8)

This challenge to condo governance is rendered more serious in a condo building since its very sustenance depends on a firm distinction between individual and common space. Here smoke nuisance reveals the balcony as interstitial in ways normally ignored and that begin to call that firm division into doubt.

The verticality of condo arrangements introduces new possibilities for smoke nuisance, especially for that morally spoiled end product of tobacco smoke, the aptly named "butt." One resident explained about what happens in the "upper units": "People sometimes fling things off the upper units that land on my terrace ... like cigarette butts ... About every other year I have to stand up and say, you know, spring time rolled around and I had to clean up cigarette butts again and please send out a notice: 'Don't throw things off your terrace'" (TO Res. 11). In New York a resident similarly related: "We've been having issues where people [were] smoking cigarettes on the roof and then throwing their cigarette butts off ... so there's the two units on the ground floor have backyards so they were thrown there or they would end up on people's balconies" (NYC Res. 9). Both noise and smoke move "through" internal physical boundaries between units and common areas. Butts, especially when combined with balconies, manage to circumvent internal borders by launching from interstitial spaces – frequented because internal smoking is banned – and then skirting the building envelope, craftily exiting one balcony, travelling vertically, and entering another, sometimes collecting together. Examples from another building show different efforts to police this common nuisance, ranging from issuing notices, to speaking with alleged perpetrators, to alerting security personnel:

> The main thing about smoking is that people ... have a bigger balcony which is over the front door. And they get cigarette butts on their balcony all the time from somebody above. And she's complained to the manager over and over and over. And one day a lighter was on her balcony. So she took it to the manager and she said, "You find out who owns this lighter. Because whoever owns this lighter is the person who's dropping all these cigarette butts on our balcony." And also sometimes, there's a big notice on our notice board, "Please do not throw your cigarette butts off your balcony because the wind can blow it in." (TO Board 27)

In another situation the nuisance's cause had to be identified through "asking around" before security would act, again showing that, in policing nuisance cases, it is usual to first generate common knowledge:

> The problem with smoking is ... most people smoke on the balcony and throw their butts. We've had a lot of problems with that. I actually had an umbrella, because I'm on the bottom, which got holes in it. And our awning at the front is filled with holes, so every year we put up notices to not throw butts ... Throwing a live butt – it could hit me on the head. So we keep trying ... There are no means [of enforcement] because we don't even know who's doing it ... I knew that it was coming from above me. I asked the lady above me if she smoked and she said no, so I figured it had to come from two stories up. I asked around and learned it was a girl and her boyfriend ... So you have to do it yourself because we [the board] don't send the concierges out to enforce anything. (TO Board 36)

This sequence was evident in another case of smoke nuisance: "I was talking with one of my friends downstairs ... and there were some cigarette butts thrown from the balcony and it seems that they had the party. They talk to the concierge and they took care of that" (TO Res. 10).

Policing butts in a New York complex also meant e-mailing reminder notices to residents: "Every once in a while, we'll see that management will send an e-mail out that says: 'People shouldn't throw their cigarettes out the window on the 40th floors'" (NYC Res. 14). A Toronto board member explained: "People complain. Like somebody will have a cigarette butt land on their patio furniture and it'll start a fire, but I think it's really impossible to figure out who did it so just a barrage of notices will go out saying: 'Don't flick cigarette butts off the balcony'" (TO Res. 40).

One presumed effect of butts, as with smoking generally, is the potential for fire or related property damage, an instance in which "just a nuisance" can be deemed a serious risk:

> You can't smoke in the building of course. You are not allowed to. You can smoke in your unit obviously, but the problems that we have are people tossing lit butts off their balcony. And they land on other balconies and do damage. I had flower pots melted on my balcony ... people up above pitching lit butts down and melting my pots. (TO Res. 39)

Elsewhere a board member similarly explained why a resident should report butts:

> One [nuisance] that is bad is people smoking on their balcony and throwing cigarette butts and they land on somebody else's balcony ... This old lady who said one day, "You know, I don't mean to bug you but is there something I could do?" I said, "Yes, please send us a letter because if you don't send us a letter we can't try to find out who is doing it, and that's a fire hazard, it's not just an annoyance, it's actually a rule not to throw cigarette butts for a very good reason." (TO Board 6)

Butts at times acquire generative powers in Latourian terms (see Chapter 1); they work as agents to assemble governance. So while tobacco cigarettes have been analyzed for their seductive power (Klein 1993), their capacity, at one end, to entice lighting and smoking, their less celebrated end has a diametrically opposed but perhaps equally significant power. In his acclaimed cultural history, Richard Klein (1993, 2) writes: "Cigarettes are not positively beautiful, but they are sublime by virtue of their charming power to propose what Kant would call 'a negative pleasure': a darkly beautiful, inevitably painful pleasure that arises from some intimation of eternity." Butts lack all such qualities: they are negative through and through. Arriving from above ugly, crooked, and spoiled by unknown outsiders' lips, even smeared with lipstick, they may be smouldering their last gasps and are of zero value. But they effectively generate activity among other agents in assemblages, whether it be residents complaining or the property management, boards, and security personnel receiving this common knowledge and then seeking to somehow confront these crafty objects appearing in interstitial spaces. One condo property manager related that "butts" were the most difficult problem to solve in her condo buildings and that, despite the use of numerous tactics, they remained defiant and unstoppable (TO Manager 7). Butts like to congregate in little communities, perhaps more than condo residents themselves, before moving on to the next balcony below. They travel vertically exceedingly well and with great stealth. And, upon silently landing, they commence sitting, as butts do, as tiny reminders to owners on cheaper floors that there is much rule violation happening above, along with blatant disregard for their aesthetic and safety concerns. Butts may be the finest example of a condo nuisance there is. Partially due to the anonymity of butts, notices in or next to elevators were the most common initial response to this variant of smoke nuisance: "We get notices ... that there are people who throw their lit cigarettes off the balcony. We know several times a year we get a little notice: 'Don't do that'" (TO Res. 41).

Nuisance and Renters

Noise and smoke are two key nuisances disproportionately blamed on renters. These nuisances rise from renters' presumed immoral lives, stemming from their failure to own property. First, renters are disproportionately identified as noise nuisance creators: "We used to have some tenants that used to be ... noisy" (NYC Res. 19). A New York owner described how she would reduce her own noise but juxtaposed it to a renter's conduct upstairs (again, at a particular time):

> Our building is older and wooden floors and ... above you ... if people walk really hard it can sound like someone's stomping ..., you have to be conscious of that so I purposely, for example, don't put on my shoes until I'm like walking out the door. I wear slippers that are light ... But my ...

> non-resident-owner upstairs, their tenant, when they first moved in it was like the guy was stomping. And I had to go up and tell him ... "Excuse me, you're walking really hard. I can hear you downstairs." And he pushed back ... It came out that they had their nephew visiting ... and the kid was running up and down at seven in the morning. That's ... the quiet hours. So it is like you have to make sure people are aware of it. If you have an issue you try to address it in a calm way ... Depending on how their gait is it can sound like they're stomping over your head. (NYC Res. 15)

Significantly, none of the noise perpetrators remarked upon in previous sections, including those visited by security personnel, were identified as renters. The interviews showed that there was a discernibly greater tendency to deploy public police and criminal legal knowledge against renters than against owners, thus pointing to an inequality in policing nuisance both in who is blamed for it and in the character of rule enforcement: "There's a tenant that lives across from me that has a family that ... used to argue all the time. At least once a week there would be some crazy arguments and they did the screaming in the hallways and I remember ... I opened the door and I'm like: 'Do I have to call the police?'" (NYC Res. 19). In another complex, an owner was quick to call public police:

> The particular noise issue that I had was with ... a rental unit ... When all the loud noise issues came about if it was worth anything it was discussed at the board level but I deal with only the property manager ... And I said to them: "I will call the police and I will follow through and that kind of thing if there's any noise issues ..." I spoke to the property manager. I've called police I think four times in a year and a half ... the guy that was renting it he had issues ... What I've said to our concierge and property manager [is]: "You can tell anybody who's renting right here that if they wake me up in the middle of the night on ... any night I will call the police and ask questions later." (TO Res. 20)

Similarly, in a New York building public police were called to enforce the city (or municipal) noise bylaw (or ordinance):

> The only issue that been divisive has to do with ... renters next door who had been there about a year or two ... and my granddaughter ... needs to be able to go to bed at ... eight o'clock ... [It was] really a pain in the neck

> ... if we can't do something with them so they will obey the noise level rules. We were doing things like calling ... the cops and bring[ing] the cops over and that was making them unhappy because ... you could get them on the noise ordinance. (NYC Res. 21)

Renters also seemed to be disproportionately associated with butts: "There has been a big issue recently ... with a lot of cigarette butts being thrown from terraces. It's a thirty-five-story building and falling cigarettes are still lit, falling on other people's terraces, and the assumption is it is probably a lot more so now with tenants who don't care maybe as much about the building" (NYC Res. 25). Like noise and butts, marijuana smoke tended to be assigned more to renters than to owners:

> He was an owner; the person above him was a renter. The renter had a niece that kept smoking marijuana and it would seep down into their apartment and ... through the pipes ... and you can smell it in the apartment. So someone went in for verification to say, "Yeah, you can smell it," and they tried to talk to the person upstairs ... How do you go about telling someone that you're going to call the cops, you know? And then the guy's like, well, isn't that the board's responsibility over my responsibility, you know? So we had to figure out like legally who was responsible for that. Was the guy responsible for calling the cops or was the board responsible for going to the person and saying, "Hey, you have to cut that out"? That was like a back and forth and I think the final answer was he was responsible ... he was supposed to call the cops if he felt that he wanted to do that. And if they did not do anything ... Legally I think after a while then the response, it could stiffen, and then we could legally give a notice saying, "If you don't stop doing that ... you can be evicted." (NYC Res. 17)

This tendency was also evident in two other New York buildings. One resident made a point of noting that it was a renter who caused the marijuana smoke nuisance: "At the last board meeting, there was ... complaining that all they could smell was pot from their neighbours constantly and ... it was a tenant, it wasn't a resident" (NYC Res. 25). Another related:

> The other thing that happens in the building is marijuana use. There's someone in the building that smokes and you ... walk to your apartment

> and you just smell all this marijuana smoke. You ... tell the person about it, you leave a note for them, but they still do it ... I haven't actually smelled it in a while, but it was a chronic problem that I had with marijuana smoke ... It was coming from his neighbour's apartment into his apartment and he has a small son, so he was very concerned about that and the resident. The renter was being sympathetic ... it was a tough situation, but it seems to have resolved itself ... People want to smoke ... their marijuana recreationally and it impacts others in their environments. (NYC Res. 15)

Elsewhere a board member related: "It was a tenant [renter] so ... I reported him several times [laughs] ... the pot-smoker and the TV noise ... and then the sponsor had to get more aggressive ... I don't know what ultimately made him ... change his habits but I have not smelled it in a while" (NYC Board 3).

For both noise and smoke nuisance, there were rare instances in which the source of the nuisance was linked to residents' imagined ethnicity, race, or national origin. For example, one resident recounted about smoke: "Her apartment is next to the stairwell and this crazy guy's girlfriend would go into the stairwell and smoke and the smoke would go into our friend's apartment. She complained to her about it and she said: 'Why don't you move back to China?'" (NYC Res. 23). Similarly, regarding noise in a building, a board member remarked: "There's people from the ... Middle East. One noise complaint that I mentioned, they're from the Middle East and the children seem to run wild. They haven't got the concept yet that this is an apartment building and you have to ... treat it like a house" (TO Board 15). However, any suggestion of disproportionate targeting on these bases was largely absent, and mention of these differences was far outnumbered by mention of renters as nuisance sources. It may be that renters were disproportionately visible minorities in the condo buildings studied and that perhaps "renter" was code for imagined ethnic/racial/national origin differences when it came to policing nuisances, but the interviews give almost no evidence for this. It is noteworthy too that, while children are sometimes mentioned, targeting children as nuisances per se in Toronto and New York condo buildings (perhaps because few seemed to house children) was also largely absent from these accounts. This contrasts with previous research on some gated communities in which children's conduct is a significant source of conflict among residents (Atkinson and Flint 2004, 884; Glaze 2013, 41).

TECHNOLOGIES, OTHER KNOWLEDGES, AND POLICING NOISE AND SMOKE NUISANCES

While legal knowledge is prominent in policing noise, smoke, and other nuisances, also prominent are numerous emerging technologies and forms of expertise to confront nuisance, all of which are being marketed to condo owners, boards, and property managers. Noise has led to a wide range of outside expertise whose purpose is to respond to issues in the condo world. This can be thought of as potentially further expanding the condo assemblage by enlisting more agents. In one instance, noise was to be reduced through the installation of new exterior windows:

> They replaced all the exterior windows right after we moved in ... and this may have been related to that original lawsuit, like dating back to the late nineties. Because ... originally it was promised that they would be noise-proof, but I guess they weren't. Something was wrong with them, so they actually took them out and put ... new ones in. (NYC Res. 1)

Most significantly, because it shows another knowledge bearing down on condo life, in some Toronto buildings board members resorted to hiring an audiologist to generate objective readings of noise levels to potentially resolve disputes:

> There was a dispute between two residents because one was making a lot of noise and the other happened to be very sensitive to it. We had a specialist come in to measure the noise level ... and do all kinds of tests. There was definitely too much noise in that apartment and it was caused by the neighbour. Finally, the resolution was that she moved out. (TO Board 26)

Yet legal knowledge is not necessarily separate from other means of policing noise nuisance and related expert knowledges. This becomes clear in a 2011 legal case involving noise nuisance in another Toronto condo building – a case that eventually led to a human rights tribunal complaint on the part of the alleged perpetrator (earlier in 2010 a "notice of dispute" was launched by another resident, and it partially concerned the alleged perpetrator of noise nuisance). In *Dalinda v. Brookfield Residential Services Ltd.*, 2011, the owner Dalinda filed a complaint alleging "discrimination and harassment in housing on the basis of family status, age and reprisal ... he alleges that the noise complaints made by England [a resident living in the unit directly below] and followed up by Brookfield [a Toronto condo property management firm] are discriminatory and reflect an anti-child (family) animus." He challenged "England's alleged intolerance of any noise coming from his apartment" and "Brookfield's response to England's noise complaints ... without any proper investigation." In the interim, an external engineering firm was contracted by the board to "have noise transmission testing done ... [that] apparently revealed that the flooring in the applicant's unit is in compliance with the rules that were in place at the time the flooring was installed." Earlier, but unresolved at the time of the above decision, England had sought to use Ontario's Condo Act process following her filing of a "notice of dispute." According to this decision, the case was not to be deferred to mediation. This case also clearly demonstrates two other themes of this chapter: (1) that noise nuisance can become more than "just a nuisance" and end up being linked to conflict and claims of serious practices of discrimination (in this case based on family status) and (2) that nuisance is policed via types of legal knowledge (in this case human rights law) in addition to the condo statute provisions. Some condo corporations have been brought before human rights tribunals in Canada and forced to compensate aggrieved owners for refusal to impose smoking regulations (Aaron 2012). This shows an ultimate reliance on public courts to resolve nuisances.

This commodification of knowledge about noise has been increasing. Another example involves an annual Toronto condo industry conference in the mid-2000s that featured a booth called "Bark Busters." The aim was to reduce dogs' barking and other nuisance behaviour in condo buildings; but, significantly, it sought to govern dogs *through* the condo owner's conduct – that is, it sought to train condo residents to properly deal with their dogs' conduct. Using behaviour therapists, Bark Busters claimed, in two to three hours, to be able to teach owners how to speak their dogs' language, essentially to say: "Stop barking please or our neighbours will complain to the board."

As with noise, smoke nuisance at times leads to the involvement of outside expertise and the deployment of technologies. A Toronto resident discussed one such incident:

> Certainly people don't smoke in the public areas, although there are a couple of heavy smokers where the odour does drift into the corridor and those individuals were asked to put air filters in their unit and also the condominium put an air filter in the common elevator corridor so that

> the odour would not permeate the furniture and then drift into the individual units. That would be the most contentious issue certainly because one of the owners felt that it was affecting her allergies. (TO Res. 44)

This expertise is of various kinds. In one instance it included engineers:

> We had a big issue. We had one [resident] that smokes like a chimney, and the people are really complaining. We have called in engineers; we've done everything we can. We think we have an obligation to do what we can, but we've done every single thing we can and we've redone the pipes, we've done everything and they're still complaining. So we're suggesting that they get filters in their units. We pay for most of it ... It's a horrible issue. (TO Board 8)

Elsewhere the ventilation was identified as needing adjustment: "We have to rebalance the whole ventilation system because I don't think it was ever done quite as it should be. So once that's done maybe there won't be a problem ... There's one person who lives next door to a very, very heavy smoker and she could smell it and then the hallways ... it's a concern" (NYC Board 2). In other instances, such filter technologies were implanted because of this expert knowledge but not always to good effect:

> One was designed to remove the harmful toxins and odors associated with cigarette and cigar smoke. Unfortunately, by turning on all three large air purifiers to the highest speed plus turning on the exhaust fans both in the washroom and the kitchen for 24 hours [we were] still unable to remove all the cigarette smoke from my unit because cigarette smoke came in every single day continuously almost 24 hours either through the gaps of my balcony door, the gaps of my bedroom window, the gaps of the entrance door from the hallway. (Condo Briefs 2012)

Efforts to police smoking and noise nuisance by paying outsiders through various means shows that condo life is less than consistent with notions of community. Commodification of policing nuisance is tantamount to a move from the common knowledges of owners toward purchased expert knowledges and technology that is mostly but not exclusively associated with governing agents beyond the board. Here policing nuisance itself becomes something of a commodity.

In early Ontario and New York State condo statutes, "police" would seem to stem almost exclusively from boards. There was little to no anticipation that these practices would be commodified through private insurance, private security, or property management, all of which are current agents of condo governance. Private insurance benefits from an increased reliance on these privatized forms that are conceived and avoided or reacted to as forms of risk. Since the 1960s, more risks associated with condo governance have been discerned, and these risks are increasingly packaged as insurance commodities. As this has occurred there is a sense in which insurance has taken over "police" practices from boards (i.e., conquered them) and from the limited scrutiny condo statutes might have provided. For example, statutory changes require board directors to acquire liability insurance as the capacity of boards to effectively manage condo life without major errors is increasingly called into question. The associated risk is then transferred to insurance, but only for a fee ultimately paid by owners and renters. Similarly, property management and private security firms can be observed working in conjunction with the dictates of private insurance as a form of commodification of "police." Governance of myriad little issues that arise in condo buildings is therefore increasingly provided through these commercial agencies, even though only boards have statutory legal authority to govern condo affairs. Where nuisances are concerned, "police" is becoming more closely tethered to the goals of commercial agencies implicated in these increasingly commodified arrangements.

CONCLUSION

Nuisances are significant features of condo life and how they are policed matters. To reside in a condo and to reside in the urban more broadly is to encounter nuisance. But policing nuisance as an exemplar of condo governance is not self-evident. Condo boards and owners govern smoke and noise as nuisance and use narrow channels of legal knowledge to navigate a relatively undeveloped legal terrain. Implementation of bylaws in some condo buildings has emerged through extolling financial benefits, including increased marketability of units to health-conscious urbanites, lower insurance costs, reduced probability of broken leases by non-smokers, and reduced maintenance costs for preventing smoke damage (Pizacani et al. 2011). But the focus here is not so much implementation of smoking and noise condo bylaws as the means that emerge when smoke and noise become intolerable to residents, including how legal knowledge is invoked to confront nuisances. Though occurring in an ostensibly private realm, the foregoing shows that policing nuisance in the condo remains dependent to some degree on municipal government bylaws, civil law, and public police and criminal law, even if only as a last resort. In these latter instances, "police" and public police become one and the same. And when private declarations, bylaws, and rules must be enforced, this often ends up in the public courts, thus showing overlap between the private and public policing of nuisance. When legal knowledge is used to confront nuisances in these instances, as with renters, it enters the condo world through other channels. This chapter further reveals that, in practice, the notion of the condo as a separate private realm is mostly a myth. It also further supports the main argument of this book, which is that condo governance is an assemblage of actors, knowledges, and techniques rather than a sealed off private world run by a board of owners.

So what has been learned about "police" and nuisance through having explored them in the condo complexes of Toronto and New York? Noise and smoke become nuisances precisely by eliminating space and spatial divisions (hallways, walls, etc.) and are therefore deemed a concern. They are found to dominate condo life and to challenge the very notion upon which the condo rests – that is, the combination of individual and common property ownership but the separation of corresponding spaces. Noise and smoke especially show that much nuisance in condo buildings is as much about olfactory and audio violations as it is about positioning and space in relation to, for example, aesthetics. These discerned foci of the condo world also suggest that the urban – the urban problem space and milieu (Lippert and Walby 2014a) – so closely associated with "police," is ultimately also about noises and smells. But noises, smells, and aesthetics share a subjectivity in condo buildings in which communication among owners is limited. This, in turn, limits possibilities for reaching a consensus and can unleash "police-informed" rules about what constitutes a nuisance. In this way, in the condo world "just a nuisance" can become something quite grave. Nuisance is found to lead to having contentious meetings, experiencing "immense paranoia," calling public police and threatening civil lawsuits, using courts usually reserved for serious matters, enacting expensive expertise and technologies, enlisting new commodified solutions, and, for residents, even ultimately moving out of a building.

This chapter shows that "police" logic has certainly not become *less* prevalent in cities since urban neoliberalization commenced; its influence continues, and not in a static way. However, to explore "police" in the condo world is not to valorize it. Since "police" is ostensibly uninterested in subjects' motivations and, in practice, operates largely without external legal or other scrutiny, Foucault (2007, 339) aptly remarks: "Police is not justice." Yet neglecting "police" and other logics in combination is a serious omission since it remains unclear whether "police" merely plays a supporting role for urban neoliberalism or whether it remains the venerable star of urban governance, including in ostensibly private domains. Neoliberalism may merely be demanding revisions to an old urban script about dealing with nuisance, at least to the extent that the "police" function in condo buildings is becoming commodified as resident common knowledge is being supplemented or buried by purchased expert knowledges and technologies. And there is a need to further examine "police" in other private urban realms where it likely flourishes.

7

Ups and Downs of Urban Governance
High-Rise Condo Elevators

RANDY K. LIPPERT with RHYS STECKLE

> The technology of elevating has become so good, fast ... So the high-rise is not a detriment anymore ... When we started, the high-rise was a detriment because they didn't have the high-speed elevators, so you had to put a lot of elevators in to take care of the number of people moving at certain times.
>
> *– TO ARCHITECT 2*

> We needed to get a new elevator. We would have to take out another loan and either just raise the common charges outright to cover the loan or make an assessment.
>
> *– NYC BOARD 5*

> There's two apartments on each floor and the elevator kind of goes up the middle ... So there's not a hallway where you like run into your neighbours, so ... you don't really see them. So we see the woman who shares the elevator ... with us.
>
> *– NYC RES. 29*

> If it's really important – the annual meeting – I'll stick it in the elevator to make sure they see it.
>
> *– TO BOARD 30*

In contrast to horizontally sprawling suburbia, the urban is vertically extending more and more via sky-scraping high-rises, built spaces in which urbanites work, consume, and reside. But rising to scrape the sky is neither effortless nor immediate: it requires vertical travel and a means to safely and swiftly move up and down. The passenger elevator (hereafter "elevator") arose in nineteenth-century cities as a transportation technology promising verticality (Gray 2000). The elevator was to be no less than "the main nerve of a building, its centre of communication, a place where we involuntarily yet pleasantly and enrichingly pass time in the rush of a breathless epoch" (Lampughnani and Hartwig 1994, 7). The elevator has since become to the current urban what the automobile is to the suburb. In permitting one to rise high, in what was once commonly called a "car," the elevator renders the urban possible. This chapter takes up how the elevator and its space as a mundane device are implicated in and exemplary of condo governance. It explores the high-rise elevator as a technology of government and an intensively regulated space within the high-rise residential condo. While seemingly banal on the surface, the elevator occupies a central place in the condo high-rise not merely in physical space, with its shafts typically close to a condo building's spine, but also in the peculiar private governing arrangements and imaginings of its ruling authorities and often isolated residents living within. The centrality of the elevator and its importance would seem to be common to condo high-rises across North America and globally. In the condo high-rise, the elevator is a technology and space commonly owned and regularly occupied by residents. Condo unit owners and renters – distant, diverse, and scattered across floors and units, with varied work and leisure schedules – are virtually guaranteed to be collected and confined in this elevator space for several minutes each day. The elevator has acquired innovative uses beyond self-evident, routine functions of transporting owners and visitors between floors to achieve the aspirations of condo boards, managers, and security personnel. As a technology of government under the immediate control of these private authorities, the elevator seeks to shape its riders into governable subjects amenable to detailed private governmental initiatives.

The condo high-rise elevator is indeed traversed and constituted by multiple governing strategies. It is not only a target of condo governance but also a means of governance, a space of resistance, and a reflection of creeping commodification. In these ways, the elevator is exemplary of high-rise condo governance, by which I mean that it offers a window on these governing relations. As explained below, as a technology the elevator is not a *defining* feature of neoliberal urban governance associated with the condo as it is also present in private rental apartment, public housing, and commercial complexes. Though there may be functional overlap, the elevator may well serve and reflect the different politics and governing arrangements of these other urban forms,[1] all of which play roles that have yet to be studied in any detail. So what follows is an exhaustive study neither of the elevator nor of the high-rise condo building but, instead, a foray into the role of the elevator in one form of governance that is of growing significance in the urban imaginary.

THE HIGH-RISE CONDO

In Toronto, almost 30 percent of all dwellings are high-rises (Statistics Canada 2017c). Most new condo buildings in Toronto are also high-rises (Rosen and Walks 2013, 164) and this city's towering skyline now has the condo high-rise as an increasingly dominant feature. New York is second behind Toronto among North American cities in new high-rise construction (CBC 2014), many of which are condo towers. As noted in the opening chapter but worth repeating here is the fact that, while the condo is usually thought of as a building, it is more accurately a legal, social, and spatial relationship among various elements and a unique blend of individually and commonly owned property. Condo units are of course managed by their owners, but common elements are to be controlled by the board and various other governing agents. Property managers and security personnel are the most visible representations of the rising commodification of condo governance, whereby their services are sold to boards rather than board members providing these services as community members themselves. Typically, even minute behaviour that risks damaging the integrity or aesthetics of common elements (or is otherwise deemed to harm property values) is to be curtailed and managed. This is to be accomplished in no small part through governmental technologies, including mobile elevator technologies and space. Of course, elevators are relevant to more traditional rental and other commercial buildings too, but in condo high-rises they exemplify condo governance as a common space and commonly owned element as well as the somewhat unexpected isolation – given the "community" moniker assigned to the condo – of owners using them. These special configurations distinguish residential condo high-rises from other vertically arranged edifices and, as shown below, also distinguish the role of the elevator therein.

The elevator promises to further illuminate and ground (so to speak) thinking about the governing arrangements of the condo discussed in earlier chapters. Several significant common spaces together comprise condo high-rises, some of which could be studied as technologies. These included mail-rooms, which all residents must occasionally enter, as well as other amenities and spaces that vary by building but can include specially designed lobbies, hallways, property manager's offices, and exercise rooms/gyms, where residents may pass or encounter one another. High-rises are "living buildings" (see Strebel 2011) and all these spaces potentially invite or force a condo building's population to momentarily share the same urban space, but arguably not as frequently, involving as great a proportion (nearly everyone), nor in such close quarters as the elevator. The AGM of owners is also specific to condo life and is absent from private rental buildings, public housing, and commercial complexes. Yet, as shown in Chapter 2, in condo buildings in Toronto and New York the AGM is often poorly attended in person (as opposed to by proxy) and, since it only occurs annually, is far less a means of governance, resistance, or a window on condo governance than is the elevator. At the same time, the residential condo high-rise presents an opportunity to study the elevator in contemporary private urban arrangements. The elevator is a technology of government that makes possible and exemplifies these governing relations and articulates with, but cannot be reduced to, urban neoliberalism.

The remainder of this chapter unfolds in four parts. First, it describes the condo subject and related vertical isolation. Second, it discusses how, simultaneously, the elevator is a target of governance and represents the increasing commodification of condo governance; is used to achieve the aspirations of boards, property managers, security personnel, and even private insurance; and is a means of fomenting owner resistance. Third, it explores how the high-rise condo elevator is exemplary of condo governance and, fourth, it looks at the implications of this for understanding urban governance and elevators, for the sociology of governance, and for verticality more broadly.

Interviews discussed in Chapter 1 provided especially detailed insight into condo owners' experiences and the efforts of boards and property managers to govern their buildings and conduct. No basic interview questions mentioned elevators. Yet elevators appeared in owner, board member, and property manager discourse organically and often. This chapter also draws on other data sources noted in Chapter 1.

VERTICAL ISOLATION

Chapter 2 describes the condo subject and the expectations of condo owners in current arrangements of governance, including the lack of community among them. Overall, owners reported little interaction with other residents of the same building. Vertical isolation is especially evident in high-rise condo buildings. Condo high-rises typically have more than a hundred units. As mentioned in Chapter 1, there has been steady growth in the number of units over the past twenty years, and things are now a far cry from the remarkably modest first townhouse condo development in Brampton in the late 1960s. However, the relative isolation of owners may have more to do with the vertically arranged living space than it does with the sheer number of units. Owners recognized this verticality as contributing to isolation. One remarked upon the lack of community this way:

> You don't have that ... same sense of community ... I suspect because we're vertical and not horizontal. I mean you meet people in the elevator and you may meet them in the party room ... but essentially you're not meeting them. Whereas on a horizontal community your backyards would butt onto each [other] and so ... you're a bit isolated, a lot more isolated than [when] we were on [Atlantic Street, a detached residence]. We knew all our neighbours. (TO Res. 18)

Another person, who had previously been a renter, explained why he had purchased a high-rise condo unit: "As a tenant I thought ... buying anything is better. I feel that you're putting your money down on long-term ... Also, I thought there would be more of a sense of community in a building that owners live versus a building that tenants live. But [it] turned out to be here that it is not the case" (TO Res. 36). A board member in another Toronto building mentioned a similar lack of interaction:

> I know people who moved in[to] ... a fifteen- to twenty-unit [horizontally arranged] townhouse condo ... where ... [you] get to know your neighbours more, like when you're out on the street somewhere. But here, it is seven hundred units, it is hard to get to know people ... and people, they just go out, down the hall, in the elevator, out, and there's not much interaction. (TO Board 30)

Consistent with this isolation, one owner could not distinguish a building resident from a visitor:

> There's normally twenty-four-hour security but there have been times where random people would follow you right to your condo. So ... when I am going to the elevator ... I always press [the floor number of] whoever's in the elevator with me first so I know where they're going. They don't need to know where I'm going until I know where they're going. So there've been times ... I'd realize there's someone behind me because they just followed me through the door ... Someone would just walk with you into the elevator. So I would go, "What floor are you going to?" And they can't answer the question and when they realize that, they step out. (TO Res. 43)

The extreme of these isolating vertical arrangements was evident in some newer condo high-rises where electronic locks prevented unit owners without the proper key fob from exiting the elevator onto any floor other than their own. Those who can enter the floor with their key fob create a digital record each time they come and go *within the building*, a record that is available to the concierge/security guard and property manager or even the board president. Thus, the elevator serves as a key data collection point along with other sites of key fob surveillance. But the vital point here is that this spatial arrangement further reduces potential for interaction among owners living on different floors, and this is less than conducive to creating a community atmosphere among residents. In many instances, occupying the same elevator space may be the only opportunity for several minutes of close contact with other owners. In one high-rise we asked the following question:

> Q: Why do you think it is that people keep to themselves?
> A: It's just the way things are arranged ... You don't really hang out in an apartment building ... You don't take out your garbage to the road. There's [sic] fewer chances of interacting. You see each other in corridors or elevators but that's about it. (TO Res. 45)

One owner was asked about the characteristics of building residents and responded: "Ethnicity I think is pretty diverse [in this building] ... based on who I take the elevator with" (TO Res. 21). Besides isolation, these comments from interviewees show the centrality of elevators in high-rise condo owner discourse. Not surprisingly, they can also be a source of owner-board conflict:

> Q: Can you give me an example [of] ... when people were hostile toward the board?
>
> A: A lot of hostility was going on because sometimes we had to deal with just one or two working elevators. (TO Res. 28)

GOVERNANCE OF ELEVATED SECURITY CONCERNS

Securitization is discussed in Chapter 3. Judging from popular culture, high-rise elevators are a source of concern over security and the potential for physical and sexual violence from other residents and (other) strangers. For example, the 2010 film *Devil* (Shyamalan 2010) underscores the apprehension of strangers stuck in an elevator and relies on the cultural trope of "stranger danger" as each passenger suspects the others of malevolent acts. This film builds on cultural foundations laid by the elevator murder in *Dressed to Kill* and the torrent of blood from the hotel elevator in *The Shining*, among many other such scenes since. Attention to elevator conduct of this sort is long-standing in scholarship, as is seen in, for example, Oscar Newman's (1972) classic *Defensible Space*, which focuses on crime prevention through environmental design in US urban public housing projects. Newman argues that "the specific area within a high-rise building that is most vulnerable [is] the elevator" (33), and he pioneered not only video (now commonplace in high-rises) but also audio surveillance of elevator space by management and residents (127–28). Yet, despite the cultural availability of physical security concerns about elevator space, the efforts of condo developers to sell security to condo corporations more broadly, and the efforts of boards to further securitize buildings, these concerns feature in the discourse of high-rise condo owners only occasionally.[2] One New York owner did recount the effects of a violent incident in the building on another resident, along with the reaction by the condo board:

> To this day, she will not go into that basement because she remembers what it was like back ... when the drug wars were going on and you couldn't go downstairs because it wasn't safe. I mean, our elevator does not go down to the basement after 9:15 p.m. because of that, and so she still refuses to do her laundry in the building ... [The board] stopped the elevator from going down at a certain hour. (NYC Res. 19)

Condo high-rise elevators are among the most intensively governed urban spaces, but this is not necessarily due to concerns about riders' physical security. Rather, the governance of condo high-rises reflects innumerable rules that target minute details of urban life and that position the elevator more as a *financial or aesthetic* concern since owners are required to pay monthly maintenance fees that cover their decoration, cleaning, upkeep, and eventual replacement. In one building the quality of the elevator was the primary concern among owners:

Q: Is there anything you like or dislike about living in this condo building?
A: It doesn't have proper elevators going from the main floor to the mezzanine floor to link up to the actual elevator system in the building ... it's under different regulations and it's a nuisance. (TO Board 31)

Elevators are a key space of nuisances; many owners complained of unsightly pet feces and urine stains consistently found on elevator floors due to resident neglect. Concern about aesthetic damage, remodelling, repairs, and replacement costs of elevators (and other amenities) dominate owner and board member discourse. The elevator is a key financial concern because it represents a portion of the value of the building and, ultimately, of individual units. Of course, the land upon which the building and elevator rest has more value than either, but interviewees and documents almost never mention land; nor do property managers and other actors mention it in relation to condo governance. The elevator as a central financial concern, even as deferred maintenance (a deferred operating expense that was twice singled out as an example of developers setting maintenance fees artificially low [see Canada's Public Policy Forum 2013c, 8, 20; Chapter 3]), was evident across condo buildings in the two cities and in the interviews. When asked about her experiences on the board, the first "big systems" one member mentioned was the elevators:

Q: What did you like about being on the board?
A: I was making a contribution to ... improve the property values to be very frank about it, and improving the quality of the building ... We tried some good work in terms of just maintaining the big systems, the elevators, the HVAC systems. All that sort of stuff needs a lot of attention and that's one area that people on boards just don't

understand ... you've got to maintain it properly, you've got to know the current regulations. (TO Board 30)

Another board member from a different Toronto condo building similarly commented:

> We've replaced half our elevators, but the other half still need to be replaced. They're old, they're creaky, they're not good, so that's about a million and a half dollars ... every board since has been promising we'll do it, we'll do it ... but ... we have a board now with this mentality: "we defer everything to next year," so ... the battle here was really over the future of this condo and ... property values. (TO Board 32)

Elevators are one source of concern regarding reserve funds. Elevator maintenance and replacement is at the centre of two competing sets of board practices, one aimed at increasing property values via aesthetic changes and restricting fees in the short term for non-resident owners and the other aimed at maintaining and, when necessary, replacing major systems such as water pipes, boilers, and other infrastructure (like elevators), and regularly raising condo fees to ensure the long-term well-being of the building for resident owners. These contrasting approaches (see Chapter 2) to fees are a source of low-level conflict between owners and boards in the condo high-rises studied.

The financial concern related to elevators more generally is reflected in their intensive governance by security personnel. As an owner related:

> They have to have a security guard on when ... moving in the elevator ... if something goes wrong ... somebody's here on the property or maybe if something breaks in the elevator. I had to pay a fee to use the elevator when I moved in ... There's a fee to ... rent the elevator but then there was a deposit after that too. (TO Res. 46)

The elevator is subject to remarkably intensive governance, a key characteristic of condo governance and "police" more broadly. For example, in one building, there was a formal program to ensure the elevator was booked seventy-two hours in advance for any movement of large personal items to units. As well, "all bookings of the elevator require[d] a one hundred and fifty-dollar ($150.00) security deposit and a non-refundable two hundred dollar ($200.00) user fee payable when moving into the building, and the owner/resident must complete the Elevator Reservation Agreement" (Toronto Condo 2014). The ten-point legal Elevator Agreement to be signed by the unit owner also required a pre-use and post-use physical inspection by the property manager and included detailed requirements concerning unauthorized entry, repair cost, liability for damage, period of use, and obstruction. In this building, transportation of bicycles to units on elevators was prohibited, as was food and beverage consumption. Finally, another rule stipulated: "residents are required to wear proper attire (shoes, shirts and bathing suit cover-up's) when using ... elevators" (Toronto Condo 2014). The aesthetics of high-rise elevator space includes the person occupying it.

Governance of an elevator's technical aspects, including maintenance and operations, is decidedly more distant from owners but nonetheless also reflects the creeping commodification of condo governance. One board member remarked: "There's a ... rule for elevators. If someone's stuck in an elevator, and it's happened here, we're supposed to write a report to whatever ministry is responsible for it" (TO Board 30). But rule enforcement for elevators no longer stems from a ministry. In Ontario, as in other North American jurisdictions, elevators are subject to detailed regulations, but the responsibility of a government regulator ended in the mid-1990s. Inspection and regulation of elevators were privatized, and the resulting governance became less a right and more a commodity to be purchased by condo corporations through hefty fees. In Ontario, regulation is now overseen by the Technical Standards and Safety Authority (TSAA), which subjects elevators to initial and periodic inspections to approve licences. This authority "licenses elevating devices and registers contractors. Publicly accessible elevating devices in Ontario require a valid licence issued by the TSSA's elevating devices safety program in order to operate legally" (Technical Standards and Safety Authority 2014). The fact that these devices and spaces are intensively regulated is perhaps most evident from the eighteen-page TSSA guide to licence application submission. Upon initial elevator inspection there is a sixty-seven-point pre-inspection checklist to be completed upon installation "for use by General Contractors or Owner on New Installations" covering all manner of details concerning design and operation of the device.[3] And even this "is not inclusive to all requirements of the applicable codes and standards" (Technical Standards and Safety Authority 2014). Ongoing compliance with these legal regulations for elevators typically falls on the shoulders of contracted property managers who are responsible for numerous legal regulations pertaining to condo buildings:

Q. You have to know the Condo Act ... what other forms of law do you have to be cognizant of?

A. Health and Safety Act, WHIMIS, the Fire Code, the Building Code, the Municipal Code, Employment Standards Act, ... the Highway Traffic Act, the Insurance Act, municipal bylaws ... this code, that code, Basketball Court code ... the same with the elevator ... TSSA regulations. (TO Manager 2)

For elevators, the property manager typically contracts, on behalf of the condo board and corporation, with an elevator maintenance contractor. Legal liability for accidents and therefore risk may remain, depending on the level of condo corporation insurance and the specific contract, with lower-cost contracts and insurance policies typically meaning the condo corporation remains potentially liable for some damages resulting from elevator accidents (Elevator Source 2015). This liability becomes clear in at least two instances in Ontario. The first is the 2013 Ontario Superior Court case of *Green v. York Region Condominium Corporation No. 834*, in which a Toronto condo owner sued the condo corporation and maintenance provider for damages under the Occupier's Liability Act when she injured her shoulder exiting the elevator. This case highlighted the liability risk inherent in elevator operations in condo high-rises for the corporation and contractors. The second instance is the fatal elevator accident involving a worker in the One King West condo and hotel complex. In this case the elevator maintenance provider had been previously fined half a million dollars for safety violations that had contributed to a previous elevator accident at another Toronto building (CBC 2016).

Elevators, like the common private pool and other spaces within high-rise condo complexes, are subjected to considerable safety regulation. The fact that this is enforced by private authorities (i.e., TSSA, property management, insurance, and subcontracted elevator maintenance companies) exemplifies how most "technical" elements of condo high-rises are increasingly governed in a manner consistent with commodification.

GOVERNING THROUGH ELEVATORS

Elevators are governed as outlined above but, crucially, governing *through* elevators also occurs in condo high-rises. These high-rises necessitate vertical rather than horizontal transportation. By temporarily forcing residents into elevator space, the governmental efforts of the building's authority become easier. Daily, elevators promise to structure the conduct of building occupants. Inhabitants cannot avoid this contact with one another; they must meet in this cramped, centrally located space (see Strakosch 1998). The only option for all but those near the high-rise's bottom is to take a much longer, typically arduous journey up and down a stairwell whenever vertical travel is required. The architectural form of the high-rise necessitates that residents regularly, if not several times daily, enter and ride one or more elevators up and down. This spatial organization of building behaviour allows the programming of condo owners' awareness and conduct through initiatives, often via property managers and security personnel, to solve many problems in the building. The elevator provides for communicating numerous house rules among what interviews revealed are often isolated unit owners. The condo high-rise, by its vertical distribution of the residential population, structures the conduct of inhabitants by requiring vertical travel in an elevator. The elevator then temporally and spatially funnels the members of the building's socially distant population into a common space and renders them receptive to governance efforts. Governing is a spatial activity, and the elevator is one of the few necessarily shared spaces of a condo high-rise.[4]

Elevators as a governmental technology are commonly coupled in condo high-rises with another mundane technology: regulatory signage (see Hermer and Hunt 1996; Lippert 2009). A key feature of regulatory signage is that it permits governing by "absent and sometimes distant centers of authority" (Hermer and Hunt 1996, 466). As one owner related: "The property manager would ... have notice boards in the elevators" (TO Board 33) to communicate administrative information. Signs, when attached to elevator space, seek to govern riders, but they are also signals that an authority elsewhere is directing conduct through the elevator. Elevators function as near perfect signposts: they permit easy positioning of signage on their uncomplicated walls, at an ideal viewing distance at or near a passenger's eye level or at control panels, thus increasing the likelihood the rule will be read (these signs are also becoming high-tech displays). Moreover, elevators are in near constant motion, thus moving these signs to the pinnacles and bowels of condo high-rises all day long. Since elevators are not instantaneous transporters between floors, they guarantee occupants will have several long minutes, especially when riding solo, in which to read signage and/or aptly named "notices" and consider their meaning in quiet, close quarters. Thus, information is spread via the elevator to make residents aware of building rules and to raise awareness of problems and nuisances the building is experiencing that may stem from a lack of resident compliance. Posting new rules or rule violations in the elevator is an inexpensive, efficient strategy since elevators have the special capacity to reach all floors and nearly all building occupants:[5] "They were talking about ... [sending notices to each unit] and then they stopped because it's too expensive so ... [they] post notices ... in the elevator" (TO Res. 47).

In a different high-rise complex the elevator was one of several means of communicating rules to residents through notices that went "up on the concierge desk, in the elevator or at the elevator" (TO Board 28). Another high-rise similarly "posted notices in ... every elevator" (TO Board 31). Notices are just that: board and property manager edicts to be noticed and acted upon by condo residents. They tend to be the visible crystallization, and sometimes convergence, of knowledges (legal, real estate, security, risk, engineering, etc.) that flow into the condo world.

One example of an elevator notice concerns a previously noted common high-rise problem: people throwing cigarette butts off balconies. Seemingly innocuous on the surface, this practice is problematic because lit or partially extinguished cigarettes land on lower-floor balconies and damage property or otherwise risk fires. One resident presented this as a significant problem:

> Q: Can you tell me a bit about your experiences living here?
>
> A: I had my [balcony] door open and we had carpet then and it had a burn hole there. Somebody threw a cigarette off. It bounced in and burned the carpet. [There] could have been a baby in the stroller, know what I mean? (TO Board 3)

The problem of residents throwing such objects onto the balconies of owners below is heightened in high-rise buildings because they tend to have hundreds of units with numerous balconies. This renders it difficult to identify culprits from above. The architectural form of the high-rise condo enables conduct detrimental to condo living, but it also enables governmental efforts that seek to curtail such conduct by way of the elevator. As the condo high-rise requires elevators to facilitate the movement of owners between floors, it also uses elevators to communicate governance problems. Notices are meant to communicate to residents for a specific end. One board member related that, for example, information is communicated when residents are "going to see some contractors coming through – so that's been posted ... in every single elevator stall ... [they] post there anything that's important ... whether you're going up and down in an elevator" (TO Board 16). The elevator serves a key role in the facilitation of everyday governmental efforts. Certain types of conduct, whether beneficial or harmful to the condo complex, are targeted through the elevator as a governmental technology. In one building, the elevator was *the* form of communication. An owner remarked: "there are notices up in the elevator. That's the only reason I'm aware of some of the things" (TO Res. 17).

When asked about surveillance in a condo complex one owner commented, "they've installed some cameras in the elevator" (TO Res. 48). In another building, a board member related that, with regard to recording owners leaving unsightly garbage: "we have cameras in the elevators and ... in the common elements but I don't have any cameras on the floors so if somebody decides to leave their pizza boxes outside the elevator door I don't know who's done it" (TO Board 32). Video surveillance in elevators is now prevalent in condo high-rises. But surveillance of condo high-rise space is also "natural" in that the elevator creates vertical visibility on its own: there is no hiding while riding. Riders' habits and hygiene are rendered visible, while olfactory and auditory (unless there is "elevator music") phenomena are similarly unhindered and unfiltered in that closed space. The elevator moves up and down the floors, and this considerable mobility translates into regular surveillance of these floors and the myriad sights, smells, and sounds emanating from them and from all who enter the elevator's space.

The elevator itself is of course sold to condo developers, as is its regular servicing to condo boards, as a commodity. But the elevator also assists property management's continued influence as commodified condo governance. Advertising is at times permitted in condo elevators, but there are also cutting-edge, high-tech programs like "MaxTV" that deploy a digital elevator screen, as was observed in two newer Toronto condo high-rises studied. In one a board member starkly remarked: "In our previous elevators, they had these things that [the] company puts in for free and [that] advertises stupid things. [They] don't work half the time and the other half they're American news. So they thought maybe they should have those in new elevators ... They get it for free, but it's not really for free" (TO Board 24). MaxTV is described as

> a system for property managers that allows you to communicate effortlessly with your residents, while making sure that the elevator displays fit perfectly to your elevator interior space and add a valuable luxurious feeling

> to the ride. Digital elevator screens offer tenants a new experience, taking away this awkward feeling that many of us have during elevator rides. You will discover that your residents engage in conversations about weather, sports, news and traffic, which in turn create a greater sense of community throughout the property ... MaxTV's digital elevator screens improve the communication and awareness in your building. (MaxTV 2014a)

MaxTV provides time between commercials for property managers to communicate rules and other governance issues to owners during the elevator ride. Owners consume by paying for condo units as well as fees for condo managers and other contractor services, but this permits the elevator to further transform riders into consuming subjects upon their leaving its confines for nearby businesses. The following appears on the webpage for these would-be advertisers:

> Targeted and Repeated Ads. By working with local condos located around your business, MaxTV can guarantee targeted and repeated exposure to local residents who may become your future customers. Exposure you can rely on. Building's residents or visitors become a captive audience to our digital elevator displays upon entering an elevator. That means a person will be exposed to your advertisements many times during their stay in a building. In fact, no other advertising media delivers the level of repetitive exposure the MaxTV network can offer your brand. (MaxTV 2014b)

Here the elevator is surveilled differently and for a separate purpose. Owners activate building notices and advertising upon entry by tripping a sensor that powers down the unit upon exit and that are premised on the elevator's promised confinement of its momentarily "captive" riders (MaxTV 2014b).

Elevators can also serve as a means of ensuring internal spatial segregation from the condo's "other," the renter. Thus, in some of the newest condo buildings elevators servicing condo units bypass affordable units on exclusively rental floors. A separate elevator permits access to those floors and thus becomes a "poor door" arrangement. These elevators become a technology of segregation and, in this way, their function differs from what it is in most other buildings, where daily, for a few minutes, they force everyone into one space. This benefits developers who typically promise municipal governments a few rental or affordable units in exchange for being allowed to build even higher towers with more floors. This new elevator arrangement permits developers to promise affluent condo owners that they need not share close quarters with risky and reviled renters.

Elevator space is therefore constituted and governed by the strategies of multiple authorities, mostly at a distance from the condo resident. This space is highly regulated through the condo board's numerous rules and intensive surveillance due to its high maintenance and replacement value (and aesthetics) for would-be purchasers. It is also at the intersection of privatized bodies garnering hefty fees for regulatory surveillance previously provided by government. However, it also serves as a means of governing for boards, property management firms, and other external corporations seeking further consumption of branded commodities ripe for the condo-residing subject. This link between the condo and consumption has not been lost on business improvement associations and others who seek to use the condo to solve the problem of stalled urban economies in retail strips.

RESISTANCE FROM DOWN BELOW

The elevator is a technology that enables boards, property managers, security personnel, and external private advertisers to govern owners' conduct from a distance. But while the elevator is appropriated by boards, managers, and others to spread information among residents to shape conduct, elevator space also has subversive possibilities. It promises to facilitate the spread of oppositional information that may ultimately undermine condo governance in various ways. The elevator, by unifying the behavioural practices of often heterogeneous residents, makes opposition in condo life possible. The elevator becomes part of a politics of vertical condo living. The distant relationship between boards and owners described earlier entails limited information dissemination. This situation is more remarkable given that condo units are sold by developers and represented in statutory reform consultations in Ontario as "communities" (Canada's Public Policy Forum 2013a); owners are supposedly equally invested not only in financial stability but also in the well-being of condo life. Undoubtedly to protect a condo building's reputation and property values, condo boards often refuse to communicate information directly to residents who have the temerity to inquire. One owner related: "If I ask, for example, [for] the board or director's phone number from the concierge ... I was told they do not give it out because the person lives here and they're not allowed to give out information about people that live in the building" (TO Res. 49). Owners reported in interviews that information about board activities and access to records that they are legally entitled to consult are at times simply refused or inexplicably delayed (see also Canada's Public Policy Forum 2013a). Moreover, there is usually only one meeting, the AGM, at which owners have only a limited opportunity to ask questions of boards and property managers (and this is sometimes filtered through the corporation's lawyer, hired at owners' expense to run the AGM). Only a minority of the high-rises studied had additional meetings that permitted more information flow between boards and owners.

Elevators create a field of governance that allows for the dissemination of knowledge from the board (above) as well as knowledge from other residents (below) and undoubtedly many actors in between. Concerning residents, the elevator can serve as a site of resistance that can counter a board's or property manager's governing efforts to control information flow within a condo assemblage. It is a space in which communication, including not only grievances and complaints but also vital facts about current governing practices among often isolated condo building residents from various floors, is unfettered and unscreened by property managers, lawyers, and boards that always demand written documentation (e.g., letters, e-mails, and suggestions via management websites) from residents about any problems or nuisances experienced. There is no written record of what is uttered and exchanged regarding all manner of activities and developments relating to a condo building's authorities as this space moves between floors. The elevator is thus a time-space of potential oppositional information: about how the last board vote was held, why fees have increased, whether Airbnb clients have entered the building, who might run for the board, potential for further communications outside the above filters, and much more. The space of the elevator will not certainly or necessarily result in resistance; it is rather what Foucault, always cognizant of contingency and uncertainty, would call a "condition of possibility" (Hunt and Wickham 1994, 6–7) rather than a "cause" of such resistance.

The elevator is also a site where the governed can confront at least some of those governing, although some governing agents operate from far beyond the condo's walls. One property manager related that "a person who ends up being on the board is no longer allowed to have a life in that condo. You go in an elevator and fifty people will ask you questions ... they'll stop here, stop you there, board members end up becoming recluses in their units" (TO Manager

3). These board members must nonetheless enter elevator space to get to their units. Managers must do likewise. Despite its vertical function in condo high-rises, the elevator is sometimes a momentary leveller of governing and power relations as board members, other owners, property managers, and security personnel must travel up and down.[6] One owner, who could identify his building's property manager and board members, related: "I may see these people in the elevator ... and we stop and chat" (TO Res. 41). Though of course mitigated by gender, ethnicity, age, and other axes of social identity in the condo world, the elevator nonetheless makes it possible to momentarily set rulers and the ruled on a similar plane, making the former spatially and temporally available to the latter. Indeed, consistent with the property manager's claim above, board members aptly described this situation using the spatial metaphor of "being cornered" by an owner in an elevator. A board member is never certain at which floors the elevator will stop to allow owners to enter or who will be already riding upon entering. That this can occur awkwardly and unexpectedly is to residents' benefit. It is the social and spatial void between boards and owners – potentially bridged through a better sense of community – that elevator space promises to reduce. One owner related: "When I interacted with the board sometimes it's one of those ... elevator grudge conversations ... I say what about such-and-such?" (TO Res. 50). Elevator space creates the possibility for owners to extract information from reluctant or distant board members and/or the property managers who shield them. Another example comes from field notes about observations in a condo building between interviews:

> On our way up the elevator to Karen's unit, we encountered Mary, another resident of the building. As I waited Karen engaged Mary and talked about what they felt needed to be included in our study of condo governance. While Karen said she knew of no serious issues with the board, Mary told Karen she had encountered serious problems from a fire started due to maintenance work the board had commissioned. She had been forced to move out of her unit for several months while her unit was repaired. Despite the fire department being called to extinguish the fire and several units being evacuated, Karen showed no prior knowledge of the fire or Mary's relocation. A serious fire had not been communicated to owners on all floors by the board or the property manager. (Field notes, November 23, 2013)

Karen learned of the fire and board negligence only in elevator space. The elevator serves not only the board and property managers but also residents in that it enables the latter to acquire and spread information about the board's administration far beyond what the board would wish. One owner viewed speaking to people in the elevator as going hand in hand with resisting condo governance, suggesting that some owners "are not ... brave enough to speak to the people in the elevator and speak up about the issues" (TO Res. 48). Resistance may at times be limited to "grumbling," as an owner asserted: "The board deliberates and resolves on a course of action which many of us in the elevator might grumble about and then carry on [with] our day ... [but] I don't think anyone has sort of malicious intent or is trying to take advantage of their board position to feather their nest" (NYC Res. 4). But the dissatisfaction is nevertheless passed along in elevator space. At other times, the elevator, in conjunction with a notice, is intentionally used to organize owners and to generate resistance. It is known that another owner in the elevator will be present for several minutes and cannot easily escape questioning. Notices serve as a regulatory tool of authorities, but here they are transformed into entry points to identify other isolated owners and to mobilize owner resistance to board governance:

> When I see them in the elevator ... I say, "Are you an owner"? And then I start to discuss, be very delicate and very gentle, and say, "What do you think of the recent thing"? Because what usually happens is you have a notice on the elevator that speaks about certain things like ... an [annual general] meeting coming up ... I will ask them, "Are you going to the meeting?" or things like that, trying to engage them basically. The aim when I speak to them is, which unit are you in? Are they happy with the board? And ultimately with them I really want to get in touch with them, get their e-mail ... to set up some kind of an owner's group and I need people on side to highlight a concern. I need to know who these owners are. (TO Res. 48)

The elevator serves as a site of resistance by facilitating communication among owners who may otherwise never interact, other than at the AGM, in this private, apparently isolating, vertically arranged residential environment. Another owner recounted how information was passed in her elevator prior to owners coming together to sign a petition to begin to identify who the board members were and to seek to oust them:

> It came on gradually, like little snippets of things ... It's my mom who talks to other people and hears things ... It was usually about the maintenance fee. Like every time, I think the petition was triggered by a note ... [about] the management fee ... and if I ... bump into you in the elevator and you're reading this, actually making a comment, you'd be like, "Yeah, so weird, that's ridiculous." Like that's how you tend to get all these conversations going [Okay, so a lot of it happens in the elevators?] Yes. (TO Res. 2)

The elevator is a space in which resistance can germinate. In one building the elevator was a site of resistance to board decisions about "every minute detail": "The board had done so many little things in the building ... Every minute detail seems to become the topic of conversation about the board's capacity to manage the building ... You couldn't just say 'hi' without it being: 'Can you believe what they've done?' It's just politics" (TO Res. 59). But it is not "just politics"; rather, it is a "politics of urban verticality" (Graham and Hewitt 2012), the content and seriousness of which varies widely across types of urban high-rises but that is undoubtedly continuously reproduced in countless elevators endlessly moving up and down the edifices of the world's cities. By enabling building occupants to have closer contact, this mobile elevator space creates an opportunity for information to spread throughout a building where it might not otherwise, and this begins to make a politics possible.

A final example of a resident obtaining oppositional knowledge through the elevator was evident in another condo high-rise. When the high-rise's security personnel came to his door late one night, supposedly answering a complaint about renovation noise (a common rule infraction), the unit owner

> asked them to check all the rooms ... and they confirmed that there was no work being done ... Next day ... in the elevator I met one of my neighbours and he said to me last night he saw ... security men at my door so he explained to me he was downstairs on the 11th floor – I'm on the 12th floor – and he ... was doing renovations there and the [guards] ... began to accuse him of making noise ... So he confirmed ... noise ... was coming from the 11th floor and ... now I have different information ... about what transpired ... So, I went ... to the manager ... He didn't know I was now aware [of] ... what transpired and I told him that "Look, I was not making noise" ... He began to apologize ... [and said] he know[s] where the noise was coming from ... but I said to him, "Look, these three so-called security

guards, their conduct got me scared ... I don't know if these are security or what was at my door. I was very, very much afraid." (TO Res. 51)

Thus, information contrary to the view of condo building authorities was made possible via the elevator, enough in this case to resist the property manager's heavy-handed, invasive rule enforcement, which typically entails a hefty "charge-back." While high-rise elevators are useful technologies of governance because of their centrality in owners' lives, they possess the potential to subvert board and manager efforts to regulate building occupants' conduct. Elevator exchanges are important instances of common knowledge flow that counter the unidirectional or purposely restricted flow of information from the board and managers to owners and renters.

CONCLUSION

The foregoing analysis demonstrates how the high-rise condo elevator exemplifies condo governance and urban governance more broadly. First, it illustrates and underscores the often touted but rarely empirically substantiated rules about the minute details of urban life and the low-level conflict between boards and owners that characterizes condo governance. Second, it reveals that this governance tends to be conducted by distant, impersonal governing agents rather than, for example, by community leaders, which is why the elevator serves as a point of resistance when some authorities are suddenly or unexpectedly thrust into the presence of the ruled, or when the ruled can exchange subversive information. Third, it demonstrates competing short-term and long-term sets of governing practices, both reflecting a preoccupation with property values. The elevator, as an exceedingly costly common element at the physical and symbolic centre of owners' lives and concerns, illustrates this ongoing, narrow debate that pervades condo owner and board discourse and renders condo units into merely isolated commodities and investments consistent with urban neoliberalism. Fourth, commodification is evident too in the activities of hired property managers in and in relation to elevators, who govern in place of community volunteers and public governments; in the emergence of MaxTV, which sells the communication of rules to owners and access to captive owners to businesses via advertisements; in the private safety regulator who charges hefty fees for elevator licensing and surveillance previously conducted by a provincial government agency; and in elevator maintenance and insurance companies that assume risk – for a price. This growing commodification increasingly defines urban governance and the urban imaginary and is exemplified by the otherwise mundane condo high-rise elevator. The elevator is not, by any means, essentially a neoliberal technology of government; however, in the condo high-rise it effectively brings this form of urban governance into being by closely articulating with this rationality at a crossroads of multiple strategies that target vertically isolated consuming urbanites.

The elevator is both a central concern in high-rise condo life and an exemplar of high-rise condo governance. Its exploration contributes to the sociology of governance and governmentality literature by underscoring the vital role of technologies in urban governance and demonstrating that they are not merely tools but, instead, help make governing practices and a corresponding politics possible. They should garner more analytical attention as a result. This chapter also begins to reveal what ought to be stated explicitly and more often in urban studies: elevators are central to and make the current urban world possible.

8

Conclusion
Law Reform, Assemblages, and Condo Futures

You know when they put that all together the resident condominium owners basically was the last group, alright?

– TO CONDO OWNER ASSOCIATION 1

I go back to community because if you can't have a community within your own building you have a problem, or at least attempt to try to form this community ... together because in the long range you're living there ... When you start bringing them together and talking and hearing the stories, it's like, okay, now I see where the issue is.

– TO BOARD 9

The historical event of a bad king or bad shepherd is [due to] the sins or faults of the community or city. So in all this we have a sort of total relationship, a common destiny, and reciprocal responsibility between the community and the person who is responsible for it.

– FOUCAULT (2007, 168)

Let's just see what tomorrow brings.

– "WHEAT KINGS," THE TRAGICALLY HIP

What might be the future of the condo and its governance considering the dissection of innards – nuisances, elevators, renters – and now that stories have been told and knowledge shared by residents, boards, and others? This chapter discusses the implications of preceding chapters about condo governance as an assemblage in relation to law reform, condo futures, and the literatures in which the condo is an object of interest. Though focused on the jurisdictions of Ontario and, to a lesser extent, New York State, these implications have relevance to condo governance and the condo across North America and possibly in other common law jurisdictions beyond. This chapter first considers recent condo statutory law reform primarily in Ontario and contemplates some future paths of the condo considering the character of statutory reform and the condo's frailty within assemblages. Three potential futures are condoization as a solution to affordable urban housing; secession of condo corporations from municipal governments; and the collapse of the condo. *Condo Conquest* concludes with a summary of main themes and arguments as well as a discussion of the implications of the foregoing analysis for the sociology of governance and socio-legal, urban, and surveillance studies.

Before proceeding to its implications for arguments about possible futures that circulate about the condo, we first need to pay attention to the fact that understanding condo governance as an assemblage has implications for condo statutory reform. This book commenced by discussing the emergence of condo statutes in Ontario, New York State, and North America, so it is perhaps fitting that this final chapter briefly returns to statutes. While the condo statute constitutes the source of only some legal knowledge that shapes and brings condo governance into being,[1] this knowledge nonetheless remains vital.

CONDO STATUTORY LAW REFORM AND ASSEMBLAGES

Early condo statutory reforms in Ontario sought to deal with ongoing problems with condo developers, but more recent bills and actual amendments have begun to target condo governance (Gardiner 2001), though not governance as broadly conceived in this book. For example, Ontario's statute was amended in 1975 to ensure full disclosure about condo units and buildings in the form of a declaration of their rules and financial statements to would-be owners (although this amendment was deemed unsuccessful in a later major review) (Ontario 1977, 93). Specifically, reforms have sought to respond to the failure of boards to manage reserve funds to ensure the long-term maintenance of condo buildings' common elements. Since those changes the legislators of many jurisdictions, including those in Ontario and New York State, have experienced rising pressure from owners' associations to do more about the seemingly perpetual problems of condo governance that remain unsolved. In Arizona, California, Florida, and Connecticut, this increased oversight through more detailed legal statutes has occurred over the past decade (McKenzie 2011, 93; Prevost 2011). This section therefore briefly discusses reforms primarily in Ontario and elaborates upon the effort to establish more government oversight of condo governance. The aim is not to determine whether and how Ontario's (or New York State's) statute is "better" for owners, renters, municipal governments, or the growing condo industry; rather, it is to lend insight into this statutory reform considering the foregoing chapters. Thus, this section elaborates a law reform assemblage, arguing that corresponding legislative Standing Committee Hearings in Ontario held to consider the new statute are a channel for legal knowledge such as the condo conference and condo law newsletters. This account raises questions about whether statutory reform can successfully tame condo governance if it is already all but conquered by commercial actors. Special attention is paid to the assemblage of agents involved in this process, empirically demonstrating their dominant presence in this realm. This section additionally elaborates upon several government responses to condo governance disputes and problems via statutory reform beyond the commodified solutions offered by commercial entities. These include a condo authority and a property management licensing regime.

As remarked upon in Chapter 2, pressure from condo owners and resident owners is growing for provincial and state governments in North America to provide more government oversight of condo governance. This is seen in the emergence of condo owner associations, such as the Canadian Alliance for Condo Owners' Rights (CAFCOR 2016) and the Condo Owners Association (COA 2016), and, in New York, the Alliance of Condo and Co-op Owners (ACCO 2016) and Council of New York Cooperatives and Condominiums (CNYC 2016). But calls for statutory reform have also been watched closely by the assembled commercial agents that form the condo industry and whose practices are dependent to some degree on how condo statutes change. They, too, have large and more powerful organizations set to influence statutory law reform on an ongoing basis, and they influence whether and how related legal knowledge flows into condo buildings for instances relating to legal governance. Of specific note in Ontario are chapters of the Canadian Condominium Institute (CCI), a national organization that comprises mostly insurance, law, and property management representatives, as well as ACMO and the Ontario

Home Builders' Association, representing property managers and developers, respectively.

While there was already pressure from condo owners, the 1998 iteration of Ontario's condo statute that came into force in 2001 began to be more seriously questioned following extensive media coverage of the most egregious case of "condo crime" (Lippert, Treffers, and Bud 2017) in Ontario's history. This brought owner pressure to a boil, triggered fear over falling property values and bankruptcies stemming from extensive corruption in condo governance, and suggested that an unpalatable and unseemly mix of elements was lurking under that otherwise shiny and desirable condo sausage. In late 2012, news media reported that, without the condo owners' knowledge, Channel Property Management owner Manzoor Khan had taken out millions of dollars of loans under the auspices of condo corporations he was contracted to manage in Toronto (Zlomislic and Aulakh 2012). This case, involving more than one thousand condo owners, soon became the most notorious condo embezzlement and fraud scheme ever publicized in Ontario. In addition to fraudulent loans, allegations against Channel and its owner included forging documents, falsifying signatures, creating phony companies, bid-rigging, and kickbacks (*MTCC No. 831 v. Khan,* 2012). Amounts misappropriated were estimated to be above CDN$20 million. For one downtown Toronto condo building managed by Channel, Khan had registered a condo bylaw on his own, allowing him to borrow up to CDN$3 million in loans against the property. The acquired funds were alleged to have then disappeared (Aulakh 2012). In other Channel-managed condo complexes, owner maintenance fees typically rose far more than the inflation rate, sometimes by more than 100 percent over only several years (Hildebrandt 2011). In a 2012 Ontario Superior Court decision, Khan was held liable for defrauding Metropolitan Toronto Condo Corporation No. 710, from which he had appropriated funds for never completed renovations (*MTCC No. 710 v. Khan,* 2012). Of the almost CDN$1.3 million in damages awarded to this condo corporation by the courts, by 2012 none had been paid (Zlomislic and Aulakh 2012). Khan's acts financially devastated many condo owners.

In addition to paying Channel's inflated monthly condo fees for years, victimized owners had to cover high legal fees to seek compensation. Special assessments to respond to huge shortfalls in reserve funds to maintain buildings were issued, sometimes approaching CDN$300,000 per building due to Channel's activities alone. Furthermore, the scandal reduced property values, making it more difficult for owners to sell their morally and financially tainted condo units and move on. The case involving Channel and Khan was unusual, partially because it was discovered to have involved the misappropriation of millions in condo corporation funds and had gained much media attention. In comments to the Standing Committee overseeing statutory reforms, for example, one presenter called it: "The 2011 high-profile fraud case ... [that] could be North America's largest condo fraud" (LePage 2015). This incident was a catalyst for the latest statutory review (Canada's Public Policy Forum 2013a, 2013b).

As with condo governance, with which it is linked, statutory law reform involves a complex assemblage of elements. The legislative hearings to consider the revised condo statute, which followed a review process by private consultants contracted by the provincial government (see Canada's Public Policy Forum 2013a, 2013b), are an example of another channel for legal knowledge. There is a sense in which these hearings close the "circuit" remarked upon previously in that legal knowledge about condo governing practices – including those directed at renters – exits condo buildings and travels to hearings through various means, including oral presentations and written briefs, to then shape what transpires. Rather than attempt to explore how the legal knowledge arriving at the hearings is transformed into statutory reform, however, what follows is a more modest but revealing examination of the organizational representation of the human emissaries who espoused such knowledge during two days of hearings held by Ontario's Standing Committee on Finance and Economic Affairs regarding the first draft of the revised Ontario condo statute, Bill 106, the Protecting Condo Owners Act.

Distribution of Representation at 2015 Standing Committee Hearings to Comment on Bill 106

The legal knowledge flowing into the Ontario Standing Committee Hearings held to examine the bill's first draft effectively assembled varied agents with seemingly diverse but mostly commercial interests. The Standing Committee comprised a chair, vice-chair, and six other members of Ontario's legislature. In total, with substitutions, eight were from the ruling provincial Liberal Party, two from the Progressive Conservative Party, and two from the New Democratic Party. Hearings were held across two days, October 22 and 29, 2015. Written submissions about the draft were also accepted, as were the numerous written briefs in 2013 (also acquired via an FOI request) to kick off the statutory review, but they were mostly represented by owners and the governing agents identified in preceding chapters. Commentary on the oral submissions were "tweeted" in real time by condo industry observers as they transpired at the hearings (another form of "excerpting" that allows this new legal knowledge to exit quickly and re-enter the condo world beyond the legislature) and were later published online as part of the provincial legislature's record in *Hansard*.

Organizations and individuals were selected to present what they thought about the bill before the Standing Committee. The distribution of presenters at these hearings is a snapshot of condo statutory law reform. During these two days full-time, paid condo industry lobbyists filled twelve fifteen-minute time slots to address the Standing Committee, and twenty such representatives attended. Key among these were ACMO, representing property managers (one slot, two reps); the Ontario Home Builders' Association, representing developers (two slots, three reps); a condo auditing firm (one slot, two reps); a property management firm (one slot, one rep); the Real Estate Institute of Canada, representing real estate firms (one slot, two reps); the Canadian Condo Institute, almost exclusively representing condo law, insurance, and property management firms (one slot, two reps); individual law firm representatives (three slots, five reps); the Alternative Dispute Resolution Institute of Ontario, representing paid mediators mandated to play a role by the 1998 statute (one slot, one rep); and the Advocacy Centre for Tenants Ontario (representing renters in condo units in Ontario and beyond) (one slot, two reps).

Striating this channel of legal knowledge were fourteen other time slots across the two days that permitted individuals representing themselves to enter its flow. These fourteen included two self-described condo owner advocates, four unit owners, a board member, a professional engineer knowledgeable about condo buildings, a condo lawyer from outside Ontario, a property manager, a real estate consultant, a condo auditor, a condo governance consultant, and a professor studying condo governance. Only four "regular" condo owners and two other owners, as either current board members or property managers, were given this standing (despite "owners" being in the act's name and the existence of hundreds of submissions from owners in the early stages of the statutory review who could have been invited). Thus, only six of fourteen time slots for individuals were allotted to the tens of thousands of condo owners and renters. Of the twenty-six slots across the two days, only six, or 23 percent, were designated for condo owners. Only six of the thirty-four, or 18 percent, of representatives permitted to orally comment directly to legislators on the bill did so as owners. This configuration mirrors and, through this dispensing of knowledge at the hearings, becomes affixed to the condo governance assemblage described in previous chapters. While the condo may not be fully tamed, the condo statutory review, like the condo conference, was conquered by commercial firms or their well-funded industry groups (e.g., ACMO, CCI) via a deluge of legal knowledge that swamped the draft statute. This occurred while only one board member, a few owners, and one person who apparently previously rented a condo unit were given standing to speak and transfer what was, in comparison, a trickle of common knowledge. This raises a question about whether statutory law reform that does not confront condo governance as an assemblage of myriad actors beyond boards, and to some extent property managers, is doomed to fail to respond to perpetual problems of condo governance. Flowing into the hearings were, almost exclusively, legal and expert knowledges dominated by representatives of firms that now form condo governing assemblages. This underscores how these assemblages extend into statutory law reform processes and enable us to begin to predict the character of statutory mutations. These changes are many, but here I briefly discuss three vital ones.

First, it is perhaps no surprise that the legislation allows for the creation of tribunals comprising agents discussed in previous chapters. The statute will create two "self-funded" bodies: the Condo Authority and the Condo Manager Licensing Authority. The revised statute allows for the formation of a condo authority responsible for administering a dispute resolution tribunal with powers to oversee disputes and require compliance with Ontario's condo statute (section 1.31 of Bill 106, 2015). But "self-funded" means owners will pay the freight for this Condo Authority through an annual fee, even though conflict resolution plainly benefits mostly commercial agents that form governing assemblages by ensuring that condo governance and the condo have future viability. As mentioned in Chapter 2, a bill in the New York State legislature (A6941) still in process after several years similarly calls for a new ombudsperson office to oversee condo disputes to be paid for via a regular fee levied on all New York State condo (and cooperative) owners (New York Senate 2012). Florida, Nevada, and Connecticut have similarly introduced, or are contemplating, condo offices to resolve condo disputes (Lasner 2012, 281). McKenzie (2011, 105) notes in passing that this "per units cost" approach was implemented in Florida and Nevada but was rejected in California. Yet paying for the Condo Authority in Ontario does not come with the opportunity to dispense the common knowledge of an owner or board member (or renter). Owners will have very little or no opportunity to play a significant role on the Condo Authority. Rather, criteria for Condo Authority board members appointed by the minister to oversee the implementation of the tribunal are as vague and as open-ended as the assemblage to which it is tethered. Section 1.9 (1)(a) of Bill 106 refers to "competency criteria for members of the board of directors" of the Condo Authority, but these competency criteria do not protect owners by preventing industry representatives from filling all board positions to the detriment of resident owners and renters. Section 1.10(3) indicates that the members appointed by the minister "may include" "representatives of the public, consumer groups, government organizations, corporations, owners or those owners who occupy units for residential purposes" (no renters need apply). While "will include" would have guaranteed owner inclusion, "may include" is vague about leaving room for this future possibility. Moreover, non-resident "owners" and "owners who occupy units for residential purposes" are given the same opportunity to participate, despite the latter having more or better knowledge of condo governance due to having resided in condo buildings more frequently than non-resident owners, who sometimes have never done so.

As noted earlier, a similar condo authority (or "Condo Office") to deal with disputes was established in previous Ontario statutory reforms (Bill 103) after having been recommended in the major 1977 statutory review (Ontario 1977), but it never came to fruition (see sections 56 and 57 of the Condo Act, 1978). Even at that time there was a sense that condo owners should be more significantly involved in the Condo Office than in its most recent iteration. Then as now the new Condo Office in Ontario would require "every condominium owner paying a small annual assessment to finance the operation" (Ontario 1978a). At the time, Minister of Consumer Affairs Grossman explained the plan for the office: "the composition of the board will be 50 per cent condominium owners chosen regionally and 50 per cent representation drawn from the private sector such as builders, developers, property managers, lenders, insurers, the legal and accounting professions" (Ontario 1978a). Concern about Bill 103 was raised in the Ontario legislature before its passage into law. Opposition member Michael Davison commented on the new office's proposed composition, albeit to no avail:

> The question, Mr. Minister, [is] about ... the makeup of Condominium Ontario, the composition of the members in the bureau? Specifically, are you at this point in time willing to guarantee in this House publicly *that the majority membership of the bureau of Condominium Ontario will be*

> *unit owners and their representatives and not some people you may pick from the other parts of the condominium world?* (Ontario 1978b; emphasis added)

The opposition legislative member Evelyn Gigantes also commented about this aspect but was more concerned about the proposed bill and lack of owner representation in the proposed Condo Office:

> As if that weren't enough, now they [owners] get told by Mr. Grossman in June [1978] that this external agency, this non-government agency, is going to be made up 50 percent of *those very professions* who have seen to it that individuals and families in this province *have been ripped off* under the Condominium Act. (Ontario 1978c; emphasis added)

At least some emphasis on representation of condo owners in dispute resolution was legislated almost forty years earlier, more so than recently, even though in 1978 already half the members were to be from the "private sector" and owners were to fund the Condo Office then too. It is also noteworthy that condo lawyers are conspicuous by their absence in the minister's elaboration of "private sector" in 1978, perhaps reflecting a lesser prominence then and the subsequent growth, consistent with juridification, since. Reflecting condo conquest by commercial agents of condo governance and the shift it represents, no such opposition from elected provincial representatives to the need to ensure some condo resident (owner and renter) representation in the new Condo Office's workings is found in *Hansard* regarding recent statutory changes or in Standing Committee Hearings. Such opposition is no longer part of condo governance discourse.

Furthermore, industry representatives and condo owners are not mutually exclusive categories. There is seemingly no means to prevent those owners – if they were to serve on the Condo Authority – from being screened out due to a serious conflict of interest. The revised statute does not recognize these phenomena, leaving much room for condo industry and possibly non-resident owner influence on the new Condo Authority supposedly designed to protect *resident* owners (if the latest iteration of the act is about more than consumer protection and is to extend to preserving condo "communities" [Canada's Public Policy Forum 2013c]) and suggests the notion that the condo is or can be more than commodified property.

Second, arrangements with (usually engineering) firms hired to conduct a reserve fund study – that is, to provide expert knowledge about a building's infrastructure – can become problematic if the same firm vying for contracts to oversee repairs or renovation projects can otherwise manipulate the reserve fund plan to suit the board's or a property manager's desires. One property manager explained:

> What the engineering firms want is not the $5,000 to do the study. What they want is the $100,000 in engineering fees for doing these projects, because they should be done under the oversight of an engineer. Where are you going to get your engineer from? From the company that did the reserve fund study. They want the $100,000 over ten years they're going to make in engineering fees for doing these major repair and replacement projects around the property that need to be done. So they ... minimize the contribution, because what they want, ultimately, is the business. (TO Manager 2)

The revised statute now takes condo board members off the liability hook (see section 1.19[1], Bill 106) when they operate in good faith regarding a reserve fund study. While this change might increase notoriously low owner-board participation levels by lowering their exposure, the statute does not require that reserve fund providers be more independent from the influence of boards and property managers.

Third, a result of the statutory reforms is, for the first time, the promise of licensing property managers and, more important, property management firms through a condo manager licensing authority. After describing the requirement in his industry not to cross the line with his clients when being asked to hide flaws in condo properties, a real estate agent remarked about the current property management situation: "In the management community, there is no line" (TO Real Estate 1). The details and veracity of this licensing have yet to be seen in the regulations. Yet it is unclear how effective this can be, given the intimate involvement of property management firms and ACMO in shaping it at the hearings. If the voluntary industry practice code called "ACMO 2000" is any example, one might be concerned to know that Channel Management of massive fraud fame was a signatory to it. It has yet to be seen whether and how this and other changes will reshape condo governing assemblages. It seems doubtful they will permit resident owners and renters to gain more control of condo governance from powerful commercial actors that have all but conquered this realm at their expense.

CONDO AS SOLUTION TO URBAN AFFORDABLE HOUSING?

Since its emergence in the 1960s, the condo has been touted as a solution to urban problems in North America. City planners, for example, have claimed the condo as an urban revitalization tool.[2] In both New York in the 1980s and Toronto in the 1990s, consumption was "promoted as the touchstone for urban economic development and as the source of urban regeneration" (Ruppert 2006, 101). To enhance consumption, especially in declining retail zones and downtowns overseen by business improvement associations (or BIAs) (Lippert 2007, 2012), the condo promised, often implicitly, to fill a blighted area with new consumers. Condo buildings are deemed a means of increasing local pedestrian consumption traffic by establishing nests of residential consumers for retail strips, and sometimes they form part of that retail strip if such space is offered by a condo building's street front base (as is increasingly seen in Toronto). In contrast, introduction of social or public housing and other rental buildings is rarely touted as a tool to revitalize downtown cores or retail areas; such phenomena are not assumed to be a source of "good" consumers (Ruppert 2006). Such gentrification has a specific purpose, which is improved consumption in surrounding areas (a notion that MaxTV sought to capitalize on via its advertisements). The location and size of a condo building thus permits some control over the wealth and volume of consumers, depending on how it is marketed. When contemplating approval by municipal planning departments the condo's developers have often offered services or infrastructure in place of necessary municipal provision or as higher-density housing to at least ease municipal service delivery costs (Nelson 2005; Warner 2011). This is a common and well-known tactic across North America, the aim of which is to achieve municipal approval of condo complexes.

But the condo is also being deployed as a new source of mixed-use residential housing for low-income people in cities or as affordable housing in Toronto and New York. This is yet another example of governing urban problems *through* the condo – that is, condo conquest. This problem is worth focusing upon here. The arrangements for this come with major tax breaks or profit-generating benefits for developers, such as receiving permission to build more units than normally allowed. In exchange for a neighbourhood accepting condo high-rises on Toronto's King Street West, for example, the developer

Urbancorp built three floors of units in the Westside Gallery condo building, and then Artscape, a non-profit organization supporting artists, sold these forty-eight units to artists (Vincent 2012). The condo rental units tend to be owned by non-profit housing agencies. Similarly, a Great Gulf Homes condo building has four units for affordable housing to be owned and controlled by Kehilla, the housing agency of the UJA Federation of Greater Toronto. The city of Toronto agreed to permit the developer greater density while Kehilla signed an agreement with the city to ensure the units remain affordable. Similarly, Ten York is a sixty-two-floor tower with 694 condo units, twelve of which will be owned and managed as cooperatives by the Co-op Housing Federation of Toronto. The developer Tridel is providing CDN$5 million for Ten York's affordable units. It arranged with the city to increase height of the sixty-two-story Ten York condo tower (Vincent 2012). The affordable units will become available for those who are "employed, and meet certain thresholds," according to a Tridel representative. Other new condo buildings will have affordable rental units, but ultimately only forty to fifty across Toronto after 2012, without specifying a timeline, according to Toronto city councillor Adam Vaughan (Vincent 2012). This councillor also claimed: "Is it going to solve the problem of people on the waiting list for affordable housing in Toronto? No, I'm not naïve. But it's better than doing nothing, and for a decade we've been doing nothing" (Vincent 2012).

Similarly, Toronto's East Bayfront projected condo building will have up to eighty "affordable" rental units separated from another 150 condo units (Vincent 2012). The city of Toronto will own the units and Artscape will manage and screen artist renters. As well, Artscape accepted terms whereby the city allowed condo-registered rental units at a building at 38 Abell Street. This last configuration is becoming more common. The city of Toronto can transfer the management costs of these programs onto not-for-profit agencies and avoid political pressure to build long overdue social or public housing or encourage more rental buildings to be constructed (Monsebraaten 2013). Using the condo this way is evident in New York too. Extell Corporation's 40 River Boulevard condo building in Manhattan has 346 units, twelve of which are affordable and available for persons with less than US$36,000 in annual income, an arrangement that permits the developer to build more projects elsewhere (*Daily Mail* 2016).

Yet there is no City of Toronto policy guide or mandate for these condo arrangements. The number of rented units is dwarfed by regular condo units in each building. Such arrangements also at times come with "poor doors."

This is evident both in Toronto (*Huffington Post* 2014) and in New York (Sorkin 2014). Of course, there is a sense in which poor doors (including segregated elevators) are merely the spatial catch-up of longer-running condo governance arrangements targeting the disparaged and scapegoated renter in the condo world. Incredibly, in New York, these poor doors have been justified as follows:

> The so called poor door actually reduces segregation by economic status; they are all in the same building, sharing the same streets. The developer benefits by getting a density bonus and more money for his units because everyone wants higher floors; the people in the lower floors actually get housing in a nice part of the west side instead of being stuck out in some project somewhere else. (Alter 2015)

Of course, how and why practices of public governments and other agents enlisted in condo assemblages gradually helped permit the emergence of the obviousness of such class segregation into "nice" urban spaces and "somewhere else" where one gets "stuck" is left unquestioned. Here segregation becomes reproduced in a single condo building in New York City via the poor door.

Private (urban) governance, especially in gated communities (e.g., Low 2003), is often associated with class (and sometimes racial/ethnic) segregation between residents who own and outsiders who do not. Consistent with this is the notion of Toronto and New York as polarized or divided cities. But condo governance arrangements also reflect practices that differ based on class-related property ownership *within* complexes being governed. Thus, renters are found to be a source of anxiety and risk and are differentially policed when it comes to nuisance. The condo industry, including non-resident owners, has become dependent on the lower-class renter. The assemblage revealed in the foregoing chapters exemplifies inequitable property relations, whereby some property owners avoid legal sanction and responsibility while profiting from those without property, and where mutually reinforcing legal, property management, and insurance firms turn lower socio-economic status renters' (and others') assumed risk, immorality, and propensity as a nuisance source into profitable commodities. But, until this recent onset of condo buildings becoming positioned as low-income housing, there has not been a means to seal renters off from regular owners. Toronto is a divided city; but its condo spaces are also divided, and those dividing them are often not physically present. Rather, their knowledge and influence passes through the external walls of condo buildings as though they were porous. But poor doors fail as spatial segregation since nuisances, if we are to believe that dissident noise and smoke stem more from renters than from resident owners, pass *through* segregating walls and sealed off floors and ceilings as though they, too, were porous. Not unlike the bowing peasant who farts as the great lord walks by (Scott 1990, v), noise and smoke nuisances drifting upward and the arrival of ugly, smoldering butts from rented units' balconies or from the building's roof onto owners' aesthetically pristine balconies may, in the condo world, well be the excluded, maligned, and exploited renters' semi-intended revenge and resistance.

Ultimately, the condo as a solution to urban affordable housing is intimately linked to condo governance. Thus, its "success" in managing lower-income renters, for example, is really a question of condo governance: Who will be responsible? Through what processes, logics, agents, and spaces will they be governed? And how will these relate to the rest of condo life? And if the few new affordable rental units are exempt from condo fee increases and special assessments given to other condo owners, rather than to the developer or the city, who will assume this financial burden when it eventually appears? If covered by a condo building's house rules, will non-profit agencies have to cover the high legal costs if renters violate these rules (as they are supposedly so adept at doing due to their assumed disregard for property and propensity for nuisance)? The foregoing chapters cast doubt on the potential of the condo to solve the affordable housing crisis.

CONDO AS SEPARATE LEVEL AND SECESSION?

One implication of seeing condo governance as an assemblage is to move away from taken-for-granted notions of "levels" of government (e.g., municipal/local, provincial/state, federal/national, international, global). Condo lawyers and other condo industry representatives have called condo governance a "fourth level of government" for some time (e.g., Silverstein 1992). This characterization has continued in Ontario's latest statutory review, which refers to the "condo sector" as "the fourth level of government" (Canada's Public Policy Forum 2013c, 15). A recent descriptive study of condo governing arrangements in Australia similarly labels condo corporations as the "fourth tier of government" (Easthope et al. 2014). Yet, other than to suggest a much smaller geographical scale and population to govern, it is unclear how much understanding is gained by referring to condo governance as a distinctive and subordinate "level" or "tier." Certainly, such characterizations hint at the complexity and influence of condo governance beyond what is suggested by the surprisingly limited scholarly attention paid to it to date. Yet condo governance is more fruitfully seen as operating alongside, borrowing from, and contributing to other levels and tiers (especially municipal) as a potential solution to urban problems than it is as operating distinctively "below" or at the bottom of urban life. Condo governance is somewhat distinct from public government to be sure, but it is not particularly useful to conceive of it as another level in a hierarchy since it has been shown to consistently involve forms drawn from these other levels to a greater or lesser extent (e.g., public police, provincial and state courts, and even the federal US Housing Authority), depending on the problem addressed. This is perhaps most evident in instances in which legal knowledges from other levels are seen to be seeping (or are invited) into condo governance as well as in instances that indicate how nuisance is policed. Rather than a hierarchy, the notion of an assemblage comprising shifting elements from these levels and private sources is more illuminating and accurate.

Related to the discussion of separate levels is the notion of "secession," previously raised in relation to gated communities (see Levi 2009; Blandy 2008; Cashin 2001; Stark 1998). With the rise of private gated communities in the US governed by home owner associations, which are similar though not equivalent to condo corporations, there has emerged discussion about civic secession from public government whereby public taxes would no longer be paid by their residents to municipal governments and, instead, the complex would be entirely self-funded and governed. All services would be privately owned and managed. Cashin (2001, 1677–78) explains this development:

> The secessionist mind set ... has crossed an intellectual firewall. In a few [US] jurisdictions, the previously accepted understanding that public tax support should not be available for facilities that are wholly private or exclusive has given way. In 1996, for example, the private gated community of Panther Valley near Hackettstown, New Jersey was allowed to set up a special taxing district for the maintenance of roads that are wholly closed to the general public. As a result, the residents of Panther Valley are able to deduct what they spend for private road maintenance from their federal and state income tax returns. Several nearly identical arrangements reportedly have been created in Florida. This and other forms of "civic secession" have been occurring across the country. At the extreme, a CID [community

> interest developments that include condo complexes] formally secedes from the surrounding city or county, forming its own incorporated municipal government. With such formal secession, the common interest community gains the regulatory powers, particularly zoning powers, that enable it to attract desired entrants and wall out populations deemed undesirable ... By giving the private property owner a formal context ... [to feel] she is "doing her part" simply by paying her way for services, it will be increasingly difficult in the 21st century to establish a mandate for governmental policy, whether federal, state, or local, that requires shared sacrifice.

In the Toronto suburb of Markham, condo corporations in recent years have formed the Markham Association of Townhouse Condominium Owners (MATCO) to lobby against what they claim is "double taxation" and to have the condo recognized as a separate class of property in so far as taxation is concerned. This happened much earlier in the US, for example, in municipalities in Texas, Missouri, and Maryland (Kennedy 1995, 774). The argument is that, since condo unit owners cover the cost of an array of services through mandatory fees delivered privately and therefore reduce costs to municipalities, when they are also required to pay standard municipal taxes, they are "double-taxed" for services (see also Stark 1998). In Markham, this "New Residential Condominium Property Class" would be taxed 10 percent less than the standard residential home owner rate, which would increase to overcome the resulting revenue reduction (MATCO 2010). Thus, the condo would be a realm in which regular taxation rules no longer apply. Influence has been accomplished through regular, formal meetings with municipal government officials (i.e., a Markham condo working group comprising MATCO and Markham municipal officials). Such meetings are of course unavailable to those, like renters, who do not own property. This ostensibly influential lobbying through condo owner organizations is historically new for Canadian condo buildings. Non-maintenance-fee-paying renters are disenfranchised in the complex governing arrangements of this form since they are restricted from serving on condo boards in practice and cannot avail themselves of these privileged spaces of influence. But having a new tax class or a reduction of municipal taxes is a far cry from civic secession, even if the latter is a long-term goal. And when condo governance is revealed as an assemblage, especially given its current dependence on statutory municipal bylaws, building standard law, and various other legal knowledges (such as criminal law as well as enforcement in the courts) – at least to some extent at taxpayer expense – the very notion of extreme secession is impossible. However, the question of the long-term harmful effects on the viability of municipal governments due to permitting rebates for the growing number of ostensibly private condo corporations that market "amenities" (rather than municipal "services"), whether in sprawling gated arrangements or equally securitized high-rises that provide their own services, will be a continuing issue. The notion of tax rebates ignores the reality of governing condo spaces and their inhabitants via owner-funded condo "authorities" (or "ombudsmen") as well as the costs of public courts and all the other public legal knowledges bearing down upon them and provided "for free." The further reach of the condo into public spheres, and calling fees "taxation," will remain problematic in the future. This is underscored when the various ways condo governance is dependent upon public authorities is considered and its assemblage surfaces.

CONDO COLLAPSE?

While secession from municipal government is unlikely, the collapse of the condo may be just as unlikely if the cost of poor construction and governance is gradually foisted, building by building, onto federal, provincial/state, or municipal governments and taxpayers in a way not unlike what occurred with the massive bailouts of Wall Street firms and auto manufacturers consequent upon the 2008 financial crisis. Put differently, it may well be that the condo world has become "too big to fail." But its potential for collapse comes from the following facts: that fees need to substantially rise and to cover government condo oversight from authorities/ombudsmen; that there is tension between non-resident owners seeking low fees and aesthetic changes to commodified property, on the one hand, and resident owners seeking a long-term home and community in which to live, on the other; that it is easy for owners who are in the know or on the board to quickly sell units at the first sign of financial crisis and move on, leaving others to clean up the mess; that there is isolation among owners that leads to the related possibility of board and property management fraud; and that the condo industry has self-interested "jackals" whose legal, security, and risk knowledges are packaged and sold at premium prices and who feed off poor governance and reluctant, self-interested, or corrupt boards. This concern over collapse is coupled with recognition of the frailty of the collective aspect of condo governance, which binds together all owners financially and spatially, but rarely socially, and which held out the promise of fomenting community.

Much media attention in Toronto has been focused on new condo towers whose poorly insulated and installed windows have, in dramatic fashion, fallen to the streets (e.g., Preville 2014):

> With all the glass disasters that you read about, what does that mean for those owners, the ones that are going to stay long term? They're going to have issues with reserve fund increases and special assessments potential and replace those windows a lot earlier than expected, so they should be aware of that and make sure that they have money set aside for that. (TO Real Estate 1)

But attention to the poor construction of newer buildings neglects a mostly hidden and uncomfortable truth prevalent in the interviews conducted in both cities, in briefs to Ontario's statutory review, and on owner advocacy websites. This truth is that there were numerous condo buildings erected in the late 1960s through the 1980s in Toronto and New York (some were condoized after being built as cooperative or rental buildings) with grossly outdated systems and infrastructure that are unable to meet newer legal regulations and standards for elevators, ventilation, fire safety, wiring, water pipes, and physical accessibility. These buildings are now reaching old age. This raises the question of whether any level of special assessment – without forcing owners to sell or declare bankruptcy – would be enough to cover the inadequate reserve funds to allow these condo buildings and communities to be salvaged. It also raises the question of whether any number or kinds of statutory amendments affecting boards and owners could still overcome this impending danger before resident owners (but not necessarily non-resident owners – see, for example, Harris and Gilewicz 2015) declare them a catastrophic loss leading to the condo corporation's dissolution.

When another great recession returns, as the regulations of Wall Street finance are dismantled under a new US regime and the lessons of 2008 (which included more stringent mortgage requirements for condo unit purchases in the US) (Browning 2011) are forgotten, and poorly constructed and maintained condo buildings start to crumble, and foreign investment in condo units is legislated against in Toronto and beyond – all of which is happening – some condo corporations and buildings will begin to topple. And when resident owners and renters can no longer pay to prop them up, this will lead to siphoning away the public monies of citizens (as happened during the first wave of condo conversions in the US in the late 1970s [see United States Congress 1981]), including those who neither owned nor could afford a condo unit, much less a detached residential dwelling in the divided cities of Toronto and New York. These are public monies that could have built and maintained social, subsidized, and non-profit cooperative rental housing but now may be spent on rescuing these complexes and corresponding assemblages one by one.

On the way to that happening, there is perhaps the last resort of exceptional special assessments and court-appointed administrators of counter-law fame, but these agents are not necessarily saviours in the waiting. Owners can abandon units if special assessments become too high and as buildings become less and less attractive due to physical and financial deterioration, and as more abandon the building, the condo corporation will move closer to collapse. Administrators are an exceptional provision with or without special assessments before collapse, but they are not always adequate when it comes to improving the long-term viability of a building. They are not all-knowing saviours and sometimes arrogantly disregard common knowledge of residents. For example, one administrator explained that, once taking over from boards, some "administrators have borrowed money far in excess ... than they should have, and made decisions on the normal maintenance and decisions that should have been left to the board" (TO Administrator 1). Furthermore, the court-appointed administrator's

> attitude ... is I'm dictator ... I can mandate whatever I want. I have the ability to special assess; I have the ability to raise the fees; I have the ability to enact a bylaw now. And this has actually happened: ... I'll do what I want and think about, but what happens is the angst and anger and frustration of owners is so high that how do you expect anyone on that board to function when you're gone? So basically at the end of three years you can say, "Well, they're still angry and frustrated and there's no community unity, so why would I suggest to you, the judge, that they are ready for self-governance?" ... because of that approach that's being heard and seen and observed, the remedy for a building that has gone "sour" financially, socially, physically is less and less a viable option. (TO Real Estate 1)

It is unclear that spirals of more and more surveillance and detailed statutory legal regulation, coupled with more and more commodified "solutions" piling up one upon another, can prevent this or, indeed, whether these on their own or collectively will soon blight anything remaining of common interest and community in condo governance and living. Whatever sharing of space and elements via common knowledge and resulting community the condo ideal promised to yield is now not so much lost as held somewhere else by agents located far from the condo's walls and residents, with renters and resident owners alike ironically paying a monthly ransom, not for its return, but for it to stay away. In many cases in Toronto and New York, when turned inside out the condo sausage's innards are found to be not so much unseemly and rife with conflict and contradiction as hollowed out and dispersed – as risk, indifference, nuisance, insecurity, commodified property, and decision making – for someone else to deal with for a price.

A related troubling question is whether the condo, if it was ever a viable long-term solution to urban issues, can break free of its conquerors if its residents are inclined to seek the community they advocate or whose loss they lament. This frailty of the condo, with its peculiar joining of individual and collective ownership, is exacerbated as more and more external governing agents shape and drain its financial and common sustenance, and this generates concern about the condo's longer-term future in Toronto, New York, and globally (see also McKenzie, 2011, 118). This book shows that there is an assemblage in place and that with it a range of legal knowledges enters the condo world. Given this, statutory reform, even if it were to stall condo conquest and influence the range of actors, is unlikely to be effective for long. Effective change requires engaging with a wider range of legal knowledges relating to these other agents. But of course, this assumes that more legal knowledge is an answer, and there is some doubt about this since such knowledge tends to foment surveillance and so to further erode trust and community.

Regardless of the above, once elements of the condo sausage are known, alternative recipes entailing other ingredients are possible. Indeed, a key feature of an assemblage is that it is not a structure: it is a contingent arrangement of elements hanging together that, in principle, lends itself to being reassembled differently or even to being dismantled. Non-profit (or non-market) cooperatives in which there is no individual ownership of units and there is an open approach to the selection of diverse residents may prove to be one alternative recipe (see, for example, McKenzie 2011, 35). However, for now a prudent (albeit chancier) approach to the condo may be to at least ensure common knowledge flourishes and flows from and to all residents (owners and renters alike) and to seek to create and maintain community in this way. This might be accomplished by altering the recipe for the condo by including fewer and fewer rather than more and more commodified elements in simpler combinations and with less detailed regulation and surveillance – an arrangement that would at once require and encourage more owner and renter participation and interaction. This would entail a move away from what Low (2003, 182), in her study of gated communities in the New York area, aptly called "moral minimalism." It may also be that Barton and Silverman's (1994, 138) assertion about rules, made more than twenty years ago following their study of condo governance in California, is relevant today for Toronto, New York, and wherever else condoization is occurring: "Rule violations are reduced by ... member participation in the association; by self-management, where people do the work of the association themselves; and by neighbors' concern for each other, whether expressed in sociability or simply in the more 'public' attitude of looking out for others even when they are not friends." Indeed, it may also mean fewer rules would be required in the first instance.

SUMMARY OF ARGUMENTS

Condo Conquest argues that condoization is an assembled means of governing people and space in cities. This condo governance is best seen as a complex assemblage of contingent, heterogeneous elements that has all but muscled out, or is relentlessly replacing, longer-standing cooperative and rental building alternatives. The foregoing chapters demonstrate the relations of these elements to condo development and renters and the role of knowledges, including governing logics such as "police," knowledges, processes, and technologies as diverse as high-rise elevators and "condo control" software. A major motivation of purchase and board participation found in owner discourse is investment and property value. As well, since the birth of the condo world in North America in the 1960s owners have mutated into two types, and the condo world is home to a range of owner-board relations.

Condo governance is more complex than it might seem when references are made to owners and boards exclusively as there are other vital agents beyond these, along with accompanying knowledges that are exercising more and more influence in condo governance and, ultimately, in urban life. Condo governance and condoization more broadly comprise at least four often overlapping processes – commodification, juridification, risk avoidance, and securitization. These processes do not merely happen: they are intimately and necessarily linked with the production, acquisition, and transfer of various knowledges about the condo world and its inhabitants. These knowledges are assembled as elements and help to assemble other elements. While some attention has been placed on structural changes in the political economy, the vital role of these knowledges has been overlooked in all previous accounts of the condo. This also implies that reforming the condo world will require other forms, or transforming proportions, of existing knowledges. A related implication is that it would be grossly inaccurate to suggest that these processes and knowledges have somehow developed and flourished due to gradually identified needs among condo owners and boards or other agents as the number of condo buildings and residents in North America have grown. Rather, these elements are better understood as going hand in hand: they render myriad aspects of condo life amenable to the exercise of powers (police, surveillance, legal adjudication), and the exercise of these powers demands these knowledges. Put simply, law firms, property management firms, insurance firms, security firms, and other agents have not operated outside the condo world, growing merely as needs for services are identified; rather, they and associated processes have become key constituents of the condo world inside and outside buildings and throughout statutory and related legal reforms.

The currently available knowledges and other elements identified bearing down on the condo world evident in accounts of owners and others presented here are neither incidental nor ephemeral: they are intimately intertwined with the production of the condo and, increasingly, with its commodified property form, shaping and making its governance possible in a number of ways. In case it is not obvious, this is also a historical claim more befitting Foucault's and the governmentality literature's historical orientation than that of the sociology of governance, but it requires more research: the condo takes its current form due to the knowledges, technologies, and other available elements as the "condition of its possibility," to use Foucauldian language (see Hunt and Wickham 1994, 6–7). Understanding condo governance and condoization as well as how one might rethink or resist its current contours demands scrutiny not only of the complex black letters of statutes and case law, of the economic forces of global capital evinced in powerful developers' decisions and municipal or higher-level planning decisions about urban intensification, and of the geographical patterns of physical building construction but also of mundane and expert knowledges, technologies, inscription devices, and various others devices available at this specific juncture.

Renters are excluded from condo governance arrangements other than as their target. Legal knowledge enters the condo world to confront this category through special channels (e.g., conferences and discussion boards) and techniques (e.g., excerpting), along with related processes. In tandem with this juridification of condo life, various forms of surveillance, some authored by security agents and consistent with securitization, are developing. These include audits of boards and other means of watching residents enter, exit, and move horizontally and vertically in condo spaces. There may be a spiral of law and surveillance occurring in the condo world, the curtailment of which is not obviously forthcoming.

Policing nuisance in the condo is a central governmental concern. Nuisance is best understood as the residue or detritus of condo governance, which can accumulate in ways that activate and illuminate other key processes of condoization, such as risk avoidance or securitization. There is a sense in which nuisance helps assemble these and other processes in a common cause. And two nuisances – noise and smoking – are exemplary of how nuisance is governed. The preoccupation with and occasional overreaction to nuisance is shaped by a "police" logic, including but not limited to a focus on positioning and flow, but that also has a neglected temporal aspect. Nuisance defies condo space, although mostly at specific times. And nuisance is either disproportionately blamed on renters or its remedies are heavier-handed when its source is deemed to be renters rather than owners. The forms that policing nuisance takes are increasingly enacted not solely by boards and residents but also by governing agents and knowledges imported and purchased from beyond the condo's walls (e.g., lawyers and insurance brokers) and are becoming further commodified.

While logics shape governing practices, as vital to condo governance are governmental technologies. The condo high-rise passenger elevator is found to have a complex, vital role as a neglected governmental technology in condo and urban life. The condo elevator is also the target of condo governance, being a major common element, and is spatially positioned in the life of condo buildings. It is enlisted in numerous strategies of governance as well as in numerous possibilities for resistance. There is, consequently, a need for more attention to what the elevator makes possible – verticality in urban governance.

IMPLICATIONS FOR GOVERNANCE, SOCIO-LEGAL, SURVEILLANCE, AND URBAN STUDIES LITERATURES

The foregoing analysis of condo governance has implications for various literatures. The concept of assemblage itself serves to bridge governance, socio-legal, surveillance, and urban studies literatures and transcend any disciplinary or subdisciplinary barriers that might exist among them. Put differently, assemblage suggests that maintaining firm boundaries among and between these literatures is not helpful. The notion of assemblage has implications for previous accounts of condo governance, as noted in Chapter 1. Recall Barton and Silverman's assertions that condo arrangements are a contradiction and those of Sherry, which suggest that this form of governance, when it comes to rendering bylaws difficult to change, has deleterious effects and is undemocratic. The now established notion of a condo governing assemblage is found to be broadly consistent with their findings, but it would also insist on considering renters in the mix as well as the contingent nature of these property relations. Assemblage suggests that the condo could be reassembled differently rather than remaining a contradiction or becoming fixed as universally undemocratic. It also points to a wider array of relations not considered by previous research, especially regarding commodification. Indeed, one means of change on both counts (i.e., contradiction and lack of democracy) is, once again, greater effort to permit the promise of community to be fulfilled. And this will certainly demand less reliance on expert knowledges and commercial agents, which is what is now found around every corner of the condo world. This assumes, too, that condo "community" is not reducible to ideological camouflage for structural changes described as urban neoliberalism or, in Toronto's case, that it is not merely the fluffy creation of crafty condo developer marketing, whereby "community is deliberately and narrowly constructed" and "predetermined" for "young, middle-class professionals" (Kern 2010a, 104). It also assumes that financial "investment" has not yet fully smothered and conquered what remains of the other lingering motivational discourses that encouraged condo owners to originally enter the condo world. Community is a root that, while shallow, damaged, and certainly undernourished in the current condo world, under the right conditions of possibility could grow and blossom into something decidedly wider and far more inclusive.

The preceding chapters also have implications specific to the sociology of governance literature and socio-legal studies in that they suggest that future research should investigate in greater detail the channels of legal knowledge (e.g., numerous legal newsletters, advice columns, phone-in programs, discussion boards, and blogs of various kinds that pertain to law's various subfields); strategies, such as excerpting, through which this knowledge enters (and returns from) private realms; and how these channels and strategies (and associated processes of juridification, commodification, and risk avoidance) together constitute and target specific categories of governance. It needs to be determined how and whether legal knowledge flows matter not only to condo governance but also to governance in other realms. Legal knowledges almost never move fully formed from courts and legislatures to instances of governance and back again into statutory reform processes and legislative hearing arenas. They flow from armchairs on stages, newsletter pages, briefs, "tweets," and via chosen human emissaries. However, in any given instance, it is more what is gained or lost along the way, what and who is squeezed in or out, and less the departure or arrival of such knowledges, that is vital in shaping a realm. As private realms continue to expand consonant with neoliberalism and yet depend on and siphon precious public resources in various ways via police and the courts, how legal knowledges shape their governance will remain a broader salient question in governance and socio-legal studies.

The conceptual tools used in the foregoing analysis are not incompatible with seeking to understand how class or other inequalities relate to instances of legal governance. This book begins to show how mostly (but not exclusively) class-based categories – the non-resident owner and the renter – in a residential realm have emerged and are constituted, thus demonstrating that analytical tools from governance and socio-legal studies could engage in a more fruitful dialogue (see also Valverde 2005; Hunt 2004). Relatedly, the foregoing underscores how legal knowledges encourage creeping surveillance and vice versa, thus showing how surveillance studies is of relevance to socio-legal studies and how the two might engage each other. This is especially evident in relation to the two types of "counter-law" (Ericson 2007) that have purchase – and that are increasingly purchased – in the condo world.

Regarding governing logics specifically, "police" logic is shown to be about the physical positioning and flow of things in condo governance, but it also targets smaller urban things (Lippert 2014) like noises and smells. Policing noise nuisance in the condo also underscores a temporal aspect of the condo world, and, going forward, its examination encourages paying more attention to temporality and how it is linked with spatiality in relation to "police." More generally, it is revealed that not only is this "police" logic alive and well in cities, despite suggestions it has been replaced by liberal sentiments, but that it is operating well beyond municipal government in condoized and undoubtedly other urban spaces. In discussing "police" logic, Mark Neocleous (2000, x), a critic of Foucault-inspired governmentality work, asserts:

> Foucauldians use the police concept so abstractly ... Foucauldians barely mention the police institution itself, to the extent that one begins to think that policing and the police have nothing connecting them at all. One searches high and low in Foucauldian texts for police officers themselves to appear and play a part in the exercise of power ... Foucauldian texts are stripped of any sense that police has anything to do with violence and thus state power.

The notion that "police" and public police are linked should receive more attention in urban and socio-legal studies.[3] This book shows that in condo arrangements, particularly where renters are concerned, they are tethered. However, it also suggests that this tie is neither strong nor uniform and that public police tend to be used as a last resort (and are often ineffective in achieving rule compliance) regarding nuisance (though sooner when complaints are against renters than against owners).

A related implication for the sociology of governance and urban studies is that there is a need to further explore the verticality that the study of condo governance underscores in relation to, for example, policing nuisance, interstitial vertically arranged balconies, and, above all, the elevator as governmental technology. This verticality is a long-standing and developing dimension of the urban and of urban governance more broadly, and yet it has not received much attention in the condo world. Future research must explore this aspect of the urban to a far greater extent in urban residential and commercial realms.

Using a Foucault-inspired sociology of governance approach to the condo world reveals that the condo form and condo governance involves multiple and shifting contingent elements, and especially the role of knowledges in urban power relations, in ways either not previously discovered or that tend to be overlooked in perspectives drawing primarily from structural or political economic approaches. Indeed, even when Foucault's governmentality concept is laudably invoked to augment approaches in urban studies focused on revitalization (Kern 2010a, 8–10; Brash 2011, 5–6), including condo development, attention to the vital role of knowledges and technologies as two of these elements is peculiarly absent, thus missing an opportunity to more fully benefit from Foucault's influence when it comes to making sense of the urban. The sociology of governance and its close attention to knowledge ought to be embraced not simply as a supplement to be cited and then moved on from. Nor should it be ignored by those who would adopt policy relevance as their lodestar, as though policy relevance appears ready-made, concept-free and without systematic thought. Rather, Foucauldian-inspired scholarship can make sense of urban assemblages that regularly include law, governance, and surveillance, providing insights into its own trajectory, though nonetheless complementary with critical approaches informed by political economy.

Much condoization has been characterized as stemming from the onset of urban neoliberalism (Kern 2010a) or as otherwise fueled by this logic's onset (McKenzie 2011). Reference to neoliberalism – whether from political economy or Foucauldian-inspired governmentality studies – advances understanding of happenings in Toronto and New York over the past few decades more broadly (see, for example, Isin 1998; Brash 2011). However, the foregoing chapters show that neoliberalism is not the whole story. For example, a tension was noted between the expectation that condo residents would actively govern themselves as individuals and an apparent increasing passive reliance on formal governance and external agents and knowledges made possible through various processes. These processes of condoization and corresponding governing logics relate to but cannot be reduced to neoliberalism. All of this reinforces the notion that shifts in urban governance more broadly should not be studied or assumed to be about neoliberalism from the outset. Condo governance is a heterogeneous and historical configuration rather than a self-evident and fixed offspring (in some accounts) of totalizing neoliberalism. Certainly some relevant processes resonate with neoliberalism, especially commodification, but others and the knowledges they entail (such as juridification, securitization, and "police" logic) predate, fail to fully befit, or are only contingently related to this concept as it is deployed in urban and socio-legal studies. It may be that neoliberalism is "variegated" (Peck and Tickell 2002, 387), but it may also be that other urban logics, such as "police," lie "between brightly coloured neoliberal spots in cities" (see Lippert 2014, 52). It may be that calling condoization and condo governance "neoliberal" is ultimately unhelpful and perhaps even a "hindrance" (O'Malley 2017, v) to fully rendering intelligible the new urban imaginary that now surely includes these phenomena.

Thus, the foregoing chapters are relevant to urban studies in that they show the complexity of residential housing as a form of urban governance. Much of what is documented, such as policing nuisances and physical security provision, is not unique to condo governance. The identified processes and knowledges are relevant to other forms of residential housing governance. However, they are likely configured differently, including with some unique elements, and this, too, ought to be the subject of future urban studies research. Indeed, another implication for urban studies of seeing condoization as multiple processes and agents loosely assembled is to begin to doubt that the invocation of broad terms like "gentrification" and "development" can fully elucidate the complex urban governance arrangements in which the condo is playing a more significant role.[4] The growth of condo investment leads to conflict that is not well captured by "gentrification" but that nonetheless occurs *within* condo governance in buildings rather than only across urban neighbourhoods. The critical political economist Mike Davis is correct when he writes that "we are dealing with a fundamental reorganization of metropolitan space, involving a drastic diminution of the intersections of the lives of the rich and the poor, which transcends traditional social segregation and urban fragmentation" (Davis 2007, 119). But in Toronto, New York, and undoubtedly other cities, this transcendence is not merely about walling off or gating urban enclaves to reflect the growing divide in cities; the condo is currently assembled in ways that enable this to happen *inside* residential, vertically arranged urban spaces. In condo conflicts, resident owners from the dwindling middle class seeking long-term community and building integrity are pitted against non-resident investors (who may never set foot in condo buildings and who seek low maintenance fees and a better aesthetic for profitable unit flips), developers typically armed with high-priced legal knowledge, and lower-income renters with nowhere else to live but whose presence investors demand.

It should be noted, too, that "gentrification" frequently entails condoization but the reverse is not necessarily true. It is not that "neoliberalism," "development," and "gentrification" are concepts that have somehow incorrectly been assigned to the condo. They certainly capture aspects of condoization in cities in relation to developers, statutory law, and related policies as well as their exclusionary effects. And this book is ideally seen as complementing rather than replacing the insightful work that embraces these concepts (e.g., Kern 2010b; Rosen and Walks 2015a). But these and related concepts tend to omit and/or fail to lend much insight into other vital and various exercises of power – at the lawyer-run AGM of owners, in the questions asked of renters by concierges at the tower's entrance, in unequal reactions to noise nuisance late at night, in the elevator on the way to the eighteenth floor as the board member enters, and/or at legislative hearings dominated by commercial agents. Such concepts do not fully anticipate the range of constituents, contingencies, and complexities of condoization; how the condo is brought into being; or how condo governance works in relation to common, individual, and even interstitial spaces. This matters partially because the condo form and its varied governing agents and subjects have inserted themselves into urban imaginaries the world over, not only in Toronto and New York but also in cities of Europe, Central and South America, Asia, and so on. Condoization is now a global, expanding phenomenon. But it matters too because it would seem we must first come to terms with condoization and the untold knowledges bearing down on, permitting the governance of, and making the condo possible before we can effectively resist, improve, reorganize along community lines, or replace this fast-growing, complex form of urban governance in cities. And there is little sign the condo's growth will soon subside. Instead, condoization keeps rolling, moving over, into, and through urban spaces and citizens' rights to the city the world over, assembling myriad agents, ways of knowing, and elements along its way, with some deeply troubling results.

Notes

CHAPTER 1: INTRODUCTION

1 While the phrases "condoized building" or "condoized unit" would be more accurate than the term "condo" (as there is nothing inherent in a building or unit that makes it a condo), I use the latter to avoid the inelegance of the former.

2 Conversions continue and are themselves complex. For example, Gallaher (2016) has studied a government program designed to support renters' right to buy their unit and revealed the complex and variable consequences of condo conversion in Washington, DC.

3 "Condoization" should be distinguished from "condoification" (Lehrer and Wieditz 2009), which, in Toronto, refers to condo development as gentrification. No doubt condoization sometimes involves gentrification – though it can also create slums when condo buildings fail – and its use here is not a critique of this revealing work. Rather, it is intended to capture, as a summary term, processes and other elements comprising this vast, largely unexplored, ostensibly private realm.

4 In the US there was some federal anticipation of the property manager role since, in the 1960s, the FHA created a model of condo governance that encouraged hiring a professional manager, but this role appears limited (see also Chapter 3 regarding New York's first statute's mention of property managers). And, as Teaford (1969, 257–58) pointed out in the late 1960s, this encouragement was based primarily on the longer-standing market cooperative experience and was not necessary for condo buildings involving lower-income owners (where "community control" would suffice).

5 McKenzie uses the broader term "common interest development" (CID), which, in his account, includes the condo, as noted elsewhere in Chapter 1.

6 I sincerely thank one anonymous reviewer for identifying the need to make this point.

7 This analysis does not preoccupy itself with what is termed "policy relevance." Proceeding under that rubric often hides or implicitly derides theoretical deployment, engagement, and refinement. Those who place the importance of policy relevance above all else or otherwise dismiss the value of theory need only be reminded that no policy is bereft of theory: the former is always premised on the latter.

8 This avoids imposing yet another expert knowledge on condo governance – that of sociology.

9 This is not to suggest that many of the condo conversions that proliferated in US cities, especially beginning in the mid-1970s, and often forced renters to purchase units or to be displaced (and that these renters and later US legislators resisted)

had a community ideal in mind. Yet, arguably, even with these conversions the promise of residential community remained a possibility.

10 This is not to suggest that broader categories into which condoized and cooperative arrangements fall cannot usefully describe broader processes pertaining to urban governance; it depends on why these elements are being studied.

11 An otherwise thorough historical account of condo development in the US (Lasner 2012) similarly lacks attention to governance.

12 Rather than concern ourselves with reasons that such a marriage is unseemly or cannot last, to the extent that these accounts are associated with political economy and governmentality, inspired at some level by the social thought of Marx and Foucault, respectively, for now they should be permitted to at least "get in bed together" (Hunt 2004; see also Brady and Lippert 2016).

13 Although there is no clear division, one difference between the sociology of governance and "governmentality" studies is that the former embraces more traditional sociological methods (such as interviews with agents) (e.g., Lippert 2006) and more closely considers actual practices, or "the real," beyond the discursive realm (Lippert and Stenson 2010).

14 Drawing from this understanding, condo *governance* is indistinguishable from condo *life* or *conduct* (see Hunt and Wickham 1994). As well, it is presumed that the condo, assembled from various elements on an ongoing basis, does not exist separately from its governance; in this special sense the condo and condo governance are also synonymous.

15 In surveillance studies assemblage similarly entails "rhizomatic" forms of surveillance analogous to weeds growing up in cracks and fissures (Haggerty and Ericson 2000) rather than reflecting centralized growth. Despite attention in surveillance studies to surveillant assemblages specifically (Ericson 2007; Haggerty and Ericson 2000; Lippert and Wilkinson 2010; Wilkinson and Lippert 2011; Lyon 2007; Lippert 2009), it is assumed here that these are largely interchangeable with or operate within governance assemblages.

16 Neoliberalism is used to refer not only to a rationality in Foucauldian influenced governmentality literature, as it is here, but also as an ideology in critical political economy. The differences have undergone much discussion (e.g., Larner 2000), and sometimes these two understandings overlap in urban studies (see Kern 2010a; Brash 2011) and other work (see Brady and Lippert 2016).

17 It was particularly difficult to secure interviews in New York despite much effort and expense. Early in the study it became clear that, given the funds and time available, a systematic comparison of condo governance in the two cities and corresponding jurisdictions was impossible.

18 There were no similar data available for New York condo buildings, but it is likely they have followed a similar pattern.

19 Additionally, commercial condo arrangements without a residential component are emerging in Toronto and New York. I focus only on residential condo governance.

CHAPTER 2: CONDO OWNERS AND BOARDS

1 The power relationships within condo high-rises produce specific kinds of governed subjects, including the condo renter.
2 Walks (2014, 33), who has closely studied the socio-spatial distribution of this process in Toronto, defines financialization as "the growing importance and influence of finance within an economy."
3 Norbert Elias similarly describes "othering" by elaborating upon established families and outsiders in a given neighbourhood (see Elias and Scotson 1994).
4 These Canadians often reside in "time-shares," the product of a legal arrangement that adds a temporal dimension to ownership and that is far more prevalent in the US than in Canada. Time-shares are ripe for further study.
5 Recently there have been efforts in Toronto and Vancouver to restrict foreign investment in urban housing, including condo units, through several legal means.
6 Harris and Gilewicz (2015) discuss an example of resident owners battling non-resident owners over dissolution, which they argue reflects differing versions of property, the former of which includes an understanding of condo property as a home or residence as it is discussed in this book.
7 See also Harris and Gilewicz (2015) for a discussion of competing understandings of condo property.
8 Connecticut similarly introduced legislation for an ombudsman office to deal with condo disputes (Prevost 2011).

CHAPTER 3: ASSEMBLING THE CONDO

1 There are other relevant agencies that are selling expert knowledge for condo governance purposes (McKenzie 2011, 20) thanks to legislative reforms that demand more surveillance of boards, including engineering (reserve fund studies) and accounting (performance audits) firms. Condo governance has become increasingly dependent upon these non-legal expert knowledges mandated through reforms to deal with building envelopes (e.g., Canada Mortgage and Housing Corporation 2003) and also, in Ontario, on impending reserve fund disasters that threaten to take the bloom off the condo rose. These reflect the fact that at least some owners and other interested agents are experiencing a growing lack of trust in boards to manage condo complexes. This is consistent with greater reliance on expert knowledge, a development that mirrors shifts in other governmental realms and institutions where, for example, the audit has become a choice means of governance (see Rose 1999).
2 Similar situations emerge in condo conversions that are more prevalent in New York.
3 A special assessment is a governmental tool that assesses each unit owner a (usually) large sum beyond regular fees to fund major repairs or purchases of roofs, elevators, boilers, or other costly "common elements."

4 Each tower had one board and two members from each board on a "shared facilities board" that governs expenditures of co-owned facilities.

5 Emphasis added, http://www.concordadex.com, site discontinued.

6 McKenzie (2011, 14) indicates that, in "many states," property managers are not required to have licences. They are regulated in at least some North American jurisdictions, however, such as British Columbia. Regulation is often limited to licensing and/or is influenced by the industry itself. For example, in British Columbia regulation is provided by the private Real Estate Council of BC, a private industry association rather than a government agency, which is responsible for the "licencing, education and discipline" of managers (British Columbia 2017).

7 Additionally, in the Toronto condo context during the late 2010s there emerged condo governance consulting firms such as "condohive" (http://www.condohive.ca/) and "condo facts" (https://www.condofacts.ca), which, for a fee, produce and transfer knowledge via research and experience to boards and owners to solve specific governance problems.

8 Recent emergence of websites like www.condos.ca, hosted by real estate firms or associations that provide detailed information about specific condo buildings, is also a source of this real estate knowledge, which will not only permit owners to make purchasing decisions but also allow boards and other owners to compare property values with similar condo buildings to inform governance decisions about their buildings (e.g., whether to upgrade amenities, whether aesthetic improvements might increase value, and whether property management fees are in line with those for buildings of similar size and quality).

9 For example, the Condominium Management and Administration Certificate Program at Humber College in Toronto. See http://www.humber.ca/education-training-solutions/condominium-management-and-administration-certificate.

10 This is not to suggest that specific lawyers or firms, in providing, for example, condo boards with legal advice regarding how to deal with a "hoarder" in their condo building purposely and systematically withhold information necessary to dealing with that resident so as to reduce liability. But it *is* to suggest that, across the condo world, numerous board decisions cannot possibly be informed in this manner without bankrupting many condo corporations due to legal fees, and that these boards are thus left uninformed or only partially informed by such knowledge.

11 See https://www.condonow.com/picasso-on-richmond/Features-Finishes.

12 See http://milannyc.com.

13 Where this mutually reinforcing convergence occurs, there is a sense in which agents are subjects, but for convenience I refer to them here as agents.

CHAPTER 4: GOVERNING CONDO RENTERS

1 Residents of condo buildings also become divided into resident owners and renters when living in the same unit (typically in townhouses with basements rather than high-rise units).

CHAPTER 5: CONDO GOVERNANCE, LEGAL KNOWLEDGES, AND SURVEILLANCE

1 This increasing reliance on such commodities in this form of housing, coupled with the condo form itself becoming something to be invested in, purchased, and consumed rather than a community in which to live, also serves as a reminder of a point made in Chapter 4, which is that residents' conduct is shaped not only by surveillance and law but also by informal social interactions that yield what governmentality theorist Nikolas Rose (1999, 166) describes as "sanctioned consumption and responsible choice, through the shaping of a lifestyle according to the grammars of living that are widely disseminated" (see also Flint 2003).

2 This requirement is less relevant to New York condo buildings since the New York State condo statute has not been similarly amended. However, for New York City condo corporations the city introduced a reserve fund requirement for all condo conversions via Local Law 70 "Reserve-Fund Law" (passed in October 1982 [Daniels 1983]), and following the 2008 financial crisis the main US federal lender Freddie Mac, operated by the FHA, introduced requirements for a 10 percent reserve fund to approve mortgages to owners through banks (Browning 2011). These requirements can initiate reserve fund studies of New York condo buildings in conjunction with approvals. For example, for Freddie Mac's guidelines, "if a [condo board's] budget does not meet these requirements, the lender can request a reserves study to gauge the building's financial stability" (Browning 2011). Requirements would be relevant to every potential condo developer or condo unit buyer in New York City.

3 Similar requirements are in place in other Canadian jurisdictions. For example, after a major review, a requirement for such studies was recently added to Manitoba's condo statute (see Hildebrand 2013, 13).

4 See, for example, *David Hyde and Associates*, http://www.davidhyde.ca/admin/pdf/213.pdf.

5 Referring to Florida's increasingly detailed condo statute, Nelson (2005, 44) quotes one critic who claims it reached the "zenith of legislative micromanagement."

CHAPTER 7: UPS AND DOWNS OF URBAN GOVERNANCE

1 See Strebel (2011) on a modernist public housing high-rise in the UK as well as Flint (2013) on vertical police patrols and tenant committee surveillance of elevator entrances in New York City public housing developments.

2 This is undoubtedly partially due to security arrangements that developers sell with condo units, including security guards (or "concierges") at entrances, thus making these complexes the urban equivalent of suburban "gated communities." The irony is that much of the illegal activity occurring in condo buildings probably has more to do with board, property management, and other service provider practices than with what occurs in elevators and other common spaces (see Lippert, Treffers, and Bud 2017).

3 Elevators must also comply with the Canadian Standard Association's B44 Safety Code for Elevators and Other Lifting Devices.
4 The argument is not that the elevator is *necessarily* a means of oppression but, rather, that it is a means of governance in the Foucauldian sense. Condo governance can become oppressive, but this is not being asserted about the condo buildings studied. Nor does a lack of oppression negate the possibility of resistance.
5 The exception is perhaps first-floor residents, unless some amenities are located on higher floors or the first level consists only of a lobby and common spaces (a spatial arrangement common in the buildings studied).
6 Service elevators in Toronto's condo high-rises are rare but would overcome this need for property managers and board members if they had access. Nor are elevator operators (who potentially complicate these relations) used in Toronto's condo buildings, unlike in many typically older condo buildings in New York. But in the latter arrangements too, as Bearman's (2005, 111) study of New York "doormen" notes in passing, "joint trips in the elevator force sociability."

CHAPTER 8: CONCLUSION

1 Arguably the condo statute is a greater source of such legal knowledge in Ontario than in New York State, considering, for example, New York City's Reserve-Fund Law.
2 Permitting commercial firms to increasingly influence condo governance at owners' (and ultimately renters') expense may also augment urban revitalization by growing the urban service economy. Though almost never explicitly stated, not only have condo buildings grown dramatically in number and size in recent decades but so have the number of what might be termed condo production *workers* (custodians, security personnel, auditors, engineers, lawyers, property managers, architects, real estate agents, developers, marketers, insurance brokers and salespeople, construction workers, etc.) constructing and servicing these spaces and arrangements in Toronto and New York in numerous ways, with the condo being their continuously assembled product.
3 Unfortunately, when one looks "high and low" in neo-Marxist work, one still finds almost no accounts of those who experience "police" as it shapes their mundane lives that are derived from empirical research.
4 Rosen and Walks (2015a, 2015b) might similarly suggest that "police" and assemblages are vital aspects of what they call "condo-ism." Thus, not all theoretically engaged previous work about the condo implies that these elements can be reduced to a unitary urban neoliberalism.

References

Aaron, B. 2012. Smoking issues plague condo corporations. *Toronto Star*, July 20. https://www.thestar.com/life/homes/2012/07/20/smoking_issues_plague_condo_corporations.html.

ACMO (Association of Condominium Managers of Ontario). 2002. Insurance case law revisited. http://acmo.org/.

Adams, J. 1987. *Housing America in the 1980s*. New York: Russell Sage Foundation.

Alliance of Condo and Co-op Owners (ACCO). 2016. Mission and methods. http://condocoopowners.org/home/mission-and-methods.

Alter, L. 2015. Should so-called "poor doors" have been banned in New York City? *Treehugger*, June 30. https://www.treehugger.com/urban-design/should-so-called-poor-doors-have-been-banned-new-york-city.html.

Arabian, A. 1995. "Condos, cats, and CC&Rs: Invasion of the castle common." *Pepperdine Law Review* 2 (1): 1–30. http://digitalcommons.pepperdine.edu/plr/vol23/iss1/1/.

Atkinson, R. 2004. "The evidence on the impact of gentrification: New lessons for the urban renaissance?" *European Journal of Housing Policy* 4 (1): 107–31. https://doi.org/10.1080/1461671042000215479.

Atkinson, R., and S. Blandy. 2013. *Gated Communities: International Perspectives*. New York: Routledge.

Atkinson, R., and S. Flint. 2004. "Fortress UK? Gated communities, the spatial revolt of the elites and time-space trajectories of segregation." *Housing Studies* 19 (6): 875–92. https://doi.org/10.1080/0267303042000293982.

Aulakh, R. 2012. Fraud forces condo owners to pay thousands. *Toronto Star*, September 3. https://www.thestar.com/news/crime/2012/09/03/fraud_forces_condo_owners_to_pay_thousands.html.

Baker, T. 2010. "Insurance in socio-legal research." *Annual Review of Law and Social Science* 6 (1): 433–47. https://doi.org/10.1146/annurev-lawsocsci-102209-152839.

Bardai, N. 2003. "Transient tenancies in condominium corporations." *Condo Law* 17: 215–6.

Barry, A., T. Osborne, and N. Rose. 1996. *Foucault and Political Reason: Liberalism, Neo-Liberalism, and Rationalities of Government*. Chicago: University of Chicago Press.

Barton, S., and C. Silverman. 1994. *Common Interest Communities: Private Governments and Public Interest*. Berkeley: Institute of Governmental Studies Press.

Bearman, P. 2005. *Doormen*. Chicago: University of Chicago Press. https://doi.org/10.7208/chicago/9780226039718.001.0001.

Beazley, D. 2013. Condo disputes: Keeping the lawyers out. Canadian Bar Association, *National: The Power of Perspectives*, November/December. http://www.nationalmagazine.ca/Articles/November/Condo-disputes-Keeping-the-lawyers-out.aspx.

Benner, K. 2016. AirBnB ends fight with New York City over fines. *New York Times,* December 3. https://www.nytimes.com/2016/12/03/technology/airbnb-ends-fight-with-new-york-city-over-fines.html.

Benson, L. 2012. About Utah: Father of modern condominiums will never live in one. *Deseret News,* November 15. https://www.deseretnews.com/article/765615708/Father-of-Modern-Condominiums-will-never-live-in-one.html?pg=all.

Berger, C. 1963. "Condominium: Shelter on a statutory foundation." *Columbia Law Review* 63 (6): 987–1026. https://doi.org/10.2307/1120421.

Bernard, A. 2014. *Uplifted: A Cultural History of the Elevator.* New York: New York University Press.

Blandy, S. 2008. "Secession or cohesion: Exploring the impact of gated communities." In *Community cohesion in crisis? New Dimensions of Diversity and Difference,* 239–58, ed. J. Flint and D. Robinson. Bristol: Policy Press. https://doi.org/10.1332/policypress/9781847420244.003.0013.

Blandy, S., J. Dixon, and A. Dupuis. 2006. "Theorising power relationships in multi-owned residential developments: Unpacking the bundle of rights." *Urban Studies (Edinburgh, Scotland)* 43 (13): 2365–83. https://doi.org/10.1080/00420980600970656.

Blandy, S., and D. Lister. 2005. "Gated communities: (Neo-)gating community development?" *Housing Studies* 20 (2): 287–301. https://doi.org/10.1080/026730303042000331781.

Blomley, N. 2004. *Unsettling the City: Urban Land and the Politics of Property.* New York: Routledge.

–. 2005. "Remember property?" *Progress in Human Geography* 29 (1): 125–27.

–. 2011. *Rights of Passage: Sidewalks and the Regulation of Public Flow.* London: Glasshouse.

Bradamore, G., and D. Spencer. 2017. Much a-doo about dogs in condos: DNA registration programs match pet waste to offending pooches. *Condo Business,* May 25. https://www.reminetwork.com/articles/dogs-in-condos/.

Brady, M., and R. Lippert. 2016. *Governing Practices: Neo-liberalism, Governmentality, and the Ethnographic Imaginary.* Toronto: University of Toronto Press.

Brash, J. 2011. *Bloomberg's New York: Class and Governance in the Luxury City.* Athens: University of Georgia Press.

Brenner, N., J. Peck, and N. Theodore. 2009. "Variegated neoliberalizations: Geographies, modalities, pathways." *Global Networks* 10 (2): 188–222.

Brenner, N., and N. Theodore. 2002. "Cities and geographies of 'actually existing neoliberalism.'" *Antipode* 34 (3): 349–79. https://doi.org/10.1111/1467-8330.00246.

British Columbia. 2017. Strata property manager licensing. https://www2.gov.bc.ca/gov/content/housing-tenancy/strata-housing/operating-a-strata/roles-and-responsibilities/strata-property-managers/licensing.

Brown, J. 2010. Condo culture. *Canadian Security Magazine,* September 7. https://www.canadiansecuritymag.com/Guarding/News/Condo-culture.html.

Brown, S. 2006. "The criminology of hybrids: Rethinking crime and law in technosocial networks." *Theoretical Criminology* 10 (2): 223–44. https://doi.org/10.1177/1362480606063140.

Browning, L. 2011. Stricter lending guidelines for condos. *New York Times*, January 13. https://www.nytimes.com/2011/01/16/realestate/mortgages/16mort.html?_r=1ands cp%3D3andsq%3Dcondominium+reservesandst%3Dnyt.
Buckley, R. 1981. *The Law of Nuisance*. London: Butterworth.
Bull, S. 2012. Two more drug labs found in Scarborough high-rise. *CBC News Toronto*, July 4. http://www.cbc.ca/news/canada/toronto/2-more-drug-labs-found-in-scarborough-highrise-1.1154201.
CAFCOR (Canadian Alliance for Condominium Owners Rights). 2016. https://ontario.cafcor.org/.
Canada Mortgage and Housing Corporation. 2003. *Re-sale of Leaky Condos: Did the Buyer Know?* Technical Series 03–108. Ottawa: Canada Mortgage and Housing Corporation.
–. 2007. *Housing Now: Greater Toronto Area*. Ottawa: Canada Mortgage and Housing Corporation.
–. 2012. *2006 Census Housing Series. Issue 16. A Profile of Condominiums in Canada, 1981–2006*. Ottawa: Canadian Mortgage and Housing Corporation.
–. 2017. *Condominium Buyers' Guide*. Ottawa: Canada Mortgage and Housing Corporation. https://www.cmhc-schl.gc.ca/.
Canada's Public Policy Forum. 2013a. *The Ontario Resident's Panel to Review the Condominium Act: An Initiative in Support of the Ontario Ministry of Consumer Services' Condominium Act Review*. Final Report, January. https://files.ontario.ca/residents_panel_report_en.pdf.
–. 2013b. *Ontario's Condominium Act Review: Stage One Findings Report*, January. https://files.ontario.ca/ontario_condo_act_review_stage_1_en.pdf.
–. 2013c. *Growing Up: Ontario's Condominium Communities Enter a New Era – Condominium Act Review Stage Two Solutions Report*, September. https://files.ontario.ca/condo_act_stage_2_solutions_report_en.pdf.
Cashin, S. 2001. "Privatized communities and the 'secession of the successful': Democracy and fairness beyond the gate." *Fordham Urban Law Journal* 28: 1675–92.
Catungal, J., and D. Leslie. 2009. "Placing power in the creative city: Governmentalities and subjectivities in liberty village, Toronto." *Environment and Planning A* 41 (11): 2576–94. https://doi.org/10.1068/a41245.
CBC (Canadian Broadcasting Corporation). 2014. 130 Highrise building projects in Toronto lead North America. *CBC News*, January 21. http://www.cbc.ca/news/business/130-highrise-building-projects-in-toronto-lead-north-america-1.2504776.
–. 2016. Hotel worker killed in elevator accident suffered serious head injuries. *CBC News*, November 16. http://www.cbc.ca/news/canada/toronto/elevator-accident-hotel-fatal-1.3853464.
Centre Court Developments. 2014. http://www.centrecourt.com.
Chambers, R. 2006. "Pushed out: A call for inclusionary housing programs in local condominium conversion legislation." *California Western Law Review* 42 (2): 355–76.
Chen, L., and M. Kielsgard. 2014. "Evolving property rights in China: Patterns and dynamics of condominium governance." *Chinese Journal of Comparative Law* 2 (1): 21–42. https://doi.org/10.1093/cjcl/cxt016.

Chen, S., and C. Webster. 2005. "Homeowners associations, collective action and the costs of private governance." *Housing Studies* 20 (2): 205–20. https://doi.org/10.1080/0267303042000331736.

Christensen, K., and D. Levinson. 2003. *Encyclopedia of Community: From the Village to the Virtual World*. Thousand Oaks: Sage. https://doi.org/10.4135/9781412952583.

COA (Condo Owners Association). 2016. http://www.coaontario.com/.

Collier, S. 2012. "Neoliberalism as big leviathan, or ...?: A response to Wacquant and Hilgers." *Social Anthropology* 20 (2): 186–95. https://doi.org/10.1111/j.1469-8676.2012.00195.x.

Condo Briefs. 2012. Anonymous written submissions to Ontario's condominium act review: Scarborough Public Information Session.

Condoplex. n.d. *Workstation Interface*. http://www.condoplex.net/products/framep.php.

Condo Control Central. 2017. About Us. https://www.condocontrolcentral.com/about-us/.

Cooper, D. 2002. "Far beyond 'the early morning crowing of a farmyard cock': Revisiting the place of nuisance within political and legal discourse." *Social and Legal Studies* 11 (1): 5–35. https://doi.org/10.1177/096466390201100175 2.

CNYC (Council of New York Cooperatives and Condominiums). 2016. "About cnyc." http://www.cnyc.coop/about.htm.

Cowan, D., and M. McDermont. 2006. *Regulating Social Housing: Governing Decline*. Abingdon: Routledge Cavendish.

Daily Mail. 2016. Revealed: The shocking disparity between the "haves" and "have nots" inside luxury Manhattan building with a "Poor Door." January 17. http://www.dailymail.co.uk/news/article-3404014/Luxury-Manhattan-building-poor-door-separating-low-income-tenants-opens.html.

Daniels, L. 1983. About real estate: City's reserve-fund law is challenged. *New York Times*, March 18. https://www.nytimes.com/1983/03/18/business/about-real-estate-city-s-reserve-fund-law-is-challenged.html.

Davies, S. 1969. They like life in a condominium. *Toronto Daily Star*, 16 August, 3.

Davis, M. 2007. *Planet of Slums*. New York: Verso.

Deacon, J. 2012. Noise and nuisance: Balancing rights to quiet enjoyment with living in the close proximity of condo unit configuration. *Condominium Manager Magazine*, Spring. https://www.acmo.org/wp-content/uploads/CMMagazineArchives/CM%E2%80%8BSpr%E2%80%8Bing%E2%80%8B%E2%80%8B20%E2%80%8B1%E2%80%8B2%E2%80%8B%E2%80%8B%E2%80%8B/L_CMSP12.pdf.

Dean, M. 1996. "Putting the technical into government." *History of the Human Sciences* 9 (3): 47–68. https://doi.org/10.1177/095269519600900303.

–. 2010. *Governmentality: Power and Rule in Modern Society*. 2nd ed. London: Sage.

Defert, D. 1991. "'Popular life' and insurance technology." In *The Foucault Effect: Studies in Governmentality*, 211–33, ed. G. Burchell, C. Gordon, and P. Miller. London: Harvester Wheatsheaf.

Dowling, R., R. Atkinson, and P. McGuirk. 2010. "Privatism, privatisation and social distinction in master-planned residential estates." *Urban Policy and Research* 28 (4): 391–410. https://doi.org/10.1080/08111146.2010.508870.

Dubber, M., and M. Valverde, eds. 2006. *Police and the Liberal State*. Stanford, MA: Stanford Law Book.

Easthope, H., J. Warnken, C. Sherry, E. Coliacetto, D. Dredge, C. Guilding, N. Johnston, D. Lamminmaki, and S. Reid. 2014. "How property title impacts urban consolidation: A life cycle examination of multi-title developments." *Urban Policy and Research* 32 (3): 289–304. https://doi.org/10.1080/08111146.2014.899210.

Eilbott, P. 1985. "Condominium rentals and the supply of rental housing." *Urban Affairs Review* 20 (3): 389–99. https://doi.org/10.1177/004208168502000308.

Elberg, A. 2001. "Remedies for common interest development rule violations." *Columbia Law Review* 101 (8): 1958–97. https://doi.org/10.2307/1123711.

Elevator Source. 2015. Elevator maintenance contracts, 13 February. http://www.elevatorsource.com/elevator-contracts.htm#legal.

Elias, N., and J. Scotson. 1994. *The Established and the Outsiders a Sociological Enquiry into Community Problems*. 2nd ed. London: Sage. https://doi.org/10.4135/9781446222126.

Ennis, T. 1965. Already popular condominium expected to gain further here. *New York Times*. December 26, W1.

Ericson, R. 2007. *Crime in an Insecure World*. Malden, MA: Polity.

Ericson, R., A. Doyle, and D. Barry. 2003. *Insurance as Governance*. Toronto: University of Toronto Press.

Ericson, R., and K. Haggerty. 1997. *Policing the Risk Society*. Toronto: University of Toronto Press.

Farias, I. 2010. Introduction: Decentring the object of urban studies. In I. Farias and T. Bender, eds., *Urban Assemblages: How Actor Network Theory Changes Urban Studies*, 1–24. New York: Routledge.

Farias, I., and T. Bender, eds. 2010. *Urban Assemblages: How Actor Network Theory Changes Urban Studies*. New York: Routledge.

Farrell, A. 1966. Condominium: A new idea in housing. *Toronto Star*, 29 July, 7.

Ferrer, A., and K. Stecher. 1967. *Law of Condominium: With Forms, Statutes and Regulation*, vol. 1. Oxford: Equity Publishing.

Fine, D. 1980. "The condominium conversion problem: Causes and solutions." *Duke Law Journal* 1980 (2): 306–35. https://doi.org/10.2307/1372272.

Fleming, D. 2011. What you need to know about condo fees. *The Grid*, 30 September. http://www.thegridto.com/index.html.

Flint, J. 2003. "Housing and ethopolitics: Constructing identities of active consumption and responsible community." *Economy and Society* 32 (4): 611–29. https://doi.org/10.1080/0308514032000107628.

–. 2013. "Policing public housing: New York and British cities." *Safer Communities* 12 (1): 13–23. https://doi.org/10.1108/17578041311293107.

Flint, J., and H. Pawson. 2009. "Social landlords and the regulation of conduct in urban spaces in the United Kingdom." *Criminology and Criminal Justice* 9 (4): 415–35. https://doi.org/10.1177/1748895809343408.

Florida, R. 2014. Toronto is a divided city. Here's how to repair it. *Toronto Star*, 29 November. https://www.thestar.com/opinion/commentary/2014/11/29/toronto_is_a_divided_city_hers_how_to_repair_it.html.

Fopp, R. 2002. "Increasing the potential for gaze, surveillance and normalisation: The transformation of an Australian policy for people who are homeless." *Surveillance and Society* 1 (1): 48–65.

Foucault, M. 1977. *Discipline and Punish: The Birth of the Prison*. New York: Vintage.

–. 1980. "The eye of power." In *Power/Knowledge: Selected Interviews and Other Writings, 1972–1977*, 146–65, ed. C. Gordon. New York: Pantheon Books.

–. 1982. "The subject and power." In *Michel Foucault: Beyond Structuralism and Hermeneutics*, 208–26, ed. H. Dreyfus and P. Rabinow. New York: Harvester Wheatsheaf.

–. 1991. "Governmentality." In G. Burchell, C. Gordon, and P. Miller, eds., *The Foucault Effect: Studies in Governmentality*, 87–104. Chicago: University of Chicago Press.

–. 1994. *The Birth of the Clinic: An Archaeology of Medical Perception*. New York: Vintage Books.

–. 2007. *Security, Territory, Population: Lecture at the Collège de France, 1977–1978*. New York: Palgrave MacMillan.

Gallaher, C. 2016. *The Politics of Staying Put: Condo Conversion and Tenant Right-to-Buy in Washington, DC*. Philadelphia: Temple University Press.

Gallun, A. 2006. "Bloodbath" ended first condomania. *Crain's Chicago Business*, June 17. https://home.chicagobusiness.com/clickshare/authenticateUserSubscription.do?CSProduct=crainschicago-metered&CSAuthReq=1:373679435535494:AID:FB390E1FFF9F3612F98BFBDC0980F9B4&AID=/20060617/ISSUE03/100026014&title=%27Bloodbath%27%20ended%20first%20condomania&CSTargetURL=http://www.chicagobusiness.com/article/20060617/ISSUE03/100026014/bloodbath-ended-first-condomania.

Gardiner, R. 2001. *The Condominium Act, 1998: A Practical Guide*. Aurora: Canada Law Book.

Geberer, R. 2011. Understanding local law 11: Keeping facades safe. *The Cooperator*, March. https://cooperator.com/articles/2229/1/Understanding-Local-Law-11/Page1.html.

Gillis, W. 2010. Condo employees arrested after police discover $2.6 million grow-op. *Toronto Star*, November 10, https://www.thestar.com/news/crime/2010/11/10/condo_employees_arrested_after_police_discover_26_million_growop.html.

Glaze, G. 2013. "The economic and political organization of private neighbourhoods." In R. Atkinson and S. Blandy, eds., *Gated Communities: International Perspectives*, 34–46. New York: Routledge.

GMA (Gardiner Miller Arnold LLP). 2015a. *GMA's By-Law Chart*. https://www.gmalaw.ca/wp-content/uploads/GMA_Condo_Documents_Packages.pdf.

–. 2015b. *GMA's Condo Document Packages*. https://www.gmalaw.ca/wp-content/uploads/GMA_Condo_Documents_Packages.pdf.

–. 2017. *The Ontario Condo Law Blog*. https://www.ontariocondolaw.com/services/.

Graham, S., and L. Hewitt. 2012. "Getting off the ground: On the politics of urban verticality." *Progress in Human Geography* 37 (1): 72–92. https://doi.org/10.1177/0309132512443147.

Grant, J. 2005. "Planned responses to gated communities in Canada." *Housing Studies* 20 (2): 273–85. https://doi.org/10.1080/026730303042000331772.

Gray, J. 2016. Condo concierges face off against tourists, partiers in Airbnb war. *Globe and Mail* November 4. https://www.theglobeandmail.com/news/toronto/condo-concierges-face-off-against-tourists-partiers-in-airbnb-war/article32683576/.

Gray, L. 2000. *From Ascending Rooms to Express Elevators: A History of the Passenger Elevator in the 19th Century*. Mobile, AL: Elevator World Inc.

Hacking, I. 1991. "How should we do the history of statistics." In *The Foucault Effect: Studies in Governmentality*, 181–96, ed. G. Burchell, C. Gordon, and P. Miller. London: Harvester Wheatsheaf.

Hackworth, J. 2008. "The durability of roll-out neo-liberalism under centre-left governance: The case of Ontario's social housing sector." *Studies in Political Economy* 81 (1): 7–26. https://doi.org/10.1080/19187033.2008.11675071.

Haggerty, K. 2001. *Making Crime Count*. Toronto: Toronto University Press. https://doi.org/10.3138/9781442676893.

Haggerty, K., and R. Ericson. 2000. "The surveillant assemblage." *British Journal of Sociology* 51 (4): 605–22. https://doi.org/10.1080/00071310020015280.

Hanes, T. 2008. Happy 40th. *Toronto Star*, February 23. https://www.thestar.com/news/2008/02/23/happy_40th.html.

Hardin, G. 1968. "The tragedy of the commons." *Science* 13 (162): 1243–08.

Harris, D. 2011. "Condominium and the city: the rise of property in Vancouver." *Law and Social Inquiry* 36 (3): 694–726. https://doi.org/10.1111/j.1747-4469.2011.01247.x.

Harris, D., and N. Gilewicz. 2015. "Dissolving condominium, private takings, and the nature of property." In *Rethinking Expropriation Law II: Context, Criteria, and Consequences of Expropriation*, 263–97, ed. B. Hoops, E. Marais, H. Mostert, J. Sluysmans, and L. Verstappen. The Hague: Eleven International Publishing.

Hermer, J., and A. Hunt. 1996. "Official graffiti of the everyday." *Law and Society Review* 30 (3): 455–80. https://doi.org/10.2307/3054125.

Herskowitz, H., and M.F. Freedman. 2001. *Condominiums in Ontario: A Practical Analysis of the New Legislation*. Toronto: Law Society of Upper Canada.

Hildebrand, D. 2013. "Bill 40: The Condominium Act and Amendments Respecting Condominium Conversions." *Manitoba Law Journal* 35 (2): 1–19.

Hildebrandt, A. 2011. Victims claim condo fraud "destroyed" lives. *CBC News*, September 15. http://www.cbc.ca/news/canada/toronto/victims-claim-condo-fraud-destroyed-lives-1.1109906.

Hirschauer, S. 2005. "On doing being a stranger." *Journal for the Theory of Social Behaviour* 35 (1): 41–67. https://doi.org/10.1111/j.0021-8308.2005.00263.x.

Hitchcock, J. 1981. *The Luxury Condominium Market in Toronto*. Toronto: Centre for Urban and Community Studies, University of Toronto.

Huffington Post. 2014. "Poor doors" in Toronto? Controversial trend appears at new condo developments. *The Huffington Post Canada*, September 4. https://www.huffingtonpost.ca/2014/09/04/poor-doors-toronto-condo_n_5767226.html.

Hunt, A. 2003. "Risk and moralization in everyday life." In *Risk and Morality*, 165–92, ed. R. Ericson and A. Doyle. Toronto: University of Toronto Press.

–. 2004. "Getting Marx and Foucault into bed together!" *Journal of Law and Society* 31 (4): 592–609. https://doi.org/10.1111/j.1467-6478.2004.00305.x.

–. 2006. "Police and the regulation of traffic: Policing as a civilizing process?" In *The New Police Science: The Police Power in Domestic and International Governance*, 168–84, ed. M. Dubber and M. Valverde. Stanford, MA: Stanford University Press.

–. 2013. "Encounters with juridical assemblages: Reflections on Foucault, law and the juridical." In B. Golder, ed., *Re-reading Foucault: On Law, Power and Rights*, 64–84. New York: Routledge.

Hunt, A., and G. Wickham. 1994. *Foucault and Law: Toward a Sociology of Law as Governance*. Boulder, CO: Pluto Press.

Huong, L., and E. Sajor. 2010. "Privatization, democratic reforms and micro-governance change in a transition economy: Condominium homeowner associations in Ho Chi Minh City, Vietnam." *Cities (London, England)* 27 (1): 20–30. https://doi.org/10.1016/j.cities.2009.11.007.

Hyman, G. 2001. Clarifying rental rules. *Toronto Star*, 27 May, 9.

–. 2005a. Questions should have received written responses; verbal answers failed to lead to satisfaction; owners entitled to correspond with president. *Toronto Star*, 27 May, 15.

–. 2005b. Courts back rules setting minimum terms for leases. *Toronto Star*, 13 August, 2.

–. 2006. Condo law. *Toronto Star*, 11 March, 5.

Isin, E. 1998. "Governing Toronto without government: liberalism and neoliberalism." *Studies in Political Economy* 56 (1): 169–91. https://doi.org/10.1080/19187033.1998.11675296.

Jaglowitz, C. 2008. "New human rights regime now in effect." *Condo Alert* 1:2.

Kane, L., and A. Bosanac. 2012. Police discover two more drug labs in Scarborough condo. *Toronto Star*, July 4. https://www.thestar.com/news/gta/2012/07/04/police_discover_two_more_drug_labs_in_scarborough_condo.html.

Katawazi, M. 2017. City of Toronto proposes crackdown on Airbnb-style rentals. *Globe and Mail*, June 27. https://beta.theglobeandmail.com/news/toronto/city-of-toronto-proposes-crackdown-on-airbnb-style-rentals/article35283256/?ref=http://www.theglobeandmail.comand.

Keil, R. 2009. "The urban politics of roll-with-it neoliberalization." *City* 13 (2–3): 230–45. https://doi.org/10.1080/13604810902986848.

Kennedy, D. 1995. "Residential associations as state actors: regulating the impact of gated communities on non-members." *Yale Law Journal* 105 (3): 761–93. https://doi.org/10.2307/797199.

Kern, L. 2007. "Reshaping the boundaries of public and private life: Gender, condominium development, and the neoliberalization of urban living." *Urban Geography* 28 (7): 657–81. https://doi.org/10.2747/0272-3638.28.7.657.

–. 2010a. *Sex and the Revitalized City: Gender, Condominium Development, and Urban Citizenship*. Vancouver: UBC Press.

–. 2010b. “Selling the scary city: Gendering freedom, fear, and condominium development in the neoliberal city.” *Social and Cultural Geography* 11 (3): 209–30. https://doi.org/10.1080/14649361003637174.

Kim, M. 1998. “Involuntary sale: Banishing an owner from the condominium community.” *John Marshall Law Review* 31 (2): 429–42.

Klein, R. 1993. *Cigarettes Are Sublime*. Durham: Duke University Press.

–. 2000. “Smoke knows no boundaries: Legal strategies for environmental tobacco smoke incursions into the home within multi-unit residential dwellings.” *Tobacco Control* 9 (2): 201–05. https://doi.org/10.1136/tc.9.2.201.

Kress, C. 1995. “Beyond nahrstedt: Reviewing restrictions governing life in a property owner association.” *University of California Law Review* 42: 837–83.

Lampughnani, V., and L. Hartwig. 1994. *Lift, Escalator, Paternoster: A Cultural History of Vertical Transport*. New York: Ernst and Sohn.

Laporte, D. 2007. Peril lurks deep. *Toronto Star*, December 8, https://www.thestar.com/news/2007/12/08/peril_lurks_deep.html.

Larner, W. 2000. “Neoliberalism: Policy, ideology, governmentality.” *Studies in Political Economy* 63 (1): 5–25. https://doi.org/10.1080/19187033.2000.11675231.

Lash, D. 2017a. *Lash Condo Law's Practical Guide to Short Term Stays (Hoteling)*. http://www.lashcondolaw.com/wp-content/uploads/2015/09/Short-Term-Stays-Lash-Condo-Law.pdf.

–. 2017b. Our Tips, Tricks, Knowledge and Links. http://www.lashcondolaw.com/#Services.

Lasner, M. 2012. *High Life: Condo Living in the Suburban Century*. New Haven: Yale University Press.

Latour, B. 1993. *We Have Never Been Modern*. London: Harvester Wheatsheaf.

Lees, L., T. Slater, and E. Wyly. 2008. *Gentrification*. New York: Routledge.

Lehrer, U. 2008. “Urban renaissance and resistance in Toronto.” In *Whose Urban Renaissance? An International Comparison of Policy Drivers and Responses to Urban Regeneration Strategies*, 147–56, ed. L. Porter and K. Shaw. London: Routledge.

Lehrer, U., R. Keil, and S. Kipfer. 2010. “Re-urbanization in Toronto: Condominium boom and social housing revitalization.” *Planning Review* 46 (180): 81–90. https://doi.org/10.1080/02513625.2010.10557065.

Lehrer, U., and T. Wieditz. 2009. “Condominium development and gentrification.” *Canadian Journal of Urban Research and Policy* 18 (1): 82–103.

LePage, T. 2013. Condo-ology: A former front line condo manager's perspective. *The Enterprise-Bulletin*, July 5. http://condo-ology.net/wp-content/uploads/2015/05/July-5.pdf.

–. 2015. Oral submission to Ontario Legislative Standing Committee on Finance and Economic Affairs re Bill 106, an act to protect the Condominium Act, October 29. http://condo-ology.net/bill-106-tom-lepage-transcript-and-handout-for-oct-29-2015-standing-committee/.

Levi, R. 2009. “Gated communities in law's gaze.” *Law and Social Inquiry* 34 (3): 635–69. https://doi.org/10.1111/j.1747-4469.2009.01160.x.

Ley, D. 1996. *The New Middle Class and the Remaking of the Central City*. Oxford: Oxford University Press.

Li, T.M. 2007. "Practices of assemblage and community forest management." *Economy and Society* 36 (2): 263–93. https://doi.org/10.1080/03085140701254308.

Lin, G., X. Li, F. Yang, and F. Hu. 2015. "Strategizing urbanism in the era of neoliberalization: State power reshuffling, land development and municipal finance in urbanizing China." *Urban Studies (Edinburgh, Scotland)* 52 (11): 1962–82. https://doi.org/10.1177/0042098013513644 http://journals.sagepub.com/doi/pdf/10.1177/0042098013513644.

Lincoln, M. 1999. *The Condominium Self-Management Guide*. 2nd ed. Kitchener: Marilyn Lincoln.

Lippert, R. 2006. *Sanctuary, Sovereignty, Sacrifice: Canadian Sanctuary Incidents, Power and Law*. Vancouver: UBC Press.

–. 2007. "Urban revitalization, security and knowledge transfer: The case of broken windows and kiddie bars." *Canadian Journal of Law and Society* 22 (2): 29–53. https://doi.org/10.1017/S0829320100009340.

–. 2009. "Signs of the surveillant assemblage: Privacy regulation, urban CCTV, and governmentality." *Social and Legal Studies* 18 (4): 505–22. https://doi.org/10.1177/0964663909345096.

–. 2010. "Mundane and mutant devices of power: Business improvement districts and sanctuaries." *European Journal of Cultural Studies* 13 (4): 477–94. https://doi.org/10.1177/1367549410377155.

–. 2012. "'Clean and safe' passage: Business improvement districts, urban security modes, and knowledge brokers." *European Urban and Regional Studies* 19 (2): 167–80. https://doi.org/10.1177/0969776411420023.

–. 2014. "Neo-liberalism, police and the governance of little urban things." *Foucault Studies* 18: 49–65.

–. 2015. "Thinking about law and surveillance." *Surveillance and Society* 13 (2): 292.

Lippert, R., and M. Brady. 2016. "Governmentalities, the ethnographic imaginary, and beyond." In *Governing Practices: Neoliberalism, Governmentality and the Ethnographic Imaginary*, 269–74, ed. M. Brady and R. Lippert. Toronto: University of Toronto Press.

Lippert, R., and M. Pyykkönen. 2012. "Contesting family in Finnish and Canadian refugee and immigration policies." *Nordic Journal of Migration Research* 2 (1): 45–56. https://doi.org/10.2478/v10202-011-0026-9.

Lippert, R., and K. Stenson. 2010. "Advancing governmentality studies: Lessons from social constructionism." *Theoretical Criminology* 14 (4): 473–94. https://doi.org/10.1177/1362480610369328.

Lippert, R., S. Treffers, and T. Bud. 2017. Condo crimes and legal prospects for confronting the unusual suspects. In Austin Sarat, ed., *Studies in Law, Politics and Society*, 25–52. Bingley, UK: Emerald Publishing. https://doi.org/10.1108/S1059-433720170000072002.

Lippert, R., and K. Walby. 2013. How the world's cities are policed, regulated and securitized. In R. Lippert and K. Walby, eds., *Policing Cities: Urban Regulation and Securitization in a 21st Century World*, 1–7. London: Routledge.

Lippert, R., and K. Walby. 2014a. "Municipal corporate security, legal knowledges, and the urban problem space." *Law and Social Inquiry* 39 (3): 720–39. https://doi.org/10.1111/lsi.12042.

Lippert, R., and K. Walby. 2014b. "Marketization, knowledge work and visibility in "users-pay" policing in Canada." *British Journal of Criminology* 54 (2): 260–80. https://doi.org/10.1093/bjc/azt074.

Lippert, R., and B. Wilkinson. 2010. "Capturing crime, criminals and the public's imagination: Assembling Crime Stoppers and CCTV surveillance." *Crime, Media, Culture* 6 (2): 131–52. https://doi.org/10.1177/1741659010369950.

Lippert, R., and J. Williams. 2012. "Taking exception: The case of financial and urban governance." *Social and Legal Studies* 21 (1): 51–72. https://doi.org/10.1177/0964663911418720.

Lister, D. 2005. "Controlling letting arrangements? Landlords and surveillance in the private rented sector." *Surveillance and Society* 2 (4): 513–28.

Loeb, A. 2001. *The Condominium Act: A User's Manual*. Toronto: Carswell.

Low, S. 2003. *Behind the Gates: Life, Security, and the Pursuit of Happiness in Fortress America*. New York: Routledge.

–. 2013. "Securitization strategies: Gated communities and market-rate co-operatives in New York." In *Policing Cities: Urban Regulation and Securitization in a 21st Century World*, 222–30, ed. R. Lippert and K. Walby. London: Routledge.

Luymes, G. 2014. "Crazy condo squabbles clogging courts; not so suite life." *Province* 26 (May): A3.

Lyon, D. 2007. *Surveillance Studies: An Overview*. London: Polity.

Mah, J., and J. Hackworth. 2011. "Local politics and inclusionary housing in three large Canadian cities." *Canadian Journal of Urban Research* 20 (1): 57–80.

Martin, R. 2002. *Financialization of Daily Life*. Philadelphia: Temple University Press.

MATCO (Markham Association of Townhouse Condominium Owners). 2010. "Financial Data." Unpublished information prepared by the Markham Association of Townhome Condominium Owners for the Condominium Working Group. Markham, ON.

Matthews, D. 2012. Condo owners lose ruling on vacation rentals. *Crain's Chicago Business*, September 25. https://home.chicagobusiness.com/clickshare/authenticateUserSubscription.do?CSProduct=crainschicago-metered&CSAuthReq=1:373679435535494:AID:78FD7D43D5A1F12A71265187EDC52930&AID=/20120925/CRED0701/120929885&title=Condo%20owners%20lose%20ruling%20on%20vacation%20rentals%20&CSTargetURL=http://www.chicagobusiness.com/realestate/20120925/CRED0701/120929885/condo-owners-lose-ruling-on-vacation-rentals.

MaxTV. 2014a. Maxtv media is a global leader in digital elevator display solutions. Maxtv, 1 July. https://maxtvmedia.com/gallery.html?show=slide.

–. 2014b. Discover "inside the box" advertising that makes an impact. Maxtv, 1 July. https://maxtvmedia.com/advertisers.html.

McCabe, B. 2005. "The rules are different here: An institutional comparison of cities and homeowners associations." *Administration and Society* 37 (4): 404–25. https://doi.org/10.1177/0095399705277137.

McCormack, J. 2009. ""Better the devil you know": Submerged consciousness and tenant participation in housing stock transfers." *Urban Studies (Edinburgh, Scotland)* 46 (2): 391–411. https://doi.org/10.1177/0042098008099360.

McKenzie, E. 1994. *Privatopia: Homeowner Associations and the Rise of Residential Private Government*. New Haven: Yale University Press.

–. 2003. "Common-interest housing in the communities of tomorrow." *Housing Policy Debate* 14 (1–2): 203–34.

–. 2006. The dynamics of privatopia: Private residential governance in the USA. In G. Glasze, C. Webster, and K. Frantz, eds., *Private Cities: Global and Local Perspectives*, 9–30. London: Routledge.

–. 2011. *Beyond Privatopia: Rethinking Residential Private Government*. Washington, DC: Urban Institute Press.

McLellan, B. 1978. "Two problem areas in condominium legislation." *University of Toronto Faculty Review* 36: 44–66.

McMahon, T. 2014. "Why condos are a living nightmare." *Maclean's* 28 (April): 36–41.

McNeill, D. 2005. "Skyscraper geography." *Progress in Human Geography* 29 (1): 41–55. https://doi.org/10.1191/0309132505ph527oa.

Miami Herald. 2009. Condo associations forced into bankruptcy as fees dry up. July 14. http://www.floridarealtors.org/NewsAndEvents/n4-071409.cfm.

Miles, M., and M. Huberman. 1994. *Qualitative Data Analysis: An Expanded Sourcebook*. Thousand Oaks: Sage.

Miller Thomson LLP. 2012. *Legal Brief to Ontario's Comprehensive Review of the Condominium Act, 1998*. Toronto: Miller Thomson LLP.

Miller, P., and N. Rose. 2008. *Governing the Present*. London: Polity Press.

Mittelbach, F., and J. Ebin. 1975. "Condominium housing: Some social and economic implications." *Journal of Sociology and Social Welfare* 3 (2): 170–80.

Monsebraaten, L. 2013. Condos becoming part of Toronto's affordable housing tool box. *Toronto Star*, May 21. https://www.thestar.com/news/gta/2013/05/21/condos_becoming_part_of_torontos_affordable_housing_tool_box.html.

Moore, D. 2007. *Criminal Artefacts: Governing Drugs and Users*. Vancouver: UBC Press.

Moore, D., and M. Valverde. 2000. "Maidens at risk: 'Date rape drugs' and the formation of hybrid risk knowledges." *Economy and Society* 29 (4): 514–31. https://doi.org/10.1080/03085140050174769.

Moran-Ellis, J., V. Alexander, A. Cronin, M. Dickinson, J. Fielding, J. Sleney, and H. Thomas. 2006. "Triangulation and integration: Processes, claims and implications." *Qualitative Research* 6 (1): 45–59. https://doi.org/10.1177/1468794106058870.

Murakami Wood, D. 2013. "What is global surveillance? Towards a relational political economy of the global surveillant assemblage." *Geoforum* 49: 317–26. https://doi.org/10.1016/j.geoforum.2013.07.001.

Nelson, R. 2005. *Private Neighborhoods and the Transformation of Local Government*. Washington, DC: Urban Institute Press.

Neocleous, M. 2000. *The Fabrication of Order: A Critical Theory of Police Power*. London: Pluto Press.

Newman, O. 1972. *Defensible Space: Crime Prevention through Urban Design*. New York: Collier.
New York Senate. 2012. Assembly Bill A6941. http://legislation.nysenate.gov/pdf/bills/2011/A6941.
New York State. 2017. Real estate broker. Department of State, Division of Licensing Services. https://www.dos.ny.gov/licensing/re_broker/re_broker.html.
New York Times. 1967. Condominium-hotel is built in Colorado: Owners of suites to profit from rental rooms. July 30, 225.
Novak, W. 1996. *The People's Welfare: Law and Regulation in Nineteenth Century America*. Chapel Hill, NC: University of North Carolina Press.
Olfene, A. 2013. "Of asthma and ashtrays: Examining the rights of and exploring ways to protect Maine tenants living in multi-unit rental housing who are involuntarily exposed to second-hand tobacco smoke in their homes." *Maine Law Review* 66 (1): 291–325.
Olson, M. 1965. *The Logic of Collective Action*. Cambridge: Harvard University Press.
O'Malley, P. 2004. *Risk, Uncertainty and Government*. London: Glasshouse.
–. 2017. Foreword. In *National Security, Surveillance, and Terror: Canada and Australia in Comparative Perspective*, v–vii, ed. R. Lippert, K. Walby, I. Warren, and D. Palmer. London: Palgrave-Macmillan.
O'Neil, L. 2017. "Snarky anti-condo signs pop up around Toronto." Blog. https://www.blogto.com/city/2017/10/snarky-anti-condo-signs-pop-around-toronto/.
Ontario. 1967a. Legislative Assembly. *Hansard*. 27th Parl., 5th Sess., April 4, 1725–26.
–. 1967b. Legislative Assembly. *Hansard*. 27th Parl., 5th Sess., April 10, 1928.
–. 1977. *Ministry of Consumer and Commercial Relations. Report of the Ontario Residential Condominium Study Group*. Toronto: Study Group.
–. 1978a. Legislative Assembly. *Hansard*. 31st Parl., 2nd Sess., June 1. Statements by the Ministry. Condominium Legislation. https://www.ola.org/en/legislative-business/house-documents/parliament-31/session-2/1978-12-07/hansard.
–. 1978b. Legislative Assembly. *Hansard*. 31st Parl., 2nd Sess., December 8. Condominium Act (Continued) Resumption of the adjourned consideration of Bill 103. An Act to revise the Condominium Act. http://www.ontla.on.ca/house-proceedings/transcripts/files_html/08-DEC-1978_L144.htm#P513_114459.
–. 1978c. Legislative Assembly. *Hansard*. 31st Parl., 2nd Sess., December 7. Condominium Act. http://www.ontla.on.ca/house-proceedings/transcripts/files_html/07-DEC-1978_L141.htm.
–. 2012. The condominium act, 1998: Ontario's comprehensive review. Toronto: Ministry of Consumer Services. http://www.kingstonrealestateblog.com/2012/07/the-condominium-act-1998-ontar.html.
Pacey, G. 1998. Oral submission to Ontario condominium act hearings. October 22. https://www.ola.org/en/legislative-business/committees/general-government/parliament-36/transcript/committee-transcript-1998-oct-22.
Pader, E. 1994. "Spatial relations and housing policy: Regulations that discriminate against Mexican-origin households." *Journal of Planning Education and Research* 13 (2): 119–35. https://doi.org/10.1177/0739456X9401300204.

Peck, J., and A. Tickell. 2002. "Neoliberalizing space." *Antipode* 34 (3): 380–404. https://doi.org/10.1111/1467-8330.00247.

Peck, J., N. Theodore, and N. Brenner. 2010. "Postneoliberalism and its malcontents." *Antipode* 41 (s1): 94–116. https://doi.org/10.1111/j.1467-8330.2009.00718.x.

Pizacani, B., D. Laughter, K. Menagh, M. Stark, L. Drach, C. and Hermann-Franzen. 2011. "Moving multiunit housing providers toward adoption of smoke-free policies." *Preventing Chronic Disease* 8 (1): 1–9.

Pow, C. 2009. "Public intervention, private aspiration: Gated communities and the condominisation of housing landscapes in Singapore." *Asia Pacific Viewpoint* 50 (2): 215–27. https://doi.org/10.1111/j.1467-8373.2009.01394.x.

Powell, B. 2017. Margaret Atwood joins fellow Annex residents to fight condo project. *Toronto Star,* 28 August. https://www.thestar.com/news/city_hall/2017/08/28/margaret-atwood-joins-fellow-annex-residents-to-fight-condo-project.html.

Power, E. 2015. "Placing community self-governance: Building materialities, nuisance noise and neighbouring in self-governing communities." *Urban Studies (Edinburgh, Scotland)* 52 (2): 245–60. https://doi.org/10.1177/0042098014525242.

Power, M. 1999. *The Audit Society: Rituals of Verification.* Oxford, UK: Oxford University Press. https://doi.org/10.1093/acprof:oso/9780198296034.001.0001.

Preville, P. 2014. Stuck in Condoland. *Toronto Life,* 11 June. https://www.torontolife.com/informer/features/2014/06/11/stuck-in-condoland/.

Prevost, L. 2011. New push for condo conciliator. *New York Times,* April 3. https://www.nytimes.com/2011/04/03/realestate/03wczo.html.

Priest, G. 1990. "The new legal structure of risk control." *Daedalus* 119 (4): 207–28.

Property Management Contract. 2014. Legal agreement between anonymous condo corporation and property management company.

Ranasinghe, P., and M. Valverde. 2006. "Governing homelessness through land-use: A sociolegal study of the Toronto shelter zoning by-law." *Canadian Journal of Sociology* 31 (3): 325–49. https://doi.org/10.2307/20058713.

Risk, R. 1968. "Condominiums and Canada." *University of Toronto Law Journal* 18 (1): 1–72. https://doi.org/10.2307/825167.

Rodkin, D. 2017. River City condos going back to apartments. *Crain's Chicago Business,* December 27. https://home.chicagobusiness.com/clickshare/authenticateUserSubscription.do?CSProduct=cred-metered&CSAuthReq=1:373679435535494:AID:20A007873CF5F7EA007356B275C49CF8&AID=/20171227/CRED0701/171229941&title=River%20City%20condos%20going%20back%20to%20apartments&CSTargetURL=http://www.chicagobusiness.com/realestate/20171227/CRED0701/171229941/river-city-condos-going-back-to-apartments.

Romney, K. 1974. *Condominium Development Guide: Procedures, Analysis, Forms. Boston.* Warren: Gorham and Lamont.

Rose, N. 1999. *Powers of Freedom.* Cambridge: Cambridge University Press. https://doi.org/10.1017/CBO9780511488856.

Rose, N., and P. Miller. 1992. "Political power beyond the state: Problematics of government." *British Journal of Sociology* 43 (2): 173–205. https://doi.org/10.2307/591464.

Rose, N., P. O'Malley, and M. Valverde. 2006. "Governmentality." *Annual Review of Law and Social Science* 2 (1): 83–104. https://doi.org/10.1146/annurev.lawsocsci.2.081805.105900.
Rose, N., and M. Valverde. 1998. "Governed by law?" *Social and Legal Studies* 7 (4): 541–51. https://doi.org/10.1177/096466399800700405.
Rosen, G. 2016. Condo-ism and urban renewal: Insights from Toronto and Jerusalem. In A. Lehavi, ed., *Private Communities and Urban Governance,* 77–94. New York: Springer International Publishing. https://doi.org/10.1007/978-3-319-33210-9_4.
–. 2017. "Toronto's condo-builders: Development approaches and spatial preferences." *Urban Geography* 38 (4): 606–25. https://doi.org/10.1080/02723638.2016.1179426.
Rosen, G., and A. Walks. 2013. "Rising cities: Condominium development and the private transformation of the metropolis." *Geoforum* 49: 160–72. https://doi.org/10.1016/j.geoforum.2013.06.010.
–. 2015a. "Castles in Toronto's sky: Condo-ism as urban transformation." *Journal of Urban Affairs* 37 (3): 289–310. https://doi.org/10.1111/juaf.12140.
–. 2015b. "Beyond Gating: Condo-ism as a new way of urban life." In *Beyond Gated Communities: Urban Gating and Soft Boundaries,* 154–69, ed. S. Bagaeen and O. Uduku. London: Routledge.
Rosenberg, A. 1972. *Condominium in Canada.* Toronto: Canada Law Book.
Rule, J. 1973. *Private Lives and Public Surveillance.* London: Allen Lane.
Ruppert, E. 2006. *The Moral Economy of Cities: Shaping Good Citizens.* Toronto: University of Toronto Press.
Rusk, J. 2008. Legal Issues: Condo conflicts on the rise, lawyer says. *Globe and Mail,* March 25. https://www.theglobeandmail.com/news/national/condo-conflicts-on-the-rise-lawyer-says/article669368/.
Schill, M., L. Voicu, and J. Miller. 2007. "The condominium versus cooperative puzzle: an empirical analysis of housing in New York City." *Journal of Legal Studies* 36 (2): 275–324. https://doi.org/10.1086/519421.
Scott, J. 1990. *Domination and the Arts of Resistance.* London: Yale University Press.
Sherry, C. 2017. *Strata Title Property Rights: Private Governance of Multi-Owned Properties.* London: Routledge.
Shum, D. 2013. Toronto police recover up to $6.25 million from seizures and forfeitures. *Global News,* September 19. https://globalnews.ca/news/850769/toronto-police-recover-6-million-63-vehicles-from-proceeds-of-crime-this-year/.
Shyamalan, M. 2010. *Devil.* Motion Picture. Directed by M. Shyamalan. Universal Pictures.
Silverstein, A. 1992. First fluffy, now old mickey, are booted out. *Toronto Star,* 10 October.
–. 2002. Condominium owners often pitted against investors: Competing interests end up in court. *Globe and Mail,* 13 December, A8.
Singleton, R., and B. Straits. 2010. *Approaches to Social Research.* Oxford: Oxford University Press.
Skaburskis, A. 1984. *National Condominium Market Study.* Working Paper No. 5. Ottawa: Canada Mortgage and Housing Corporation.
Skayannis, P. 2010. Is urban underground space luxury? Paper presented at the 24th AESOP Annual Conference: Association of European Schools of Planning, Helsinki.

Smith, N. 1996. *The New Urban Frontier: Gentrification and the Revanchist City*. New York: Routledge.
–. 2002. "New globalism, new urbanism: Gentrification as global urban strategy." *Antipode* 34 (3): 427–50. https://doi.org/10.1111/1467-8330.00249.
Sorkin, M. 2014. What's behind the "poor door"? Inclusionary zoning laws are among the few tools left to ensure the creation of affordable housing. *The Nation*, April 2. https://www.thenation.com/article/whats-behind-poor-door/.
Stark, A. 1998. "America, the gated?" *Wilson Quarterly* 22:58–79.
Statistics Canada. 2011. Condominium Dwellings in Canada. http://www12.statcan.gc.ca/nhs-enm/2011/as-sa/99-014-x/99-014-x2011003_1-eng.cfm.
–. 2017a. Condominiums in Canada, 2016 Census of Population. http://www.statcan.gc.ca/pub/11-627-m/11-627-m2017030-eng.htm.
–. 2017b. Housing in Canada: Key results from the 2016 Census. The Daily. http://www.statcan.gc.ca/daily-quotidien/171025/dq171025c-eng.htm.
–. 2017c. Dwellings in Canada. http://www12.statcan.gc.ca/census-recensement/2016/as-sa/98-200-x/2016005/98-200-x2016005-eng.cfm.
Steele, M. 1993. "Conversions, condominiums and capital gains: The transformation of the Ontario rental housing market." *Urban Studies (Edinburgh, Scotland)* 30 (1): 103–26. https://doi.org/10.1080/00420989320080071.
–. 2009. "Capital gains rollovers and the two-sector rental housing market: A simulation study of Toronto." *Canadian Tax Journal* 57 (3): 460–88.
Strakosch, G., ed. 1998. *The Vertical Transportation Handbook*. New York: Wiley. https://doi.org/10.1002/9780470172865.
Strebel, I. 2011. "The living building: towards a geography of maintenance work." *Social and Cultural Geography* 12 (3): 243–62. https://doi.org/10.1080/14649365.2011.564732.
Swat Protection Services. n.d. *Condominiums*. https://www.swatprotection.ca/condominiums/.
Teaford, S. 1969. "Home ownership for low-income families: The condominium." *Hastings Law Journal* 21: 243–86.
Tippens, G. 2009. "Smokers: Nuisances in Belmont City, California – in their homes, but not on public sidewalks." *Minnesota Consortium on Law and Values in Health, Environment and the Life Sciences* 10 (1): 413–40.
Toronto Condo. 2014. Building rules. Anonymous Toronto condominium corporation.
Toronto Star. 1967. Condominium not the answer to the housing crisis, opposition critics charge. *Toronto Star,* April 11.
Technical Standards and Safety Authority. 2014. Licensing and registration. https://www.tssa.org/regulated/elevating/elevatingLicensing.aspx#sthash.HcZuAmQU.dpuf.
Tridel. 2017. "Built green." https://www.tridel.com/about-tridel/our-purpose-promise/built-green/.
–. 2018. "Tridel Group of Companies." https://www.tridel.com/about-tridel/tridel-group-companies/.

United States Department of Housing and Urban Development. 2011. *American Housing Survey for the United States: 2009*. https://www.census.gov/prod/2011pubs/h150-09.pdf.

United States Census Bureau. 1991a. American housing survey for the United States.

–. 1991b. American housing survey for the New York-Nassau-Suffolk metropolitan area.

–. 2004. American housing survey for the New York-Nassau-Suffolk-Orange metropolitan area.

–. 2013a. American housing survey for the United States.

–. 2013b. American housing survey for New York City.

–. 2018. "2015 New York City: General Housing Data – All Occupied Units New York-Newark-Jersey City, NY-NJ-PA MSA (2013 OMB definition)." https://www.census.gov/programs-surveys/ahs/data/interactive/ahstablecreator.html#?s_areas=a35620&s_year=m2015&s_tableName=Table1&s_byGroup1=a3&s_byGroup2=a1&s_filterGroup1=t1&s_filterGroup2=g1&s_show=S.

United States Congress. 1981. *Condominium and Cooperative Conversion: The Federal Response*. Hearings before a subcommittee of the Committee on Government Operations, House of Representatives, 97th Congress, First Session, March 30 to April 1. http://www.planningcommunications.com/housing/Testimony_condominium_conversion_1981.pdf.

Valverde, M. 1996. "Despotism and ethical liberal governance." *Economy and Society* 25 (3): 357–72. https://doi.org/10.1080/03085149600000019.

–. 2003. *Law's Dream of a Common Knowledge*. Princeton: Princeton University Press.

–. 2005. "Authorizing the production of urban moral order: Appellate courts and their knowledge games." *Law and Society Review* 39 (2): 419–56. https://doi.org/10.1111/j.0023-9216.2005.00087.x.

–. 2009. "Jurisdiction and scale: Legal technicalities as resources for theory." *Social and Legal Studies* 18 (2): 139–57. https://doi.org/10.1177/0964663909103622.

–. 2011. "Seeing like a city: The dialectic of modern and premodern ways of seeing in urban governance." *Law and Society Review* 45 (2): 277–312. https://doi.org/10.1111/j.1540-5893.2011.00441.x.

–. 2012. *Everyday Law of the Street: City Governance in an Age of Diversity*. Chicago: University of Chicago Press.

–. 2016. "Ad hoc governance: Public authorities and North American local infrastructure in historical perspective." In M. Brady and R. Lippert, eds., *Governing Practices: Neo-liberalism, Governmentality, and the Ethnographic Imaginary*, 199–217. Toronto: University of Toronto Press.

Vincent, D. 2012. Downtown Toronto condo building set to include affordable rental units. *Toronto Star*. 14 December. https://www.thestar.com/news/gta/2012/12/14/downtown_toronto_condo_building_set_to_include_affordable_rental_units.html.

Walby, K. 2007. "Contributions to a post-sovereigntist understanding of law: Foucault, law as governance, and legal pluralism." *Social and Legal Studies* 16 (4): 551–71. https://doi.org/10.1177/0964663907082735.

Walby, K., and R. Lippert. 2011. "Spatial regulation, dispersal, and the aesthetics of the city: Conservation officer policing of homeless people in Ottawa." *Antipode* 44 (3): 1015–33. https://doi.org/10.1111/j.1467-8330.2011.00923.x.

–. 2015. *Municipal Corporate Security in International Context*. New York: Routledge.

Walks, A. 2014. "From financialization to sociospatial polarization of the city? Evidence from Canada." *Economic Geography* 90 (1): 33–66. https://doi.org/10.1111/ecge.12024.

Walters, W. 2012. *Governmentality: Critical Encounters*. New York: Routledge.

Warner, M. 2011. "Club goods and local government: Questions for planners." *Journal of the American Planning Association* 77 (2): 155–66. https://doi.org/10.1080/01944363.2011.567898.

Webb, B., and S. Webber. 2017. "The implications of condominium neighbourhoods for long-term urban revitalization." *Cities (London, England)* 61: 48–57. https://doi.org/10.1016/j.cities.2016.11.006.

White, M. 2005. "To rent or not to rent? That is the question!" *Condo Voice* 9: 20–1.

Wilkinson, B., and R. Lippert. 2012. "Moving images through an assemblage: Police, visual information, and resistance." *Critical Criminology* 20 (3): 311–25. https://doi.org/10.1007/s10612-011-9141-0.

Williams, J. 2012. *Policing the Markets: Inside the Black Box of Securities Enforcement*. New York: Routledge.

Wills, T. 1967. Act would ease condominium living. *Globe and Mail*, 23 March, 5.

Wright, J., A. Glasbeek, and E. van der Meulen. 2015. "Securing the home: Gender, CCTV and the hybridized space of apartment buildings." *Theoretical Criminology* 19 (1): 95–111. https://doi.org/10.1177/1362480614544210.

Zhang, L. 2008. Private homes, distinct lifestyles: Performing a new middle class. In L. Zhang and A. Ong, eds., *Privatizing China: Socialism from Afar*, 23–40. London: Cornell University Press.

Zlomislic, D., and R. Aulakh. 2012. Property manager bilked $20M in condo fraud. *Toronto Star*, September 15, https://www.thestar.com/news/gta/2011/09/15/property_manager_bilked_20m_in_condo_fraud_victims_claim.html.

LAWS AND STATUTES

Canada (Ontario)

Condominium (Condo) Act, S.O., c. 12. (1967).

Condominium (Condo) Act, S.O., c. 84. (1978).

Condominium (Condo) Act, S.O., c. 19. (1998).

Protecting Condo Owners Act. Bill 106. Ontario. (2015).

Occupiers' Liability Act, RSO (1990), c O.2. Available at https://canlii.ca/t/1hwc.

Toronto Municipal Code (2013). 629–25 Property Standards (Occupancy Standards). Available at https://www.toronto.ca/legdocs/municode/1184_629.pdf.

United States

National Housing Act, 75 Stat. 160, 12 U.S.C. (1961).

New York Article 9-B Condominium Act.

New York City 1998 Local Laws of the City of New York No. 11. Available at http://www1.nyc.gov/assets/buildings/local_laws/locallaw_1998_package.pdf.
New York City 1982 Local Law 70 (Title 26, Chapter 8 of the New York City Administrative Code, 26–701).

CASES CITED

Canada

Syndicat Northcrest v. Amselem, [2004] 2 SCR 551, 2004 SCC 47.

Ontario

Apartments International Inc. v. Metropolitan Toronto Condominium Corporation No. 1170 O.S.C.J. (2002).
Dalinda v. Brookfield Residential Services Ltd., 2011 HRTO 1371.
Dyke v. Metropolitan Toronto Condo. Corp. No. 972, 2013 ONSC 463.
Green v. York Region Condominium Corporation No. 834, 2013 ONSC 5004.
Italiano v. Toronto Standard Condominium Corporation No. 1507, 2008 (ON SC).
MTCC No. 710 v. Khan, 2012 ONSC 5494.
MTCC No. 831 v. Khan, 2012 ONSC 5037.
Ottawa-Carleton Condominium Corporation No. 961 v. Menzies, 2016 ONSC 7699.
Peel Condominium Corporation No. 16 v. Vaughan, 34 C.C.L.I. (2d) 245(O.C.J.G.D.) (1996).
Peel Condominium Corporation No. 11 v. Caroe et al., 4 O.R. (2d) 543 (Ont. H.C.) (1974).
Skyline Executive Properties Inc. v. Metropolitan Toronto Condominium Corporation No. 1280, [2001] O.J. No. 3512.
York Condominium Corporation No. 122 v. Sibblis (Dist. Ct.), ONSC 4098 (1989).

Index

Note: A "t" after a page number indicates a table.

Printed and bound in Canada by Friesens

Set in Gilam and Minion by Artegraphica Design Co. Ltd.

Copy editor: Joanne Richardson

Proofreader: Lauren Cross

Indexer: Laryssa Brooks